# Jamie Oliver's
# CHRISTMAS
# COOKBOOK

FLATIRON
BOOKS
NEW YORK

*This book belongs to . . .*

. . . . . . . . . . . . . . . . . . . . . . . . . . . . . . . . . . . . . . . . . . . . . . . . . . . . . .

. . . . . . . . . . . . . . . . . . . . . . . . . . . . . . . . . . . . . . . . . . . . . . . . . . . . . .

. . . . . . . . . . . . . . . . . . . . . . . . . . . . . . . . . . . . . . . . . . . . . . . . . . . . . .

. . . . . . . . . . . . . . . . . . . . . . . . . . . . . . . . . . . . . . . . . . . . . . . . . . . . . .

*Dedicated to*

# my Nan

## BETTY MARJORIE PALMER

### AKA TIGER

26 JANUARY 1920–27 SEPTEMBER 2013

What a perfect book to remember my dear old Nanny, who was such a kind, gentle soul. This time of year is all about bringing your loved ones together and, of course, remembering those who can't be with us, and Nan was always on great form at Christmas. One year, she was so excited to get her mitts on the stuffing that her paper crown caught fire on a candle, in turn setting fire to her heavily hair-sprayed blue rinse. I clearly remember recoiling in horror at what Dad had to do to put her out, but we were all relieved when the fire was extinguished, and the meal soon carried on with gusto. And that's Christmas for you—it never goes according to plan. But as long as you keep laughing, it will all be alright.

Love you, Nan—merry Christmas xxx

# Contents

# Happy Christmas

And thank you so much, dear reader, for picking up this book. My single ambition here is to give you as much inspiration as possible to ensure you have the best Christmas ever, and I've put this book together with a great deal of love, thought, care, and consideration.

In the two decades since *The Naked Chef*, I've learnt a lot from all of you about what it is that can make Christmas stressful when it comes to food, so let me fix that for you. I'm only ever going to do this book once, so I've made sure that it's the absolute best it can be. Have faith that you're in safe hands with these recipes, every one of which has been rigorously tried and tested to ensure it'll work for you at home, every single time.

I want to be there for you not only this year, but for every year going forward. Christmas doesn't have to be stressful if you delegate to friends and family (see page 76). Timing, organization, and lists, while perhaps a little boring, are really important. There's no such thing as luck when it comes to a really well done Christmas meal. Planning ahead will give you not only wonderful, tasty food, but also the ability to surprise and wow people, delivering the unexpected to mind-blowing levels and getting them almost fighting over the best roast potatoes, the perfect stuffing, or the most succulent, juicy bird you've ever slapped bang in the middle of your table—turn the page for more of my top advice.

So down to business. This book contains 17 years of my ultimate, beautifully indulgent, festive recipes—it's got all my old favorites from over the years, plus loads of new ideas to really tickle your taste buds and ramp things up on the flavor front. This is the food that makes me and my family about as happy as can be, and it provides the perfect excuse to bring all your loved ones together. I've got all the bases covered, with everything you need for the big day and any feasting meals over the festive period, as well as party fare, edible gifts, teatime treats, cocktails, and, of course, exciting ways to celebrate those lovely leftovers. Wherever possible, I've designed the recipes to be cooked at the same oven temperature, so you can be efficient with your time and oven space, and it'll be super-easy for you to mix and match the different elements and build your own perfect Christmas meal.

I haven't held back. This book is the greatest hits, all wrapped up in one Christmas parcel. Look through, pick your recipes, build your plan, and above all, have a good one, my friends.

# A little pep talk

Now hopefully you've landed on this page having just read the main intro, so you're already starting to think about the important process of preparation. What I'm saying, guys, is if you can get yourself into the mindset of doing a little pre-Christmas homework, it's only going to serve you well over the festive period, making your life much easier.

Throughout this book, you'll pick up lots of tips and hints on how to get organized, putting yourself in the best possible position for a stress-free Christmas. When there are recipes or elements of recipes you can easily get ahead with, I've flagged it on the recipe pages, so you'll be armed with the knowledge to be super-organized, should you wish to be.

When it comes to shopping, look out for seasonal offers on pantry staples, dry goods, and heavy items like booze in the weeks and months leading up to Christmas, so you can stock up and spread the cost. Buying online can be helpful, too, as it saves you carting around heavy items. Things like condiments and sauces, spices, olive oil, grains and pulses, nuts, baking ingredients, jams, pickles and preserves, organic bouillon cubes, tins, jars, and bottles, as well as all those things you're bound to run low on, such as bin bags, paper towel, aluminum foil, and dish soap, as well as containers for your leftovers.

Meal planning is always a brilliant idea, and I'm not just talking about the big day. Think about where you'll be and who you'll be entertaining on Christmas Eve, on Boxing Day, and on those days between Boxing Day and New Year when shops are a bit scarce or, let's be honest, you don't want to leave the comfort of your cozy house! Have you got what you need? Can you make stuff ahead and freeze it? If you've got family and friends staying, are you covered for all those other bits we tend to forget about, like breakfast? Stock up and plan ahead and you'll be super-thankful for it come the craziness of the festive period.

Of course, you should always have room for a bit of flexibility, and that's where your freezer is your best friend. Be prepared for unexpected guests dropping by for a holiday tipple and a bite to eat. Freeze trays of Mince pies (see page 264) or Sausage rolls (see page 342) ready for nibbles, or make a batch of Curry sauce (see page 82) ready to knock up a quick festive meal with a moment's notice. Things that keep well in an airtight container, such as Biscotti (see page 294), Brownies (see page 280), and Billionaire's shortbread (see page 276), will always come in handy and I can guarantee they'll be gratefully received, too. Good luck!

# Check your equipment

One of the best bits of advice I can give you to avoid big-day stress is to check your equipment a few weeks in advance and make sure you have all the kit you need. I can't tell you how many stories I hear about people going to cook their turkey and realizing that they don't have a pan big enough for it, or that they've gone the other way and bought a pan that doesn't fit in their oven! Good, basic kitchen equipment is widely available, so it's easy to get kitted out. Give yourself enough time to shop around and find the best prices, choosing better-quality items wherever you can—they'll last much longer, maybe even a lifetime.

To the right you'll find a list of everything I think is helpful to ensure all your bases are covered. By no means am I suggesting it's essential for you to buy everything listed here, but I hope it will help you do a recce of your own cupboards and have a think about the kit that will help you out over the festive period. Happy cooking!

| | |
|---|---|
| Food processor | Mandolin |
| Blender | Vegetable peeler |
| Electric mixer | Box grater |
| Pestle & mortar | Fine grater |
| Saucepans | Colander |
| Frying pans | Sieve |
| Casserole pans | Wooden spoons |
| Grill pans | Slotted spoon |
| Roasting pans | Ladle |
| Baking pans | Heavy-duty tongs |
| Tart pans | Meat thermometer |
| Cake pans | Potato masher |
| 12-cup muffin pan | Slotted spatula |
| 12-cup cupcake pan | Garlic crusher |
| Baking dishes | Pastry brush |
| Mixing bowls | Rolling pin |
| Measuring cups | Kitchen scissors |
| Measuring spoons | Kitchen towels |
| Weighing scales | Paper towels |
| Chopping boards | Kitchen string |
| Chef's knife | Parchment paper |
| Paring knife | Strong aluminum foil |
| Bread knife | Quality plastic wrap (non-PVC) |
| Carving knife | |
| Knife sharpener | |

# Smart
## STARTERS

# SHRIMP COCKTAIL

## MARIE ROSE SAUCE, SMOKED SALMON, SHRIMP, & ICEBERG

An American prohibition classic; I made thousands of these in my parents' pub in the '80s. Shrimp cocktail is nostalgic, retro, and just a tiny bit naff, but in a really brilliant way. People love it and, if it's done well, it's always memorable.

**SERVES 4**

**20 MINUTES**

olive oil

1 clove of garlic

cayenne pepper

8 large raw shell-on jumbo shrimp

½ an iceberg lettuce

1 ripe avocado

2 ripe tomatoes

½ an English cucumber

2 sprigs of fresh mint

1 cup sprouting cress

3½ oz peeled cooked salad-size shrimp

3½ oz brown shrimp

6 oz quality smoked salmon

**MARIE ROSE SAUCE**

3 tablespoons mayonnaise

3 tablespoons plain yogurt

1 tablespoon tomato ketchup

1 splash of Worcestershire sauce

1 splash of brandy

1 lemon

Place a large pan on a medium heat with 1 tablespoon of oil and crush in the unpeeled garlic through a garlic crusher. Sprinkle in a good pinch of cayenne and add the jumbo shrimp (butterfly them first, if you like). Cook for 3 to 4 minutes, or until cooked through, turning halfway, then remove from the heat.

To make the Marie Rose sauce, simply mix together the mayo, yogurt, ketchup, Worcestershire sauce, and brandy, then add a little cayenne pepper and lemon juice, to taste, and season to perfection with sea salt and black pepper.

Finely slice the lettuce. Peel and pit the avocado, then dice with the tomatoes and cucumber and divide between cute glasses, plates, or bowls. Pick and add the smaller mint leaves and snip over pinches of cress. Divide up the salad shrimp, brown shrimp, and delicate waves of salmon, then spoon over the Marie Rose sauce and sprinkle with a pinch of cayenne from a height. Add 2 jumbo shrimp to each portion for a grand finish, and serve with lemon wedges for squeezing over. Some buttered bread on the side is always going to go down a treat, too.

### MIX IT UP

The lovely thing about this recipe is that it's very flexible. You can use everyday frozen shrimp, which are very delicious, or even get yourself some lobster or freshly picked crabmeat and really dress it up—it's up to you. Enjoy!

| CALORIES | FAT | SAT FAT | PROTEIN | CARBS | SUGARS | SALT | FIBER |
|----------|-----|---------|---------|-------|--------|------|-------|
| 451kcal | 32.1g | 4.8g | 29.7g | 7.7g | 6.6g | 3.0g | 1.5g |

# BEEF CARPACCIO

## ROASTED SQUASH, CHESTNUTS, & WINTER LEAVES

I love this delicate warm salad for a festive starter or lunch. It really embraces winter squash, leaves, and chestnuts, with a fiery mustard dressing that sets it all off nicely. Brilliant served on a big platter to impress your guests.

**SERVES 6**

**1 HOUR**

1 butternut squash (2½ lbs)

1 teaspoon fennel seeds

1 teaspoon coriander seeds

½ teaspoon dried red chili flakes

1 pinch of ground cinnamon

olive oil

5 oz vac-packed chestnuts

3 sprigs of fresh rosemary

1¼-lb piece of beef tenderloin

1 heaping tablespoon Dijon mustard

extra virgin olive oil

2 lemons

6 handfuls of mixed seasonal salad leaves, such as mustard cress, radicchio, watercress

Parmesan cheese

Preheat the oven to 350°F. Wash the squash and carefully cut it in half lengthways. Remove and reserve the seeds, then cut each half lengthways into six thin wedges and arrange in a roasting pan. In a pestle and mortar, bash the fennel and coriander seeds, dried chili flakes, cinnamon, 1 teaspoon of sea salt, and a pinch of black pepper until fine, then sprinkle over the squash. Drizzle with just enough olive oil to lightly coat everything and toss well. Roast for 45 to 50 minutes, or until golden and cooked through, sprinkling the chestnuts and reserved squash seeds into the pan to roast for the last 10 minutes.

Finely chop the rosemary leaves on a board with a good pinch of salt and pepper. Rub the beef with 1 tablespoon of olive oil, then roll it around on the board until it's well coated in the seasoned rosemary. Put a pan on a high heat and, once it's screaming hot, sear the beef for 2 to 3 minutes, turning until browned all over, then remove to a board to rest. Remember you're searing it, not cooking it.

Mix the mustard, 6 tablespoons of extra virgin olive oil, and the lemon juice in a bowl to make a dressing, then taste and season to perfection. Use a really sharp knife to slice the beef as thinly as you can, then use the flat blade of the knife to flatten out each slice. Arrange the slices on a large platter and season from a height with a little salt. Place the roasted squash wedges on top, then scatter over the roasted chestnuts and toasted seeds from the pan. Drizzle over most of the dressing, then lightly dress your salad leaves with the remainder, and sprinkle them on top. Serve with a block of Parmesan, for shaving over at the table.

| CALORIES | FAT | SAT FAT | PROTEIN | CARBS | SUGARS | SALT | FIBER |
|---|---|---|---|---|---|---|---|
| 412kcal | 23.9g | 5.4g | 24.7g | 26.9g | 11.6g | 1g | 4g |

# ROASTED APPLE & SQUASH SOUP

## CHILE, FRESH HERBS, & CAYENNE-SPIKED TOASTED SEEDS

A bit of an old favorite of mine, this wonderful soup is a real celebration of the humble eating apple. Making the most of the incredible depth of flavor achieved by roasting, this super-comforting soup is the perfect festive bowlful.

SERVES 6

1 HOUR 30 MINUTES

1 butternut squash (2½ lbs)

3 Cox's or Braeburn eating apples

1 large onion

1–2 fresh red chiles

4 cloves of garlic

olive oil

1 pinch of coriander seeds

4 sprigs of fresh rosemary

4 tablespoons raw pumpkin seeds

1 pinch of sweet cayenne pepper

4 cups vegetable or chicken stock

optional: ⅔ cup heavy cream

optional: edible flowers or flowering herbs

Preheat the oven to 350°F. Wash the squash, then carefully cut it in half lengthways and remove the seeds. Cut the flesh into 1-inch chunks and put them into your largest roasting pan. Peel and quarter the apples, removing the cores, peel and roughly chop the onion, then add both to the pan. Halve, seed, and add the chiles, then squash and add the unpeeled garlic cloves. Drizzle with 2 tablespoons of oil, add the coriander seeds and a good pinch of sea salt and black pepper, then strip over the rosemary leaves. Toss well, then roast for around 45 to 50 minutes, or until it's all cooked through, intensely golden, and delicious. Toss the pumpkin seeds with salt, pepper, a little oil, and the cayenne. Spread out on a baking sheet and roast for 10 to 15 minutes, then put aside.

Squeeze the soft roasted garlic flesh into a blender, discarding the skins. Spoon in half the roasted veg, add half the stock, put the lid on, cover with a kitchen towel, then, holding the lid in place, blitz until smooth. Pour into a large pan, blitz the rest of the veg and stock, then add that to the pan with most of the cream (if using). Bring to a simmer on a medium-low heat, then taste and season to perfection, adjusting the consistency with a little more stock, to your liking.

Divide the soup between warm bowls and add an extra swirl of cream for a retro finish, then sprinkle over the toasted seeds. You can also delicately decorate with flowering herbs or edible flowers, if you like. Good with warm crusty bread.

| CALORIES | FAT | SAT FAT | PROTEIN | CARBS | SUGARS | SALT | FIBER |
|---|---|---|---|---|---|---|---|
| 200kcal | 7.9g | 1.2g | 7g | 26.9g | 16.9g | 1.2g | 5.9g |

# SEAFOOD SMÖRGÅSBORD

## A SENSATIONAL SEASONAL CELEBRATION OF THE SEA

Every part of the world offers up a different bounty of seafood. So embrace the wonderful diversity of our seas and have fun with what's available where you are, mixing up raw, smoked, pickled, and cured—your taste buds will thank you.

### 30 MINUTES

The glorious page of beauty you see on the right here is a brilliant principle to embrace during the festive season or, frankly, at any sociable get-together at any time of year. There's not much work involved—it's all about the art of assembly. It's beautiful for two or four people, but you can easily scale it up for eight or ten, if you want to.

Simply buy an interesting mixture of wonderful fresh, raw, smoked, pickled, and cured seafood, which you can find at all good fishmongers—ask their advice on what's best right now. Get yourself a large rustic board or platter, then take a bit of pride in delicately arranging all your favorite things. Here's what's made it onto my smörgåsbord:

Quenelles of Smoked salmon pâté (see page 25)

Freshly shucked oysters, lightly drizzled with cider vinegar and extra virgin olive oil, sprinkled with finely chopped Bramley apples, and a pinch of fresh chervil

Tasty piped lashings of Taramasalata (see page 338)

Smoked king shrimp, which you can ask your fishmonger to get in for you, or do yourself by heating a large handful of wood chips in a pan over a medium heat. Pop a wire rack on top, lay in your raw shell-on shrimp, put the lid on, wrap the pan in aluminum foil, and smoke until they're pink and delicious—do this outside on the barbecue if you can

Roses of quality smoked salmon or slices of gorgeous Gravlax (see page 34)

A handful of clams, mussels, or periwinkles, popped into a pan on a medium heat with the lid on and heated for a few minutes with a small splash of white wine and 1 knob of unsalted butter (discard any clams or mussels that remain closed)

Cooked, shelled cockles, lightly dressed with nice oil, vinegar, and herbs

With some freshly buttered brown bread and a few lemon wedges on the side for squeezing over, this is a feast fit for any festive king or queen. Enjoy.

# SMOKED SALMON PÂTÉ

## SHRIMP, WHITE CRABMEAT, SALMON CAVIAR, & CAYENNE PEPPER

This is a real winner to have prepped and ready in the fridge to enjoy as a starter or as part of a buffet. The blend of seafood is sublime, giving you silkiness and nice meaty texture, and the salmon caviar adds a real flavor pop of the sea.

SERVES 16–20

30 MINUTES

**PÂTÉ**

5 oz cooked peeled shrimp

5 oz quality smoked salmon

5 oz white crabmeat

9 oz cream cheese

1 oz salmon caviar,
    plus extra to serve

1 lemon

new season's extra virgin olive oil

cayenne pepper

**GARNISHES**

1 small red onion

1 fresh red chile

1 celery heart

½ a bunch of fresh dill (½ oz)

2 lemons

1 loaf of sourdough bread

Finely chop the shrimp and smoked salmon and place in a bowl with the crabmeat, cream cheese, and caviar. Finely grate in the zest from quarter of a lemon and squeeze in the juice from 1 lemon. Add a good pinch of black pepper and mix together well. Spoon into an appropriately sized dish and smooth out nice and evenly—I use a palette or butter knife dipped in hot water to make this process easier. Cover and pop into the fridge until needed.

To prep your garnishes, peel the red onion and chop as finely as you can. Seed and finely slice the chile. Click the outer stalks off the celery and save for another day. Cut the inner part in half and finely slice it, leaves and all. Pick and roughly chop the dill. Cut the lemons into wedges. Slice and toast the bread.

Before serving, use a regular butter knife to lightly score a criss-cross pattern into the top of the pâté, then drizzle with a little oil and sprinkle from a height with a pinch of cayenne. Either take everything to the table and let people tuck in and help themselves, or take a bit of pride in delicately plating everything up, giving each lucky guest a beautiful quenelle of pâté surrounded by all the garnishes.

| CALORIES | FAT | SAT FAT | PROTEIN | CARBS | SUGARS | SALT | FIBER |
|----------|-----|---------|---------|-------|--------|------|-------|
| 103kcal | 5g | 2.5g | 6.5g | 8.1g | 1.4g | 0.7g | 0.4g |

# BEET CARPACCIO

## BALSAMIC, LEMON, WORCESTERSHIRE SAUCE, & DIJON

It's amazing how incredibly elegant, silky, and delicate beets can be. Invest in a decent mandolin and you can transform root veg like this into beautiful things. This take on a classic carpaccio is nothing short of a joy to eat.

**SERVES 4**

**20 MINUTES**

4 large raw beets

2 tablespoons thick balsamic vinegar

extra virgin olive oil

1 lemon

2 heaping teaspoons Dijon mustard

1 tablespoon Worcestershire sauce

1 heaping tablespoon fat-free plain yogurt

1¾ oz arugula

Scrub the beets clean and trim them, then, on a mandolin (use the guard!), finely slice them about ¹⁄₃₂-inch thick and place in a large bowl—it's a good idea to wear gloves for this. Drizzle with the balsamic vinegar, add 1 tablespoon of oil and a good pinch of sea salt, then squeeze over half the lemon juice. Toss together until every sliver is well coated—this will flavor and tenderize the beets.

To make your dressing, whisk the mustard, Worcestershire sauce, and yogurt with the remaining lemon juice and ¼ cup of oil, then taste, season to perfection, and pour into a jar or pitcher.

Arrange the beets over a large serving platter and sprinkle over the arugula. From a height, drizzle the dressing over the top, serving any extra on the side. With some warm crusty bread, good goat's cheese, and a glass of wine, it's pure happiness.

### MIX IT UP

There are some amazing heirloom beets around these days—white, yellow, candy striped—and they're fantastic in this recipe. All I would suggest is swapping out the balsamic vinegar for a quality herb vinegar so you can enjoy the colors without it all getting dark.

| CALORIES | FAT | SAT FAT | PROTEIN | CARBS | SUGARS | SALT | FIBER |
|----------|-----|---------|---------|-------|--------|------|-------|
| 184kcal | 15.9g | 2.3g | 2.3g | 8.2g | 7.5g | 1.8g | 1.2g |

# SILKY PÂTÉ

## FLAMED CHICKEN LIVERS, SWEET ONIONS, SAGE, & THYME

This silky smooth pâté is super-satisfying to make. The ingredients are cheap, you get an amazing freshness, and you have complete control over flavor, so you can pimp it and make it really luxurious. It makes a great gift, too.

SERVES 12–14
50 MINUTES
PLUS SETTING

2¼ cups unsalted butter

2 onions

2 cloves of garlic

olive oil

½ a bunch of fresh thyme (½ oz)

2 lbs chicken livers, cleaned, trimmed

1 whole nutmeg, for grating

½ cup brandy

½ a bunch of fresh sage (½ oz)

### GET AHEAD

Make the pâté up to 1 week in advance, simply keeping it in the fridge until needed.

To make your clarified butter, place 1 cup + 2 tablespoons of butter in a pan on a very low heat and let it slowly melt, then tick away until it separates. Use a ladle to remove the golden butter from the top into a separate small pan, leaving the whey behind.

Peel and finely chop the onions and garlic and place in a large pan on a medium heat with 1 tablespoon of oil and the leftover whey. Strip in the thyme leaves and fry fast for 5 minutes, tossing regularly, until soft and starting to color. Add the chicken livers and a pinch of sea salt and black pepper, then finely grate in half the nutmeg. Cook for 4 minutes, or until the livers are blushing pink in the middle—don't overcook them. Add the brandy to the pan for the last minute and let it cook off, ideally flaming it, if you feel confident enough to do so.

Tip everything straight into a food processor or blender with all the juices, and blitz until smooth. You'll notice that the smell changes straight away. Taste and season to perfection, then add a little more because the seasoning seems to reduce when it gets cold, which is how you'll serve it. Dice the remaining butter, add to the processor or blender, and blitz until silky smooth and the mixture starts to shine. Taste again to check the seasoning, then whiz for a final 2 minutes. You can serve the pâté in individual terrines or in a big bowl or platter. Pop into the fridge, covered with a sheet of parchment paper, until set.

Put the pan of golden butter on a medium heat and add 1 sage leaf—this will act as your gauge so you know when it's hot enough. When the leaf just becomes crispy, pick in the remaining sage leaves and take the pan off the heat. They'll go crispy, snappy, and delicious. Use a slotted spoon to pop the sage leaves on top of the chilled pâté, then pour over the clarified butter. Put back into the fridge and the butter will go hard and opaque, acting as a seal. You don't have to eat the butter, but it will have amazing flavor. I like to serve this with toast, radishes, cornichons, watercress, and lemon wedges, and wash it down with a glass of wine.

| CALORIES | FAT | SAT FAT | PROTEIN | CARBS | SUGARS | SALT | FIBER |
|---|---|---|---|---|---|---|---|
| 372kcal | 32.1g | 19.3g | 13.3g | 2.7g | 1.8g | 0.4g | 0.8g |

# GRAVLAX

## BEETS, HORSERADISH, VODKA, & DILL

◇◇◇◇◇◇◇◇◇◇◇◇◇◇◇◇◇◇◇◇◇◇◇◇◇◇◇◇◇◇◇◇◇◇◇◇◇◇◇◇◇◇◇◇◇◇◇◇◇◇◇◇◇◇◇◇◇◇◇◇◇◇◇◇◇◇◇

A firm favorite from my travels, this beautiful, delicate dish sums up everything I love about Swedish food: it's elegant, clean, and fresh, it looks incredible, and is a doddle to make. You'll be so proud when you see the finished result.

SERVES 10
20 MINUTES
PLUS CURING

**FISH**

7 oz raw beets

3½ oz rock salt

¼ cup demerara sugar

¼ cup vodka

1 big bunch of fresh dill (2 oz)

1 lemon

1¾ oz fresh or jarred grated horseradish

1 x 1½-lb side of salmon, skin on, scaled, pin-boned

Peel and trim the beets and place in a food processor with the salt, sugar, vodka, and dill. Finely grate in the lemon zest, add the horseradish, finely grating it if fresh, then blitz until combined. Rub a little mixture onto the salmon skin, then place the salmon on a large tray, skin-side down, and pat the remaining mixture all over it so that the flesh is completely covered. Cover the tray tightly with plastic wrap. Pop a weight on top to help pack everything down evenly, then put the whole thing into the fridge for 36 hours. Please use your instincts here—if you have a particularly chunky side of salmon, you may want to leave it for up to 48 hours to allow for proper penetration.

Once cured, unwrap the fish, then, holding the fillet in place, pour the juices down the sink and rub away all the salty topping (it's messy, so you might want to wear gloves). Pat the fillet dry with paper towel, then tightly wrap in plastic wrap (sometimes I like to cover the salmon with freshly picked dill before wrapping, for bonus flavor). Put back into the fridge until needed, where it will keep happily for up to 2 weeks.

To serve, use a long sharp knife to slice the salmon thinly at an angle and, as the knife touches the skin each time, kink it off, lifting away the salmon. Arrange the slices on a board or platter as you go. Delicious with a simple salad and good whole-grain sourdough, as part of a Seafood smörgåsbord (see page 24), served up at a party, or even as part of a festive brekkie spread.

| CALORIES | FAT | SAT FAT | PROTEIN | CARBS | SUGARS | SALT | FIBER |
|---|---|---|---|---|---|---|---|
| 128kcal | 7.1g | 1.5g | 15.5g | 0.4g | 0.4g | 0.9g | 0.1g |

# PORK TERRINE

## SMOKY BACON, FRAGRANT HERBS, CLOVES, & NUTMEG

This is a real treat and you'll get a fantastic sense of achievement from making your own terrine. And, unless you buy one from a truly amazing artisan producer, you really won't get any better than one you've made yourself.

SERVES 10–12

2 HOURS
PLUS COOLING
& CHILLING

3 lbs pork—a mixture of neck, shoulder, and a tiny bit of leg

3½ oz pork or chicken livers, cleaned, trimmed

3½ oz smoked bacon lardons

½ a bunch of fresh thyme (½ oz)

1 whole nutmeg, for grating

1 bunch of fresh Italian parsley (1 oz)

3 fresh bay leaves

1 large handful of bread crumbs

½ teaspoon ground cloves

1 level teaspoon white pepper

Ask your butcher to coarsely grind the pork, or pulse it in a food processor, slicing and finely chopping a few bits to give you a nice range of textures and making the terrine more interesting to eat.

Take the meat out of the fridge 20 minutes before you want to cook, so it can come up to room temperature. Preheat the oven to 325°F. Blitz the livers and lardons to a purée in a food processor, then tip into a large bowl with the ground pork mixture. Strip in the thyme leaves, then finely grate in half the nutmeg. Finely chop the parsley (stalks and all). Pull the stalks out of the bay leaves, roll the leaves up, and finely chop them, then add both to the bowl with the bread crumbs, cloves, white pepper, and 3 really good pinches of sea salt. Scrunch and mix it all together well with clean hands.

Get yourself a round ovenproof earthenware dish, about 10 inches in diameter and 2 inches deep (I prefer to use a dish here, rather than a traditional terrine mold, which is where the recipe gets its name). Overfill the dish first, then really push and squash the mixture down and right out to the edges.

Place the dish in a large roasting pan, put into the oven, and carefully pour in enough boiling kettle water to come halfway up the side of the pan. Cook the terrine for 1 hour and 15 minutes. To check it's done, insert a knife into the center—if the juices run clear, it's perfect. It will shrink a bit during cooking, but that's normal. Carefully remove from the oven and leave to cool in the pan. Don't drain off any liquid—that'll keep it juicy once the terrine has cooled. When cool, cover with plastic wrap and chill in the fridge. Kept in the dish you cooked it in, with all the fat around the edge and properly covered, it will keep happily for up to 1 week.

I like to serve it with dressed cornichons, radishes, and chicory. A dollop of mustard, hot toast, and a glass of French Malbec on the side, and you're laughing.

| CALORIES | FAT | SAT FAT | PROTEIN | CARBS | SUGARS | SALT | FIBER |
|---|---|---|---|---|---|---|---|
| 348kcal | 26.7g | 9.2g | 25.4g | 1.8g | 0.1g | 0.8g | 0.2g |

# The
# MAIN EVENT

# ROAST GOOSE

## SLOW-COOKED WITH CHRISTMAS SPICES

If you've never had roast goose before, it's an absolute must. This method is reliable and will give you an experience you definitely won't forget, whether it's the first meal from it, or using up the lovely leftovers it gives you (if there are any!).

**SERVES 8**

**3 HOURS 30 MINUTES**

1 large goose (9–11 lbs), halved lengthways by your butcher

2½-inch piece of fresh gingerroot

6 large sticks of cinnamon

6 star anise

2 teaspoons whole cloves

olive oil

2 oranges

red wine vinegar

Get your meat out of the fridge and up to room temperature before you cook it. Preheat the oven to 350°F. Peel and finely slice the ginger, then, keeping everything quite coarse, lightly crush it in a pestle and mortar with the cinnamon sticks, star anise, cloves, and a good pinch of sea salt and black pepper. Rub into the skin of the goose halves, then put both halves skin-side up in your biggest deep-sided roasting pan and drizzle with a little oil. Roast for 3 hours (depending on the size of your goose), basting every hour. After the goose has been in for 2 hours, slice the oranges and carefully add to the pan.

The goose is cooked when the leg meat falls easily off the bone. Now you've got two choices. Leave it to rest, covered, for 30 minutes, then serve up while it's hot and crispy-skinned, in which case simply remove the meat to a board, shred the leg meat, and slice the breast. Pour all the fat into a jar, cool, and place in the fridge for tasty cooking another day, such as my Best roast potatoes (see page 108). Stir a good swig of vinegar into the pan to pick up all the sticky goodness from the base, then drizzle over your meat. Serve with spuds, veg, and all the usual trimmings.

Your second choice is to let everything cool in the pan, then place it in the fridge for up to 2 days, with the goose submerged and protected in its own fat, ready to reheat when you need it, getting you ahead of the game and saving you time and oven space another day. To reheat, put the whole pan back in a preheated 350°F oven and let the goose crisp up for around 30 minutes, or until hot through, then shred, slice, and serve as above.

### LOVE YOUR LEFTOVERS

They'll be delicious shredded into a salad or stew, or used in place of leftover turkey meat for recipes in the Leftovers chapter. Blitz any leftover skin with bread crumbs, then toast, and use as an epic sprinkle.

| CALORIES | FAT | SAT FAT | PROTEIN | CARBS | SUGARS | SALT | FIBER |
|---|---|---|---|---|---|---|---|
| 487kcal | 34.4g | 10.5g | 43.5g | 1.8g | 1.8g | 0.6g | 0.5g |

# ROAST BEEF

## WITH A DELICIOUS PULLED MEAT GRAVY

Forerib is such an exciting and beautiful cut of meat to cook. The subtle seasoning of ground ginger is absolutely sublime, and with tender pulled meat and Barolo gravy on the side, this meal is a real celebration of brilliant beef.

**SERVES 12**

**3 HOURS 30 MINUTES**

1 x 9-lb forerib of beef, French trimmed, chine bone removed, cap removed and reserved, fat tied back on

olive oil

4 teaspoons ground ginger

2 onions

2 carrots

2 stalks of celery

2 fresh bay leaves

4 sprigs of fresh rosemary

Worcestershire sauce

1 glass of red wine, ideally Barolo

1 heaping tablespoon all-purpose flour

Buy your beef from the butcher, and ask for local, grass-fed, well-marbled meat. Put in your order a month in advance so they can hang the meat for you, for better flavor and tenderness. Ask for a French-trimmed forerib with the chine bone removed and the fat tied back on, and ask them to reserve the removed cap meat for you, too. Get your forerib and cap out of the fridge 2 hours before you want to cook them, to let them come up to room temperature.

Preheat the oven to 350°F. Drizzle both pieces of meat with oil. Mix the ground ginger with 2 teaspoons each of sea salt and black pepper, then rub all over both pieces of meat. Place the cap meat in a large roasting pan. Peel the onions, wash the carrots, then roughly chop with the celery and scatter into the pan with the bay leaves, rosemary sprigs, a good few dashes of Worcestershire sauce, the red wine, and the flour. Mix everything up, then place the pan on the bottom shelf of the oven. Sit the forerib directly on the bars above, so the cap pan catches all the flavorsome fat that drips out. Roast the forerib for around 2 hours to 2 hours 15 minutes for medium, or give it up to an extra 30 minutes if you prefer it more well done (if using a meat thermometer, you want to reach an internal temperature of 140°F or 160°F). Roast the cap meat for the same time.

Remove the forerib to a platter, cover with aluminum foil and leave to rest for 1 hour 30 minutes before serving. Skim away most of the fat from the cap pan into a jar, cool, and place in the fridge for tasty cooking another day. Pick out and discard the bay leaves and rosemary sprigs, add 3 cups of boiling kettle water, cover with aluminum foil, and return to the oven for around 1 hour 15 minutes, or until the meat is pullable—the time can vary depending on the animal, so use your instincts. Use two forks to pull and shred the meat in the pan, discarding any sinew and wobbly bits, then either mix the pulled meat back through the flavorsome veggies and gravy, or sieve and serve the gravy in a pitcher on the side, loosening if needed. Carve the forerib, and serve both meats with all the usual trimmings, particularly Yorkshire puds (see page 170) and Horseradish sauce (see page 160).

| CALORIES | FAT | SAT FAT | PROTEIN | CARBS | SUGARS | SALT | FIBER |
|---|---|---|---|---|---|---|---|
| 571kcal | 26.6g | 11.5g | 74.2g | 6.7g | 3.7g | 1.1g | 1.5g |

# JERK HAM

## RUBBED WITH SPICES & GLAZED WITH RUM-SPIKED MARMALADE

These days, if I'm going to do a baked ham, it's got to be this recipe. The contrast of gorgeous juicy ham with the outer crust of incredible jerk flavors and the sweet rummy marmalade glaze that finishes it off is just brilliant. Heaven.

**SERVES 16–20**

**3 HOURS 40 MINUTES**

1 x 9-lb piece of middle-cut ham (uncooked), with knuckle

1 tablespoon black peppercorns

1 bouquet garni

1 onion

JERK

3 cloves of garlic

3 red shallots

3 fresh Scotch bonnet chiles

½ a bunch of fresh thyme (½ oz)

3 fresh bay leaves

½ a bunch of fresh chives (½ oz)

1 tablespoon liquid honey

1 tablespoon each ground allspice, ground nutmeg, ground cloves

6 tablespoons golden rum

6 tablespoons malt vinegar

GLAZE

1 orange

⅔ cup golden rum

3 tablespoons quality bitter orange marmalade

Get your meat out of the fridge and up to room temperature before you cook it. Preheat the oven to 325°F. Place the ham in a deep roasting pan with the peppercorns and bouquet garni. Peel the onion, cut into wedges, and add to the pan. Pour in enough water to come halfway up the side of the pan, then cover it with aluminum foil. Bake for 1 hour 30 minutes, then remove from the oven and leave for 30 minutes, keeping it covered. Now, while it's still warm, carefully remove the skin, keeping the fat attached to the ham. With a clean utility knife, score the ham by making lots of diagonal cuts across the leg.

Turn the oven up to 350°F. To make the jerk seasoning, peel the garlic and shallots, seed the chiles, and place them all in a food processor. Strip in the thyme leaves, tear the bay leaves off the stalks, and add the leaves to the processor with all the other jerk ingredients and 1 tablespoon of sea salt. Blitz it up until smooth, then brush or rub (wearing gloves!) it all over the ham and scored fat. Bake the ham for 1 hour.

For the glaze, squeeze the orange juice into a bowl and mix with the rum and marmalade. Remove the ham from the oven, pour over the glaze, then roast for another 30 to 40 minutes, basting with a brush every 10 minutes, or until cooked thoroughly, sticky, and golden. Remove the ham to a board, ready to slice hot, cold, or at room temperature. Pour all the spicy fat into a jar, cool, and place in the fridge for tasty cooking another day.

❖

### LOVE YOUR LEFTOVERS

Use them in my Pea soup (see page 206), serve with my Bubble & squeak (see page 198), or at a party with pickles, condiments, and nice bread.

| CALORIES | FAT | SAT FAT | PROTEIN | CARBS | SUGARS | SALT | FIBER |
|---|---|---|---|---|---|---|---|
| 311kcal | 15.4g | 5.1g | 35.6g | 5g | 4.2g | 5.5g | 0.5g |

# PORCHETTA

## ROLLED PORK LOIN STUFFED WITH BEAUTIFUL THINGS

Porchetta is a thing of complete joy. You can cook this as the epic centerpiece of a big feast with all the trimmings, or serve it up on a board with a carving knife at a party with buns, condiments, salad, and gravy for dunking. Just wow.

**SERVES 16–20**
**5 HOURS 30 MINUTES**

1 x 11-lb pork loin with belly attached, skin on (ask your butcher to remove the bones and butterfly open the loin meat)

4 red onions

15 slices of smoked pancetta

olive oil

¼ cup unsalted butter

1 tablespoon fennel seeds

14 oz chicken livers, cleaned, trimmed

1 bunch of fresh sage (1 oz)

1 bunch of fresh rosemary (1 oz)

½ a bottle of white wine

7 oz mixed dried apricots, cranberries, raisins, sultanas

1¾ oz pine nuts

3½ oz Parmesan cheese

7 oz bread crumbs

½ cup Vin Santo

8 carrots

2 heaping tablespoons all-purpose flour

2 cups chicken stock

Get your meat out of the fridge and up to room temperature before you cook it. For the stuffing, peel and finely chop the onions, finely slice the pancetta, then place in a large frying pan on a medium-high heat with 6 tablespoons of oil, the butter, and fennel seeds. Cook for 5 minutes, stirring regularly, while you finely chop the chicken livers and herb leaves. Stir the livers into the pan, followed by the herbs and 3 tablespoons + 1 teaspoon of wine. Roughly chop and add the dried fruit, along with the pine nuts. Cook and stir for 5 minutes, then remove from the heat and leave to cool. Finely grate over the Parmesan. Toast the bread crumbs and use your hands to mix them into the cool stuffing.

Place the pork loin on a board, skin-side down, open it out, and push it down flat. Season generously with sea salt and black pepper, then pour over and massage in half the Vin Santo. Scatter over the stuffing, pour over the remaining Vin Santo, then roll up the pork, patting on and compacting the stuffing as you go. Sit it with the seam underneath and tie with butcher's string to secure it, then score the skin and into the fat with your knife. Season generously and rub all over with oil.

When you're ready to cook, preheat the oven to full whack (475°F). Wash the carrots and place in a large roasting pan. Sit the porchetta on top, then pour in 2 cups of water and the remaining 1⅓ cups of wine. Place in the hot oven for 30 minutes, then reduce the temperature to 350°F and leave to cook for 4 to 5 hours, or until the meat is really tender, basting now and again.

Remove the porchetta to a board to rest for at least 30 minutes. Meanwhile, place the roasting pan over a medium heat on the stove. Skim away most of the fat from the surface into a jar, cool, and place in the fridge for tasty cooking another day. Stir the flour into the pan, mashing the carrots and scraping up all those gnarly bits from the base. Pour in the stock, and simmer until the gravy is the consistency of your liking, stirring occasionally. Strain the gravy through a coarse sieve, pushing all the goodness through with the back of a spoon, then season to perfection. Carve up the beautiful porchetta, and serve it as you wish.

| CALORIES | FAT | SAT FAT | PROTEIN | CARBS | SUGARS | SALT | FIBER |
|----------|-----|---------|---------|-------|--------|------|-------|
| 725kcal | 49.1g | 16.9g | 48.1g | 19.6g | 11.8g | 0.8g | 3.2g |

# The

# TURKEY

THIS BIRD DESERVES RESPECT

# PREPPING THE TURKEY

For me, prepping the turkey a day in advance and taking the time to get it to the stage where it's ready to cook is a joy. I take real pleasure in giving this illustrious bird the focus it deserves, plus saving myself a bit of stress on the big day.

SERVES 12
WITH LOTS OF
LEFTOVERS
30 MINUTES

1 x 15-lb higher-welfare turkey (I use a Paul Kelly bird)

1 clementine

1 fresh red chile

1 bunch of fresh rosemary (1 oz)

1 bunch of fresh sage (1 oz)

12 fresh bay leaves

8 oz Meat or Veggie stuffing (see page 166 or page 168)

1 cup unsalted butter

1 whole nutmeg, for grating

12 rashers of smoked bacon

GRAVY TRIVET

optional: turkey giblets

2 onions

2 carrots

2 stalks of celery

½ a bulb of garlic

Check the main turkey cavity for the bag of giblets, and if they're in there, remove and tip them into your roasting pan, discarding the bag. The added flavor they'll give your gravy will be incredible—trust me. Peel the onions, wash the carrots, and roughly chop with the celery, then add to the pan with the unpeeled garlic cloves. Halve the clementine and chile and place in the turkey cavity with most of the herbs—not filling it too full allows hot air to circulate, cooking the bird from the inside out and from the outside in.

Place the stuffing in the neck cavity, then pull the skin back over it and tuck it under the bird. You'll get a good contrast between the soft, juicy stuffing here inside the turkey, and the crispier stuff you can bake in a dish as well.

Scrunch and warm the butter in your hands so it's soft enough to spread all over the bird, getting into all the nooks and crannies. The butter layer serves two purposes—natural basting, plus keeping the seasoning away from the meat until it hits the oven, so the bird stays nice and juicy. The butter will melt off as it cooks, adding to the flavor of the gravy, and you'll also be able to skim off that tasty fat and save it in a jar in the fridge for delicious cooking another day.

Generously sprinkle the turkey from all sides with sea salt and black pepper, pick over the remaining herb leaves and pat them onto the butter, then finely grate over a nice coating of nutmeg. Cover the turkey snugly with aluminum foil and place it on top of the trivet in the pan. You can now either leave it for 1 hour until the bird comes up to room temperature, ready to cook, or pop it into the fridge or another cold place until you need it. Have a clear down, and your prep is done.

TURN THE PAGE FOR HOW TO COOK . . .

| CALORIES | FAT | SAT FAT | PROTEIN | CARBS | SUGARS | SALT | FIBER |
|----------|-----|---------|---------|-------|--------|------|-------|
| 734kcal | 38g | 16.2g | 91.9g | 6.8g | 3.5g | 1.3g | 1.5g |

# COOKING THE TURKEY

It's game time, and your timings are key. Remembering to work out enough time for the bird to come up to room temperature, to cook, and to rest for 2 hours will determine when you start cooking and when you eat. Plan ahead!

## THE FIRST STEP IS KEY

You must let your bird come up to room temperature after being in the fridge. It'll give you more reliable cooking times, as well as juicier, more tender meat, as the bird isn't shocked when it hits the heat of the oven.

## WHY WE REST THE BIRD

Don't be under the illusion that when you remove the turkey from the oven it stops cooking. The residual heat will continue to cook the bird, giving the juices time to travel back throughout the meat, meaning a juicier bird all round. Piping hot meat is not a clever thing—warm, juicy meat, hot gravy, and hot plates is the holy grail.

Preheat the oven to 350°F. If you've made and frozen my Get-ahead gravy (see page 152), now's a good time to get it out of the freezer. You want to cook a higher-welfare bird for 12 to 14 minutes per pound, and a standard bird for 16 to 18 minutes per pound (see my Guide to roasting meat on page 382 for more info). Higher-welfare birds generally have more intramuscular fat, which means they cook quicker than standard, lean birds. If you've got a 15-lb bird, like I had here, do it for just over 3 hours, based on the guideline timings above.

Just under 1 hour before the time is up, get the pan out of the oven and remove the aluminum foil. Cover the bird with your **12 rashers of smoked bacon**, stretching and weaving them into a criss-cross pattern however you like. Return the turkey to the oven for the remaining time, or until golden and cooked through.

The simplest way to check it's cooked is to stick a knife into the thickest part of the thigh—if the juices run clear, it's done. If you're worried, use a meat thermometer. You want to reach an internal temperature of 150°F for a top-quality bird, such as Paul Kelly's turkeys, or 160°F for a supermarket higher-welfare or standard bird.

Use heavy-duty tongs to lift up your bird so all the juices run from the cavity into the pan, then transfer the turkey to a platter, cover with a double layer of aluminum foil and a clean kitchen towel, and leave to rest for up to 2 hours while you crack on.

Use your pan of trivet veg and juices to make your gravy. If you've made my Get-ahead gravy, follow the last two paragraphs on page 152 to finish it off. Otherwise, place the turkey pan over a medium heat on the stove. Skim away most of the fat from the surface into a jar, cool, and place in the fridge for tasty cooking another day. Stir **2 heaping tablespoons of all-purpose flour** into the pan, mashing up all the veg and scraping up all the sticky bits from the base. Pour in up to 8 cups of boiling kettle water and simmer until the gravy is the consistency of your liking, then stir in **2 tablespoons of Cranberry sauce** (see page 158). Strain the gravy through a coarse sieve, pushing all the goodness through with the back of a spoon, then season to perfection. Keep warm over the lowest heat until needed, adding any extra resting juices from the turkey before serving.

TURN THE PAGE FOR HOW TO CARVE ...

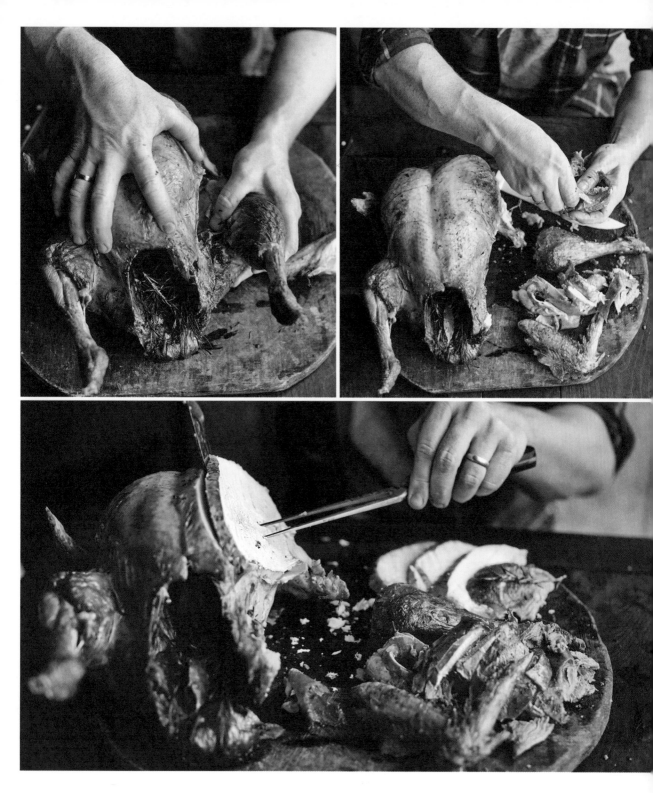

 CARVING
METHOD

Use your hands to disjoint the wings and legs, using a good, sharp carving knife to chop and help you pull them away. You can either slice or pull this brown meat—it's so tasty. Keep it warm while you move on to the breast meat. Use the full length of the knife in a smooth action to slice through the meat, transferring it to a warm platter as you go.

 CARVING
METHOD

Again, use your hands to disjoint the wings and legs, using a good, sharp carving knife to chop and help you pull them away. Now, feel where the backbone is and cut with the length of your knife all the way down beside it until you hit the carcass, and lift the whole breast off the bone. Slice on a board, transferring it to a warm platter as you go.

# TURKEY WELLINGTON

## PARMA HAM, MIXED MUSHROOM STUFFING, & GOLDEN PUFF PASTRY

A delicious alternative to cooking a whole bird at Christmas, this play on your classic beef Wellington is really tasty, looks the part, and will get everyone really excited when you cut into it. It's a little more prep, but much easier to serve.

**SERVES 10**

**2 HOURS**
**PLUS COOLING**

1 x 3½-lb turkey breast, skin off

olive oil

½ a bunch of fresh thyme (½ oz)

1 oz dried porcini mushrooms

1¼ lbs mixed mushrooms

2 tablespoons unsalted butter

3 sprigs of fresh rosemary

1¾ oz sun-dried tomatoes

1 teaspoon truffle oil

all-purpose flour, for dusting

26 oz all-butter puff pastry (cold)

8 slices of Parma ham

1 large egg

Get your meat out of the fridge and up to room temperature before you cook it. Preheat the oven to 350°F. Rub the turkey breast all over with 1 tablespoon of olive oil and a good pinch of sea salt and black pepper. Rinse the thyme in hot water to reawaken it, then strip the leaves all over the meat. Place in a pan and roast for 45 minutes, then remove from the oven and leave to cool.

Meanwhile, just cover the porcini with boiling kettle water. Roughly slice the fresh mushrooms and place in a casserole pan on a high heat with the butter and 1 tablespoon of olive oil. Add the porcini and most of the soaking water (discarding the last gritty bit), strip in the rosemary leaves, then add the sun-dried tomatoes and truffle oil (using just a little oil imparts brilliant depth of flavor). Cook and stir for 15 minutes, or until lightly golden and the water has evaporated. Pulse in a food processor until fairly fine, then season to perfection and leave to cool.

To assemble the Wellington, on a clean flour-dusted surface, roll out each pastry block to the size of a shoe box, then make one 25% larger than the other. Lay a sheet of parchment paper on a large baking sheet, dust with flour, then add the smaller piece of pastry. Spread half the mushroom stuffing in the middle, roughly the same size and shape as your turkey breast. Place the turkey on top, then use a knife to evenly cover it with the rest of the stuffing. Lay over the slices of Parma ham, overlapping them slightly. Brush the edges of the pastry with beaten egg. Lay the larger sheet of pastry over the top, then gently mold it round the shape of the breast, pushing out the air, and seal. Trim the edges to a width of 1½ inches, then confidently twist, tuck, and pinch in the pastry. Brush the whole thing with beaten egg, and either cook straight away or keep in the fridge overnight.

Cook from room temperature in a preheated oven at 350°F for 50 minutes to 1 hour, or until puffed up and golden, and the turkey is piping hot throughout—you want the internal temperature to be 160°F if you're using a meat thermometer. Leave to rest for 10 minutes, then carve into 1-inch-thick slices and serve with gravy, Cranberry sauce (see page 158), and all the usual trimmings.

| CALORIES | FAT | SAT FAT | PROTEIN | CARBS | SUGARS | SALT | FIBER |
|---|---|---|---|---|---|---|---|
| 605kcal | 33.6g | 17g | 47.4g | 27.6g | 1.6g | 1.4g | 2.2g |

# ROAST CHICKEN

## WITH YOUR CHOICE OF FLAVORED BUTTER

Here's a really solid recipe for roast chicken, using flavored butter to ring the changes, mix up the flavors, and, in turn, influence the flavor of your gravy too, as well as what you choose to serve the chicken with. I hope this inspires you.

SERVES 6

2 HOURS
PLUS RESTING

1 x 4-lb whole chicken

3½ oz Flavored butter
(see page 66)

1 lemon

GRAVY

2 onions

2 carrots

2 stalks of celery

1 bulb of garlic

½ a bunch of mixed woody herbs
(½ oz)

2 tablespoons all-purpose
flour

⅔ cup red or white wine

2½ cups chicken stock

optional: 1 teaspoon berry jam

Get your chicken out of the fridge 1 hour before you want to cook it, cover it, and leave it to come up to room temperature. Preheat the oven to 350°F.

Choose and make your Flavored butter (see page 66), then remove 3½ oz for the chicken, returning the rest to the freezer. Warm and scrunch the butter in your clean hands, then rub it all over the chicken. Halve the lemon and place inside the cavity, then sit the chicken in a sturdy roasting pan. Peel the onions, wash the carrots, then roughly chop with the celery, smash up the bulb of garlic, and add it all to the pan. Scatter over the herbs, pushing a few sprigs into the cavity.

Cook the chicken for 1 hour 30 minutes, or until golden and cooked through, basting occasionally, and turning the veg when you do so. To check it's cooked, use tongs to lift up the chicken—if the juices run clear out of the cavity, happy days. You can also check by pinching the thigh meat—if it comes away easily from the bone, you're good to go. Remove to a platter, cover with aluminum foil and a clean kitchen towel, and leave to rest for 30 minutes while you make your gravy.

Put the pan on a medium heat on the stove, skimming away most of the fat. Stir in the flour, mashing all the veg and scraping up all the sticky bits from the base. Pour in the wine and leave to bubble and cook away, then pour in the stock and simmer for 10 minutes, or until the gravy is the consistency of your liking. Strain the gravy through a coarse sieve into another pan, pushing all the goodness through with the back of a spoon, then taste and season to perfection. It's nice to balance the flavors with a little jam, then you can leave it ticking away on the lowest heat, until needed.

Serve the chicken and gravy with Baked bread sauce (see page 156) and steamed seasonal greens, or your favorite spuds (see pages 106 to 123) and veggie side dishes (see pages 124 to 147).

| CALORIES | FAT | SAT FAT | PROTEIN | CARBS | SUGARS | SALT | FIBER |
|----------|-----|---------|---------|-------|--------|------|-------|
| 789kcal | 52.1g | 17.6g | 61.5g | 14.3g | 6.6g | 1g | 2.5g |

# FLAVORED BUTTERS

Flavored butters are a fun thing to make and have available in your freezer, ready to add an incredible flavor injection to anything you're cooking: steaks, bread, fish, grilled meat, seafood, veggies, pasta—you name it, they'll all benefit.

10 MINUTES
PLUS FREEZING

Blitz up your chosen flavor combo as below, spoon it onto a sheet of parchment paper, roll it up, shape it into a log and twist the ends like a Christmas cracker, then freeze for 1 hour. Get it out of the freezer, unwrap it, and slice it ½ inch thick, then rewrap and keep frozen until needed. This means you'll be able to easily click off what you need, as and when you want it.

### GREEN BUTTER

Peel **2 cloves of garlic**, and blitz in a food processor with **1 cup of unsalted butter**, **1 bunch of fresh Italian parsley (1 oz)** and **1⅓ oz of watercress**, **1 tablespoon of jarred grated horseradish**, and a pinch of sea salt and black pepper.

### MEDITERRANEAN BUTTER

Peel **2 cloves of garlic**, and blitz in a food processor with **1 cup of unsalted butter**, 3½ oz of **sun-dried tomatoes**, **6 olives (pitted)**, **1 heaping tablespoon of harissa paste**, and a pinch of sea salt and black pepper.

### CURRY BUTTER

Peel **2 cloves of garlic**, and blitz in a food processor with **1 cup of unsalted butter**, **2 tablespoons each of medium curry powder**, **dried curry leaves**, **black mustard seeds**, and a pinch of sea salt and black pepper.

### SAGE & ONION BUTTER

Peel **2 cloves of garlic**, peel and roughly chop **1 medium onion**, pick the leaves from **1 bunch of fresh sage (1 oz)**, then blitz it all in a food processor with **1 cup of unsalted butter** and a pinch of sea salt and black pepper.

---

### JAZZ UP YOUR CHICKEN

If you're using one of these for your Roast chicken (see page 64), let what you need come up to room temperature before use.

---

| CALORIES | FAT | SAT FAT | PROTEIN | CARBS | SUGARS | SALT | FIBER |
|---|---|---|---|---|---|---|---|
| 164kcal | 17.5g | 10.9g | 0.6g | 1.4g | 0.7g | 0.3g | 0.3g |

# ROAST DUCK

### CRANBERRY HOISIN, CRISPY SKIN, CHILE, FRESH HERBS, & PANCAKES

This is a massive Oliver family favorite—everyone loves building their own pancakes, and roast duck is such a treat. I get my pancakes from a Chinese supermarket or online, but if you can't find them, use iceberg lettuce leaves instead.

SERVES 6

2 HOURS 20 MINUTES

1 x 4¼-lb whole duck, giblets reserved

1 red onion

olive oil

Chinese five-spice powder

1 clementine

GARNISHES

4 scallions

4 small carrots

½ an English cucumber

1 fresh red chile

1 mixed bunch of fresh mint and cilantro (1 oz)

1 lime

18 Chinese pancakes

HOISIN

2 cloves of garlic

2-inch piece of fresh gingerroot

7 oz frozen cranberries

2 tablespoons reduced-sodium soy sauce

2 tablespoons rice wine vinegar

2 tablespoons liquid honey

2 clementines

Get your meat out of the fridge and up to room temperature before you cook it. Preheat the oven to 350°F. Peel the onion, cut into wedges, and place in a roasting pan with the giblets and a splash of water. Rub the duck all over with 1 tablespoon of oil, 1 tablespoon of Chinese five-spice and a really good pinch of sea salt. Halve the clementine and place in the cavity, then sit the duck directly on the bars of the oven, with the pan of onions and giblets underneath to catch the tasty fat. Roast for 2 hours, or until the duck is crispy and cooked through, turning the onions occasionally to prevent them from catching.

While the duck cooks, prep the garnishes. Trim and halve the scallions and carrots, then finely slice lengthways, scratch a fork down the cucumber, and finely slice it with the chile. Pick the herb leaves. Cut the lime into wedges.

Remove the cooked duck to a platter, cover, and rest for 30 minutes. Pour all the fat from the pan into a jar, cool, and place in the fridge for tasty cooking another day. Now you've got a choice: you can make a dark hoisin utilizing the bonus flavor from the pan, or you can do it separately in a pan to achieve the vibrant color you see in the picture—both ways are super-tasty, it's purely personal preference. Using the pan, remove and discard the giblets, leaving the onions behind. Place over a medium heat on the stove, peel, roughly chop, and add the garlic and ginger, add 1 teaspoon of five-spice, then stir in the cranberries, picking up all the sticky goodness from the base of the pan. Cook for 2 minutes, then add the soy, rice wine vinegar, honey, clementine juice, and a splash of water. Simmer for 5 minutes, or until thick and glossy. Pour into a blender and blitz until smooth, then taste and season to perfection. If you're doing it in a pan, just follow the instructions above, adding a splash of oil to the pan before the garlic, ginger, and five-spice.

In batches, warm the pancakes in a bamboo steamer over a pan of simmering water for just 1 to 2 minutes. Slice the duck meat, or get two forks and ravage it all off the bone. Serve everything in the middle of the table so everyone builds their own. The crispy duck skin will be an absolute treat dotted on top!

| CALORIES | FAT | SAT FAT | PROTEIN | CARBS | SUGARS | SALT | FIBER |
|---|---|---|---|---|---|---|---|
| 734kcal | 54.9g | 15.7g | 31g | 29.4g | 12.9g | 1.1g | 3.2g |

# ROAST VENISON

### WRAPPED IN PROSCIUTTO, SERVED WITH A BAROLO, & CHOCOLATE SAUCE

This is a phenomenally delicious way to roast venison, and the method is foolproof, too. Protected by the fatty, crispy prosciutto as it cooks, then served blushing with this outrageously good, silky sauce, it's hard to beat.

**SERVES 10**

**3 HOURS 15 MINUTES**

**SAUCE**

2 lbs venison bones
 (ask your butcher)

1 red onion

1 carrot

1 stalk of celery

1 tablespoon all-purpose
 flour

½ a bottle of Barolo

1 oz quality dark chocolate (70%)

2 tablespoons unsalted butter

**VENISON**

1 level tablespoon coffee beans

1 teaspoon white peppercorns

2 sprigs of fresh rosemary

2 cloves of garlic

1 orange

2 tablespoons balsamic vinegar

2 x 1½-lb venison tenderloins,
 trimmed

14 slices of prosciutto

olive oil

Preheat the oven to 350°F. Place the venison bones in a large, deep roasting pan. Peel the onion, wash the carrot, then roughly chop with the celery, add to the pan with the flour, and toss together. Roast for 1 hour, then use tongs to transfer everything to a big pot. Add enough boiling kettle water to the pan to scrape up the sticky goodness from the base, then pour that into the pot with the wine. Just cover with boiling water, then simmer on a low heat for 2 hours, skimming the surface and topping up the water occasionally, if needed. Carefully remove the bigger bones, then strain the sauce through a coarse sieve into a pan. Simmer on a low heat to the consistency of your liking, then turn the heat off.

Get your meat out of the fridge and up to room temperature before you cook it. Crush the coffee beans and peppercorns in a pestle and mortar until fine, pick and pound in the rosemary leaves, then peel and crush in the garlic to make a rough paste. Finely grate in the orange zest and muddle in the balsamic. Cut each venison loin in half to give you four pieces, then rub the paste all over the meat.

Divide the prosciutto between two large sheets of parchment paper, slightly overlapping the slices. Place two pieces of venison on top of each other on each one, spooning the meat so the thick and thin ends even each other out. Roll up in the prosciutto, tucking in the ends, tie with string at regular intervals to secure the prosciutto in place, then put on a roasting pan.

To cook, drizzle the loins with a little oil, then roast in a preheated oven at 350°F for 30 minutes, turning every 10 minutes. Remove and rest for 10 minutes. Meanwhile, bring the sauce back up to a simmer, snap in the chocolate, add the butter, and whisk until smooth. Leave for a few minutes, then season to perfection. Remove the string from the venison, then carve and serve with the sauce. Delicious with Jerusalem artichoke and celery root mash and steamed seasonal greens.

| CALORIES | FAT | SAT FAT | PROTEIN | CARBS | SUGARS | SALT | FIBER |
|---|---|---|---|---|---|---|---|
| 298kcal | 9.4g | 4.2g | 42.2g | 5.8g | 3.4g | 1.2g | 0.8g |

# MEATLOAF

## SWEET ROASTED FENNEL, CRISPY SMOKED BACON, HERBS, & JUICES

There's nothing more comforting than a gorgeous meatloaf made with top-quality meat, lightened up with festive flavors. It's a delicious, easy way to feed a big group of people. And when it comes out in a big pan it looks amazing, too.

**SERVES 12**

**2 HOURS**

4 medium bulbs of fennel

olive oil

2 onions

2 carrots

½ a bunch of fresh sage (½ oz)

½ a bunch of fresh rosemary (½ oz)

1 x 4½-oz ball of mozzarella cheese

7 oz sourdough bread crumbs

2 lbs ground pork

2 lbs ground beef

2 teaspoons whole-grain mustard

2 large eggs

12 rashers of smoked bacon

2 cups chicken stock

2 tablespoons quality blackcurrant jam

1 tablespoon sun-dried tomato paste

Preheat the oven to 350°F. Trim each fennel bulb and chop into eight wedges, then place in a large roasting pan, drizzle with oil, season with sea salt and black pepper, and roast for 30 minutes.

Meanwhile, peel and dice the onions and carrots, place in a large pan with 1 tablespoon of oil on a medium-low heat, and cook for 20 minutes, stirring occasionally. Pick the herb leaves, finely chop half of them, and add to the veg pan, saving the rest for later. Leave the veg to cool completely, then tear in the mozzarella and add the bread crumbs, ground meat, mustard, eggs, and a good pinch of sea salt and black pepper. Scrunch and mix well, then shape into a loaf.

Make a space in the middle of the fennel pan and sit the meatloaf in the center. Criss-cross the smoky bacon over the meatloaf, drizzle with a little oil, then cover the pan with aluminum foil. Roast for 30 minutes, then remove from the oven and discard the foil. Mix the chicken stock, jam, and tomato paste together in a pitcher until smooth, then pour into the pan. Toss the reserved herbs with a little oil and scatter into the pan, then return to the oven for a final 45 minutes, or until cooked through. If the juices need thickening at this stage, simply put the pan on the stove to reduce for a few minutes, until they're the consistency of your liking, skimming away any fat from the surface, if needed.

Serve the meatloaf, sweet fennel, and juices with mash and seasonal greens.

| CALORIES | FAT | SAT FAT | PROTEIN | CARBS | SUGARS | SALT | FIBER |
|---|---|---|---|---|---|---|---|
| 448kcal | 22.1g | 8g | 44.1g | 18.4g | 9.1g | 1.8g | 1.8g |

# RACK OF LAMB

## WITH A GARLIC, PARSLEY, & PISTACHIO CRUST

Lamb like this is a total treat—it looks dramatic, and gives you tender blushing meat with an irresistible feisty crumb. It's also easy to scale up or down for two, six, or eight, just tweak the timings instinctively.

SERVES 4

50 MINUTES
PLUS RESTING

2 x French-trimmed 7-bone racks of lamb (caps, fat, and sinews removed)

olive oil

unsalted butter

3 cloves of garlic

3½ oz unsalted shelled pistachios

1 bunch of fresh Italian parsley (1 oz)

2½ oz bread

1 whole nutmeg, for grating

Dijon mustard

GREEN BEANS

12 oz fine green beans

1 tablespoon white wine vinegar

extra virgin olive oil

½ a lemon

3 sprigs of fresh tarragon

Get your meat out of the fridge and up to room temperature before you cook it. Preheat the oven to 350°F. Drizzle the lamb racks with olive oil and sprinkle generously with sea salt and black pepper, patting the seasoning all over the meat. Sear in a hot frying pan on a high heat with a little extra oil and 1 knob of butter for 2 to 3 minutes, turning with tongs until golden all over, then remove the racks to a roasting pan and let them cool.

Peel 2 cloves of garlic and place in a food processor with the pistachios and parsley (stalks and all). Tear in the bread, finely grate in half the nutmeg, and blitz into a fine green crumb. Generously brush each lamb rack with mustard, then cover with the herby crumb, patting it all over the top and sides. Roast for 25 minutes, until the crust is crisp, to give you beautifully blushing lamb. Remove from the oven and leave the lamb to rest for 10 minutes.

Meanwhile, trim just the stalk ends off the green beans and cook for 6 to 7 minutes in a pan of boiling salted water. Crush the remaining unpeeled clove of garlic through a garlic crusher into a jar and mix with 1 teaspoon of mustard, the vinegar, 2 tablespoons of extra virgin olive oil, and the lemon juice, then taste and season to perfection. Finely chop and add the tarragon leaves. Drain the beans and toss with the dressing. Carve up the lamb and serve with the dressed green beans and my Potato al forno (see page 112).

### BONUS FLAVOR

Sometimes I like to ask my butcher, when he's removing the cap meat, to trim and chop the cap. I then fry it with some finely chopped onions and flour until golden, adding stock to make a simple gravy. You can leave it chunky, or pass it through a sieve before serving.

| CALORIES | FAT | SAT FAT | PROTEIN | CARBS | SUGARS | SALT | FIBER |
|---|---|---|---|---|---|---|---|
| 693kcal | 57.2g | 19.6g | 29.5g | 16g | 4.3g | 2g | 5.5g |

# Delegation

## IS THE NAME OF THE GAME

Christmas is about everyone having fun with each other, and as the host you need to make sure you're a part of that. Delegate jobs, whether it's getting the kids to set the table and make place settings, tasking everyone with a different prep job, or asking any friends or family members who can't cook to bring the cheese or take control of washing-up duties. If everyone chips in and does their bit, you'll have dinner on the table with minimum stress and, most importantly, a room full of happy, well-fed faces.

# SALMON EN CROÛTE

## WITH AN HERBY SPINACH-STUFFED CRUST & A GORGEOUS CHEESY SAUCE

I couldn't resist the opportunity to go a bit retro and include my version of salmon en croûte here—it's such a nostalgic dish for many of us, and making it yourself is not only super-satisfying, it creates a brilliantly exciting centerpiece.

SERVES 8

1 HOUR 10 MINUTES
PLUS COOLING

2 onions

2 cloves of garlic

olive oil

¼ cup unsalted butter

½ a bunch of fresh oregano (½ oz)

2 lbs frozen chopped spinach

12 oz all-butter puff pastry (cold)

1 x 2-lb side of salmon, skin off, pin-boned (ask your fishmonger for a fillet from the top end of the fish)

1 large egg

SAUCE

1 leek

1¾ oz sun-dried tomatoes

6 tablespoons white wine

1 tablespoon all-purpose flour, plus extra for dusting

1 cup reduced-fat (2%) milk

1¾ oz Red Leicester cheese

cayenne pepper

Peel and finely slice the onions and garlic, then place in a large pan on a medium heat with 1 tablespoon of oil and half the butter. Pick in the oregano leaves and cook for 10 minutes, stirring regularly. Add the spinach and cook for a further 15 to 20 minutes, or until the liquid has evaporated, still stirring regularly. Remove from the heat, taste, season to perfection and allow to cool.

Meanwhile, make the sauce: wash, trim and finely slice the leek, then place in a large pan on a medium-low heat with 1 tablespoon of oil, the remaining butter, and the sun-dried tomatoes. Cook for 15 minutes, or until sweet and tender, stirring regularly. Pour in the wine and let it cook away, then stir in the flour and, splash-by-splash, stir in the milk. Leave it to simmer for 5 minutes, then liquidize in a blender until silky smooth. Grate in the cheese, add a pinch of cayenne, and blitz again. Taste and season to perfection, then leave to cool completely.

On a large sheet of flour-dusted parchment paper, roll out the pastry so it's 4 inches bigger than your salmon all the way round. Pour away any excess liquid from the cooled spinach mixture, then spoon it onto the middle of the pastry and spread it across the surface, leaving a 1¼-inch border at the edges. Place the salmon in the middle, then roll up the sides of the pastry to create the crust, going right up to the salmon and pinching it at the corners to secure it in place. Lightly score the top of the salmon in a criss-cross fashion, then pour the cool cheesy sauce over the fish. Brush the exposed pastry with beaten egg, and you're ready to cook. You can cook it now, or cover and pop it into the fridge overnight if you want to get ahead.

When you're ready to cook, preheat the oven to 425°F and place a large baking sheet in there to heat up. Carefully lift the parchment and salmon en croûte onto the preheated pan and bake at the bottom of the oven for 30 to 40 minutes, or until golden and cooked through. This is delicious served with a garden salad and lemon wedges on the side, for squeezing over.

| CALORIES | FAT | SAT FAT | PROTEIN | CARBS | SUGARS | SALT | FIBER |
|---|---|---|---|---|---|---|---|
| 657kcal | 43.5g | 14.8g | 37.3g | 36.7g | 7.1g | 1.2g | 2.9g |

# FISH PIE

### LUXURIOUS FISH, CREAMY PROSECCO SAUCE, & RED LEICESTER MASH

◇◇◇◇◇◇◇◇◇◇◇◇◇◇◇◇◇◇◇◇◇◇◇◇◇◇◇◇◇◇◇◇◇◇◇◇◇◇◇◇◇◇◇◇◇◇◇◇◇◇◇◇◇◇◇◇◇◇◇◇◇◇◇◇◇◇◇◇◇◇◇◇◇◇◇◇

Christmas in the UK, if the weather's not too rough for the fishermen to go out, can and normally does bring us the most wonderful bounty of gorgeous fish from cold, clean glorious waters, and this is a classic that celebrates them all.

**SERVES 10**

**2 HOURS 20 MINUTES**

1 x 3-lb whole live lobster

2½ cups reduced-fat (2%) milk

1 onion

1 large carrot

1 bulb of fennel

1 leek

olive oil

¼ cup unsalted butter

2 tablespoons all-purpose flour

2 teaspoons English mustard

⅔ cup Prosecco

1¾ oz Lancashire or Cheddar cheese

4¼ lbs Yukon Gold potatoes

2½ oz Red Leicester cheese

cayenne pepper

7 oz seasonal greens, such as kale, cavolo nero, chard

2 lbs mixed fish fillets and seafood, such as smoked haddock, scallops, salmon, bass, gurnard, lemon sole, skin off and pin-boned

10 raw peeled king shrimp

Buy your lobster on the day you want to cook it. Ask your fishmonger to kill it for you, or if you're happy doing it yourself, place the live lobster in the freezer for 30 minutes, so it's docile. When ready to cook, carefully and swiftly place the lobster in a large pan of boiling water head first, pop the lid on, and cook for 8 minutes. Remove, cool, and carefully halve the lobster, then remove the meat to a bowl—save the claws to decorate, if you like, or, even better, crack, pull out the meat, and add it to the bowl. Put all the shells back into the empty pan you cooked the lobster in and bash with a rolling pin, then pour in the milk and simmer on a low heat for 15 to 20 minutes to impart unbelievable flavor.

Meanwhile, peel the onion and carrot, trim the fennel, wash the leek, finely chop it all, and place in a large casserole pan on a medium heat with 1 tablespoon of oil and half the butter. Cook for 15 minutes, or until soft and sticky, stirring regularly. Stir in the flour, followed by the mustard and Prosecco. Let the alcohol bubble and cook away, then strain and gradually stir in the milk and simmer until you have a nice, loose, silky consistency. Remove from the heat, grate in the Lancashire or Cheddar cheese, taste, season to perfection and leave to cool.

Peel the potatoes, cutting up any larger ones so they're all a similar size, then cook in a large pan of boiling salted water for 15 to 20 minutes, or until cooked through. Drain in a colander and leave to steam dry, then return to the pan and mash well with the remaining butter and the grated Red Leicester. Season to perfection with sea salt and cayenne, loosening with a splash of milk, if needed.

Remove any tough stalks from the greens, then finely chop and sprinkle into a baking dish (14 x 12 inches). Slice all the fish into bite-sized pieces and add to the dish, halve and add the shrimp (deveining, if needed), then dot the lobster meat in and around. Pour over the sauce, top with the mash, then drizzle lightly with oil and poke in your lobster claws (if using). Bake for 1 hour in a preheated oven at 350°F, or until golden, bubbling, and the fish is cooked through.

| CALORIES | FAT | SAT FAT | PROTEIN | CARBS | SUGARS | SALT | FIBER |
|----------|-----|---------|---------|-------|--------|------|-------|
| 552kcal | 19.3g | 7.8g | 45.2g | 50.3g | 9.1g | 1.8g | 5.5g |

# FISH CURRY

### FRAGRANT SAUCE, FLUFFY RICE, & PAPPADAMS

Delicious, gentle, and fragrant, this curry sauce can hero any wonderful fish. I've kept it simple and accessible with salmon and shrimp, but you can also flake in crabmeat, lobster, bass, or whatever is at its seasonal best. Enjoy.

**SERVES 10**

**1 HOUR 10 MINUTES**

4 cups brown basmati rice

1 x 2-lb side of salmon, scaled, skin off and reserved, pin-boned

14 oz frozen raw peeled shrimp

10 uncooked pappadams

2 lemons

**CURRY SAUCE**

4 fresh green chiles

4 cloves of garlic

4 x 2-inch pieces of fresh gingerroot

1 bunch of fresh cilantro (1 oz)

4 onions

vegetable oil

1 tablespoon black mustard seeds

2 teaspoons fenugreek seeds

1 large handful of curry leaves

1 stick of cinnamon

4 whole cloves

2 teaspoons ground turmeric

2 x 14-oz cans of plum tomatoes

2 x 14-oz cans of light coconut milk

2 tablespoons mango chutney

Preheat the oven to 350°F. To make the sauce, seed the chiles, peel the garlic and ginger, and finely chop it all with the cilantro stalks (reserving the leaves). Peel and finely chop the onions, keeping them separate. Heat ¼ cup of vegetable oil in a large casserole pan on a medium heat. Add the mustard seeds and once they start to pop, add the fenugreek seeds, curry leaves, cinnamon, garlic, ginger, cilantro stalks, and most of the chile. Stir and fry for 5 minutes, then stir in the onions. Cook for another 10 minutes, or until the onions are soft and golden, then stir in the cloves and turmeric. Tip in the canned tomatoes, breaking them up with a wooden spoon, pour in the coconut milk with 1 can's worth of water, and add the mango chutney. Bring to a boil, simmer for 10 minutes, or until slightly thickened and creamy, then taste and season to perfection.

Cook the rice in a pan of boiling salted water, according to the package instructions, then drain. Meanwhile, halve the salmon and place in the sauce with the shrimp, making sure it's all submerged. Lightly rub the salmon skin with oil and lay on a baking sheet. Put the curry and the pan of skin in the oven for 20 to 25 minutes, or until the salmon is just tender and the skin is crisp and golden. One-by-one, puff up your dry pappadams in the microwave for around 30 seconds each.

Serve the curry with the rice, pappadams, the snapped-up crispy skin, lemon wedges, and the reserved chile and cilantro leaves, then tuck in.

---

### GET AHEAD

Make the sauce, let it cool, then cover and place in the fridge ready to cook the next day. Simply bring it up to a good simmer, pop in the salmon and shrimp, and cook as above. You can even freeze the sauce, reheating it in a pan with a splash of water.

| CALORIES | FAT | SAT FAT | PROTEIN | CARBS | SUGARS | SALT | FIBER |
|---|---|---|---|---|---|---|---|
| 732kcal | 32.7g | 9g | 38.2g | 76.1g | 12.1g | 1.6g | 6.3g |

# SALT CRUST SALMON

### FENNEL, LEMON, & HERBS GALORE

Baking salmon in a salt crust creates a natural cave that helps the salmon retain maximum moisture as it cooks, as well as imparting a very delicate seasoning. It's not only a showstopper, you'll get the most perfectly cooked flaky fish, too.

**SERVES 8**

**1 HOUR**
**PLUS COOLING**

1 x 4¼-lb whole salmon, gutted, gills removed, scales left on

4 lemons

1 bulb of fennel

½ a bunch of fresh Italian parsley (½ oz)

½ a bunch of fresh marjoram (½ oz)

½ a bunch of fresh chives (½ oz)

9 lbs rock salt

2 large eggs

**BASIL YOGURT**

½ a bunch of fresh basil (½ oz)

1 teaspoon English mustard

2 cups Greek yogurt

extra virgin olive oil

**CHILE SALSA**

3 fresh red chiles

1 bunch of fresh mint (1 oz)

liquid honey

2 teaspoons cider vinegar

Preheat the oven to 350°F. Wash the salmon well both inside and out, then pat dry with paper towel. Finely slice 1 lemon and the fennel and stuff into the salmon cavity with the parsley, marjoram, and chives.

Combine the rock salt, eggs, and 1 cup of water in a large bowl, then evenly spread one-third of the mixture over a large baking sheet (18 x 14 inches). Make a slight hollow in the middle to hold the salmon snugly, lay the salmon diagonally in the pan, then spoon over the remaining salt mixture, heaping it around and onto the salmon to create an even ¾-inch-thick layer all over the fish. Bake for 35 minutes. To test if the salmon is ready, push a skewer through the salt into the thickest part of the fish—if it comes out warm after 5 seconds, it's done. Remove from the oven and leave aside in the crust for just 1 hour.

Meanwhile, make the basil yogurt. Pick the basil leaves into a blender and add the mustard, the juice of 1 lemon, and half the yogurt. Blitz until smooth, then fold back through the rest of the yogurt with ¼ cup of extra virgin olive oil, and season to perfection. To make the salsa, seed the chiles and very finely chop with the mint leaves and a drizzle of honey. Scrape into a bowl, add 2 tablespoons of extra virgin olive oil and the vinegar, and season to perfection.

Lightly crack the salt casing and pull it away from the salmon, brushing any excess from the top. Gently loosen and carefully transfer the fish to a large platter. Pull the skin away, then use a regular butter knife to scrape away any darker fish, leaving you with beautifully cooked pink salmon, which you can rustically remove in flakes and lobes. Serve with the basil yogurt, salsa, and lemon wedges for squeezing over, plus your favorite side dishes.

| CALORIES | FAT | SAT FAT | PROTEIN | CARBS | SUGARS | SALT | FIBER |
|----------|-----|---------|---------|-------|--------|------|-------|
| 410kcal | 29.5g | 7.3g | 32g | 4.6g | 4.1g | 1.1g | 0.1g |

# VEGGIE
# & VEGAN

*plates*

# NUT ROAST

## SQUASH, QUINOA, CHESTNUTS, & SPICED TOMATO SAUCE

A good old faithful, nut roast has become the cliché for veggie Christmas dinners these days. So, I decided to celebrate that and share my most scrumptious take on this vegetarian classic for all of you out there who love and adore it.

SERVES 8

1 HOUR 45 MINUTES

olive oil

½ cup quinoa

2¼ cups butternut squash

2 onions

2 stalks of celery

7 oz vac-packed chestnuts

2 sprigs of fresh rosemary

1 teaspoon sweet smoked paprika

1 teaspoon dried oregano

2 large field mushrooms

1 lemon

⅓ cup fresh bread crumbs

4 oz dried apricots

5 oz mixed unsalted nuts

4 large eggs

1½ oz mature Cheddar cheese

SPICED TOMATO SAUCE

3 fresh red chiles

1 stick of cinnamon

2 cloves of garlic

½ a bunch of fresh thyme (½ oz)

2 large peeled roasted red peppers

2 x 14-oz cans of plum tomatoes

1 tablespoon balsamic vinegar

Preheat the oven to 350°F. Scrunch up a wet sheet of parchment paper, then use it to line all sides of an oiled loaf pan (9 x 5 inches), leaving a bit of overhang at the ends to help you lift out your nut roast later.

Cook the quinoa according to the package instructions, drain, tip into a mixing bowl, and leave to cool. Meanwhile, wash and seed the squash, peel the onions, trim the celery, and chop it all into ¾-inch chunks. Place in a large roasting pan, crumble in the chestnuts, strip in the rosemary, add the paprika, oregano, a pinch of sea salt and black pepper, and 2 tablespoons of oil, then toss well. Roast for 40 minutes, roughly chopping the mushrooms and adding for the last 10 minutes.

Remove the pan from the oven and tip everything into the quinoa bowl. Finely grate in half the lemon zest, add the bread crumbs, then chop and add the apricots and nuts. Crack in the eggs and mix well, then transfer to the lined loaf pan, piling it up high. Roast for 45 minutes, or until golden and gnarly.

With 30 minutes to go, make the sauce. On the stove, heat 1 tablespoon of oil in a roasting pan on a medium heat. Leaving them joined at the stalk, halve the chiles lengthways, then add to the pan with the cinnamon for 5 minutes, stirring regularly. Meanwhile, peel and slice the garlic. Scoop the chiles and cinnamon out of the pan and put aside, then add the garlic, strip in most of the thyme leaves, and cook for 5 minutes. Drain, chop, and add the peppers, pour in the canned tomatoes and 1 can's worth of water, breaking up the tomatoes with a wooden spoon, then add the balsamic and a pinch of salt. Bring to a boil, then simmer for 20 minutes, or until thickened and reduced, stirring occasionally.

Lift the nut roast out of its pan and sit it in the sauce, discarding the paper. Grate over the cheese, pop a chile on top with the remaining thyme sprigs, and drizzle with a little oil. Return the other chiles and cinnamon to the sauce. Roast for a final 15 minutes, then leave to sit for 5 minutes. Finely chop and stir as much of the chile as you like into the sauce, slice up the nut roast, and tuck in.

| CALORIES | FAT | SAT FAT | PROTEIN | CARBS | SUGARS | SALT | FIBER |
|----------|------|---------|---------|-------|--------|------|-------|
| 464kcal | 21.2g | 4.4g | 16.9g | 55.5g | 23.8g | 0.9g | 7.9g |

# CHEESE PIE

## CHESNUT PASTRY, BRUSSELS SPROUTS, & HAZELNUTS

◇◇◇◇◇◇◇◇◇◇◇◇◇◇◇◇◇◇◇◇◇◇◇◇◇◇◇◇◇◇◇◇◇◇◇◇◇◇◇◇◇◇◇◇◇◇◇◇◇◇◇◇◇◇◇◇◇◇◇◇◇◇

This super-indulgent, gorgeous homemade pastry pie is filled with a wonderful array of cheeses, which pair beautifully with our humble friend the Brussels sprout. Finished with a hazelnut bread crumb topping, this is insanely delicious.

SERVES 8–12

1 HOUR 40 MINUTES
PLUS CHILLING, COOLING,
& SETTING

### PASTRY

1 cup + 1 tablespoon unsalted
  butter (cold), plus extra
  for greasing

2 cups all-purpose
  flour, plus extra for dusting

7 oz vac-packed chestnuts

1 large egg

### FILLING

2 onions

1 lb Brussels sprouts

2 tablespoons unsalted butter

1 bunch of fresh thyme (1 oz)

1¾ oz Cheddar cheese

1¾ oz Gruyère cheese

8 oz ricotta cheese

3 large eggs

1 cup heavy cream

1 thin slice of whole-grain bread
  (1¼ oz)

1¾ oz blanched hazelnuts

Preheat the oven to 350°F. Lightly grease a deep, 10-inch loose-bottomed tart pan. To make the pastry, blitz the cold butter, the flour, a pinch of sea salt, and the chestnuts in a food processor, then pulse in the egg until it comes together into a ball of dough, wrap in plastic wrap, and chill for 30 minutes. Roll out on a clean flour-dusted surface until just under ¼ inch thick, then loosely roll up around the rolling pin and unroll over the tart pan, easing it in and pushing it carefully into the sides. Trim off any excess, prick the base with a fork, cover, and chill in the fridge for 30 minutes. When the time's up, line the pastry case with quality plastic wrap (non-PVC), then fill with rice, making sure you pack it right out to the sides. Bake blind for 20 minutes, remove the plastic wrap and rice, and bake for another 15 minutes, or until lightly golden, then leave to cool.

For the filling, peel the onions, wash and trim the sprouts, clicking off any tatty outer leaves, then run them through the fine slicing attachment on your food processor. Tip into a casserole pan on a medium heat with the butter. Strip in half the thyme leaves and cook for 20 minutes, or until soft but not colored, stirring occasionally. Remove from the heat and leave to cool.

Once cool, grate over the Cheddar and Gruyère, add the ricotta, eggs, and cream, and mix together well, then season with sea salt and black pepper. Pour the filling into the pastry case and spread out evenly. Bake for 20 minutes. Meanwhile, tear the bread into the processor, add the hazelnuts, and pulse into chunky crumbs. Take out your pie, sprinkle the hazelnut crumb over the top with the remaining thyme, and return to the oven for another 15 minutes, or until golden and cooked through. Remove and let it sit and set for 45 minutes, then serve at room temperature. Good with a fresh garden salad.

| CALORIES | FAT | SAT FAT | PROTEIN | CARBS | SUGARS | SALT | FIBER |
|----------|-----|---------|---------|-------|--------|------|-------|
| 492kcal | 32.6g | 17.7g | 13g | 39.1g | 7g | 0.5g | 3.8g |

# BAKED SQUASH

## STUFFED WITH NUTTY CRANBERRY-SPIKED RICE

Based on a beloved old recipe of mine, this method really takes advantage of stuffing and slow-roasting the sweet, versatile squash. You get wonderful flavors exchanging in the center, great textures, and the slices look amazing.

**SERVES 6**

**2 HOURS 30 MINUTES**

1 butternut squash (2½ lbs)

olive oil

1 red onion

1 clove of garlic

1 bunch of fresh sage (1 oz)

10 sun-dried tomatoes

2½ oz vac-packed chestnuts

⅓ cup basmati rice

2½ oz unsweetened dried cranberries

1 pinch of ground allspice

red wine

Preheat the oven to 350°F. Wash the squash, carefully cut it in half lengthways, then remove and reserve the seeds. Use a spoon to score and scoop some flesh out, making a gully for the stuffing all along the length of the squash. Finely chop the scooped-out flesh with the seeds and put into a frying pan on a medium heat with 2 tablespoons of oil. Peel, finely chop, and add the onion and garlic, stirring regularly while you pick the sage leaves and finely chop them with the sun-dried tomatoes and chestnuts. Stir into the pan with the rice, cranberries, and allspice, add a good pinch of sea salt and black pepper and a swig of red wine, and mix well. Fry for 10 minutes, or until softened, stirring occasionally.

Pack the mixture tightly into the gully in the two squash halves, then press the halves firmly back together. Rub the skin of the squash with a little oil, salt, and pepper, and if you've got them, pat on any extra herb leaves you have on hand. Place the squash in the center of a double layer of aluminum foil, then tightly wrap it up. Bake for around 2 hours, or until soft and cooked through.

Once ready, take the squash to the table and open up the foil in front of everyone, then carve into nice thick slices and serve with all the usual trimmings.

### CHANGING COURSES

This tasty squash also makes a delicious veggie side dish, in which case you should be able to feed about 10 to 12 people with this recipe.

| CALORIES | FAT | SAT FAT | PROTEIN | CARBS | SUGARS | SALT | FIBER |
|----------|------|---------|---------|-------|--------|------|-------|
| 300kcal | 8.9g | 1.3g | 5.1g | 51.1g | 22.2g | 1.2g | 6.5g |

# VEGAN M'HANNCHA

## SAVORY STYLE WITH PEARL BARLEY, SQUASH, & SPICES

I love the Moroccan m'hanncha (snake). It's a wonderful way to wrap up gorgeous smashed veg and grains to make a beautiful-looking dinner, while also adding amazing texture—crunchy on the outside, soft in the middle. Yum.

SERVES 8

2 HOURS
PLUS COOLING

½ cup pearl barley

1 butternut squash (2½ lbs)

2 red onions

2 cloves of garlic

2 red peppers

1 big bunch of cilantro (2 oz)

olive oil

½ teaspoon dried red chili flakes

1 heaping teaspoon fennel seeds

1 heaping teaspoon cumin seeds

1 teaspoon ground coriander

3½ oz mixed dates and dried
    apricots

½ a lemon

10 sheets of phyllo pastry

1 tablespoon unsalted shelled
    pistachios

confectioner's sugar, for dusting

Cook the pearl barley according to the package instructions, then drain. Wash the squash, then carefully cut it in half lengthways and remove the seeds. Peel the onions and garlic, and seed the peppers. Chop the squash, onions, and peppers into ½-inch dice. Finely chop the garlic with the cilantro stalks (reserving the leaves). Place it all in a pan on a medium-low heat with 2 tablespoons of oil, the chili flakes, fennel, and cumin seeds, and the ground coriander. Sweat with a lid on for 25 to 30 minutes, or until soft but not colored, stirring occasionally. Pit the dates and finely chop the flesh with the apricots and cilantro leaves. Fold into the veg pan with the drained pearl barley, squeeze in the lemon juice, season to perfection, then leave to cool.

Preheat the oven to 350°F. Lay out two clean damp kitchen towels on a large work surface, side-by-side, with the longest edges facing you. Working quickly but taking care, lay out 3 sheets of phyllo side-by-side with the short edges towards you, overlapping each one by 1 inch and brushing between the overlaps with water. Lightly brush the sheets with oil, place 3 phyllo sheets directly on top, then repeat with another 3 sheets. Save the remaining sheet for patching up.

As evenly as possible, spoon your filling in a line along the long edge closest to you. Brush the opposite long edge with a little oil. Now, I'd recommend finding a friend to help you roll it up. Working slowly and carefully, use the kitchen towels to help you roll it up and away from you into a giant cigar, keeping it on the damp kitchen towel at all times. Roll it into a large pinwheel, working quickly but handling it gently to avoid too many cracks. Gently slide it into a large greased baking sheet, and patch up any gaps, if needed. Brush all over with more oil and bake for 45 to 50 minutes, or until gorgeous, crisp, and golden. Ten minutes before the end, smash and sprinkle over the pistachios and an extra pinch of each of the spices, if you like. Serve with a super-light dusting of confectioner's sugar. Delicious with all the usual trimmings, or served with Spiced tomato sauce (see page 88).

| CALORIES | FAT | SAT FAT | PROTEIN | CARBS | SUGARS | SALT | FIBER |
|---|---|---|---|---|---|---|---|
| 363kcal | 8.7g | 1.1g | 8.6g | 67.2g | 19.7g | 0.5g | 6.9g |

# CRACKER RAVIOLI

## SPINACH PASTA, SWEET SQUASH, CHESTNUTS, SAGE, & RICOTTA

I've always thought of ravioli as the ultimate edible present—something made with love and wrapped up like a Christmas cracker. The Italians would call this caramelle because it looks like a giant sweet, but I like to think of it as crackers!

SERVES 6
OR 12 AS A STARTER
3 HOURS

### FILLING

1 butternut squash (2½ lbs)

8 oz ricotta cheese

½ teaspoon dried red chili flakes

1 whole nutmeg, for grating

olive oil

7 oz vac-packed chestnuts

½ a bunch of fresh sage (½ oz)

¾ oz Parmesan cheese,
    plus extra to serve

### PASTA

1 x Royal pasta dough
    (see page 188)

2½ oz baby spinach

semolina, for dusting

### BUTTER SAUCE

½ cup unsalted butter

4 clementines

### TO SERVE

1¾ oz skin-on almonds

Preheat the oven to 350°F. To make your filling, wash the squash, carefully cut it in half lengthways and remove the seeds, then chop into eight big chunks and place in a large roasting pan. Add the whole ricotta, sprinkle over the chili flakes and a pinch of sea salt and black pepper, then finely grate over half the nutmeg. Drizzle with oil and gently toss together. Roast for 1 hour. Crumble up the chestnuts, pick the sage leaves, toss both in a little oil, then sprinkle into the pan. Roast for another 15 minutes, or until the squash is tender and golden, and the ricotta is gnarly-looking. Finely grate the Parmesan into the pan, season and mash it all together, as chunky or smooth as you like. Leave to cool completely.

Make the pasta dough in a food processor (see page 188), blitzing the spinach and egg yolks together before adding the dry ingredients. Wrap the dough in plastic wrap and pop into the fridge for 30 minutes.

Divide the pasta in half, saving one half for another day. Cut the remaining piece in two (wrapping one piece back up momentarily), and roll out into sheets that are just 1/16 inch thick—use a pasta machine, or do it by hand with a rolling pin. Cut into rectangles 6 x 5 inches. Spoon 2 tablespoons of filling along the length of each one, near the bottom edge, leaving ¾ inch at either end. Brush the exposed pasta with a damp brush, then roll up and pinch in the sides to seal and create cracker shapes. Repeat with the remaining pasta and filling to make 24 crackers in total. Transfer to semolina-dusted parchment paper as you go.

For the sauce, melt the butter in a large frying pan, then, once foamy and starting to darken, squeeze in the clementine juice and swirl to create a creamy butter sauce. Season with pepper and keep warm over a very low heat until needed.

Cook the pasta in a large pan of boiling salted water for 3 to 4 minutes, transferring it to the buttery sauce when cooked, with a splash of cooking water. Work in batches (the first will happily sit in the sauce while you cook the rest). Finish with a grating of nutmeg and Parmesan, and a scattering of toasted, crushed almonds.

| CALORIES | FAT | SAT FAT | PROTEIN | CARBS | SUGARS | SALT | FIBER |
|---|---|---|---|---|---|---|---|
| 917kcal | 46.4g | 17.9g | 27.6g | 101g | 17.3g | 0.6g | 9g |

# ROASTED CELERIAC

## WINTER HERBS, BUTTER, GARLIC, & CREAMY TRUFFLED MUSHROOM SAUCE

Big, brave, and bold in flavor, this amazing veggie main is ridiculously simple to make. So much of the flavor is gained by leaving the celeriac skin on, packing it tightly with butter, garlic, and herbs, then slow-roasting it like a joint of meat.

**SERVES 6**

**3 HOURS 10 MINUTES**

### CELERIAC

1 large celeriac with roots (2½ lbs)

5 tablespoons unsalted butter

1 bunch of mixed fresh woody herbs, such as thyme, rosemary, sage, bay (1 oz)

4 cloves of garlic

1 whole nutmeg, for grating

### SAUCE

1 oz dried porcini mushrooms

1 small onion

2 cloves of garlic

olive oil

1½ lbs mixed mushrooms

¼ of a veg bouillon cube

⅔ cup heavy cream

1 heaping teaspoon English mustard

3½ oz vac-packed chestnuts

truffle oil

Preheat the oven to 350°F. Take pride in scrubbing the celeriac clean. Tear off a double layer of wide aluminum foil and place the celeriac in the middle, root-side up. Evenly rub with the butter (this looks like a lot of butter, but you'll remove most of it for use another day once it's done its job here), season with sea salt and black pepper, then pick and press on all the herb leaves. Squash the unpeeled cloves of garlic and scatter over, then finely grate over half the nutmeg. Pull the sides of the foil up really tightly around the celeriac and wrap up to seal. Place in an ovenproof dish and roast for around 3 hours, or until tender.

Meanwhile, for the sauce, cover the porcini with boiling kettle water in a little bowl. Peel and finely slice the onion and garlic and fry in a large frying pan on a medium-low heat with 1 tablespoon of olive oil for 10 minutes, or until softened, stirring occasionally. Finely slice the porcini (reserving the liquor), along with the fresh mushrooms, and pile into your pan. Cook for 30 minutes, or until golden, stirring occasionally. Crumble in the bouillon cube, then pour in ¾ cup + 5 teaspoons of boiling water and the soaking liquor (leaving the gritty bits behind). Simmer and reduce until the liquid has nearly gone, then stir in the cream and mustard, crumble in the chestnuts, and simmer for a further 5 minutes. Taste and season to perfection with salt, pepper, and just a few drips of truffle oil, then remove from the heat, simply warming through when needed.

For the last 10 minutes of roasting, carefully open up the foil and baste the celeriac every 2 minutes with the melted butter to give it extra color. Remove the celeriac to a board, pouring the butter into a jam jar to use another day. Carve up the celeriac and serve with the sauce and all the usual trimmings.

| CALORIES | FAT | SAT FAT | PROTEIN | CARBS | SUGARS | SALT | FIBER |
|---|---|---|---|---|---|---|---|
| 297kcal | 20.6g | 9.6g | 7.4g | 21.8g | 8.4g | 1.9g | 10.8g |

# PARTY SQUASH SOUP

## MASSAMAN STYLE WITH CARAMELIZED ONIONS, CHICKPEAS, TOFU, & RICE

This brilliant, hearty soup will go down a treat at any time of year, but a warming, spicy bowlful is particularly comforting right now. It's big on flavor and texture, and perfect when you've got a bunch of mates coming over.

**SERVES 8–10**
**1 HOUR 45 MINUTES**

1 tablespoon fennel seeds

1 tablespoon coriander seeds

5 cloves

1 teaspoon ground cinnamon

3 cloves of garlic

2-inch piece of fresh gingerroot

3 fresh red chiles

2 stalks of lemongrass

½ a bunch of fresh cilantro
   (½ oz)

2 limes

vegetable oil

1 butternut squash (2½ lbs)

4 onions

2 tablespoons chunky peanut
   butter

2 tablespoons tamarind paste

2 tablespoons tomato paste

optional: 1 tablespoon fish sauce

1 x 19-oz can of chickpeas

1⅓ cups basmati rice

1 x 14-oz can of light coconut milk

8 cups veg stock

12 oz firm silken tofu

For the paste, put the fennel and coriander seeds, the cloves, and cinnamon into a dry pan and toast on a medium heat until smelling amazing, then tip into a food processor. Peel the garlic and ginger, destalk 2 chiles, bash the lemongrass and remove the tough outer layer, then add it all to the processor with most of the cilantro leaves and all of the stalks (reserve the rest of the leaves in a cup of cold water for later). Finely grate in the zest of 1 lime and squeeze in the juice, add a splash of water and 1 tablespoon of vegetable oil, then blitz into a paste, stopping halfway to scrape down the sides and help it along, if needed.

Preheat the oven to 350°F. Wash the squash, then carefully cut it in half lengthways, remove the seeds, and chop into ½-inch slices. Peel the onions, cut into quarters, then break those apart into petals. In a large ovenproof casserole pan, toss the squash and onions in the paste really well. Roast for 1 hour.

Transfer the pan to a medium heat on the stove. Stir in the peanut butter, tamarind paste, tomato paste, fish sauce (if using), chickpeas (juice and all), rice, coconut milk, and stock. Simmer for 15 minutes, or until the rice is just cooked through. You can mash some of it up with a potato masher for a creamier texture, or loosen with a little water if you like, though it is intended to be a lovely, thick soup.

Taste and season to perfection with sea salt, black pepper, and lime juice—a touch of liquid honey can be nice, too, if you've got it. Cube up and stir in the tofu, then divide between your cups or bowls. If you're serving this at a party, simply leave it ticking away on the lowest heat, loosening with a little water when necessary. Place a stack of cups alongside it so guests can serve themselves. Serve with a sprinkling of sliced fresh chile, if you like, and the remaining cilantro leaves.

| CALORIES | FAT | SAT FAT | PROTEIN | CARBS | SUGARS | SALT | FIBER |
|---|---|---|---|---|---|---|---|
| 370kcal | 10.4g | 3.4g | 17g | 54.2g | 13.4g | 0.8g | 8.7g |

# VOL AU VENT

### CREAMY GARLIC MUSHROOMS & GRUYÈRE

Beautiful and comforting, this is a super-simple veggie main, and you could even make smaller ones to enjoy as a starter. The recipe is solid but, of course, the more exciting your mushrooms, the better the finished dish will be.

**SERVES 4**

**45 MINUTES**

all-purpose flour, for dusting

13 oz all-butter puff pastry (cold)

1 large egg

2 tablespoons raw sesame seeds

2 lbs mixed mushrooms, such as shiitake, oyster, chestnut, enoki

olive oil

2 cloves of garlic

⅔ cup white wine

1 tablespoon whole-grain mustard

¼ cup heavy cream

1 bunch of fresh Italian parsley (1 oz)

½ oz Gruyère cheese

truffle oil

Preheat the oven to 350°F. On a clean flour-dusted surface, roll out the pastry until just under ¼ inch thick. Cut out four 5-inch rounds. Brush with beaten egg and evenly scatter over the sesame seeds, then transfer to a flour-dusted baking sheet and bake for 25 to 30 minutes, or until golden and puffed up.

Meanwhile, randomly slice, chop, and tear up the mushrooms, placing them in a large frying pan on a medium-high heat with 1 tablespoon of olive oil as you go. Peel, finely slice, and add the garlic, then cook for 30 minutes, or until soft and golden, stirring occasionally. Add the wine and let it bubble away, then add the mustard and cream for 2 minutes while you pick and finely chop the parsley leaves. Stir most of the parsley into the pan, remove from the heat, finely grate and stir in the cheese, then taste and season to perfection with sea salt, black pepper, and just a few drips of truffle oil to add a subtle depth of flavor.

To serve, slice or pry apart the pastry circles like you see in the picture, then pile the creamy mushroom filling inside and sprinkle over the remaining parsley.

---

### ✤ MIX IT UP

Feel free to add a little chopped spinach or chard to the mix when you add the wine, to get your veg count up.

| CALORIES | FAT | SAT FAT | PROTEIN | CARBS | SUGARS | SALT | FIBER |
|----------|-------|---------|---------|-------|--------|------|-------|
| 590kcal | 38.8g | 20g | 14.3g | 39.8g | 2.9g | 1.2g | 5.6g |

# EGGPLANT CURRY

## BOMBAY MIX, FLUFFY RICE, MANGO CHUTNEY, & PAPPADAMS

Don't go thinking this is a dish just for our veggie friends—guys, this curry is supremely delicious, and if you're not a certified eggplant lover yet, I believe this is the dish to convert you. Soft, spiced and totally irresistible.

SERVES 4

1 HOUR 10 MINUTES

2 eggplants

2 cloves of garlic

2-inch piece of fresh gingerroot

2 fresh red chiles

½ a bunch of fresh cilantro (½ oz)

vegetable oil

2 teaspoons black mustard seeds

2 teaspoons fenugreek seeds

2 level teaspoons ground turmeric

2 tablespoons unsweetened desiccated coconut

2 red onions

2 tablespoons mango chutney

7 oz ripe cherry tomatoes

1 x 14-oz can of light coconut milk

1½ cups basmati rice

4 uncooked pappadams

1¾ oz Bombay snack mix

¼ cup plain yogurt

Halve the eggplants lengthways, place flesh-side down in a colander over a pan of simmering water, cover with a lid, and steam for 30 minutes, or until soft.

Preheat the oven to 350°F. Peel the garlic and ginger, then finely chop with the chiles and cilantro stalks (reserving the leaves). Place a large ovenproof casserole pan on a low heat with 2 tablespoons of vegetable oil, the mustard and fenugreek seeds, and the turmeric. Stir for 1 minute, then add the garlic, ginger, chiles, cilantro stalks, and desiccated coconut. Peel the onions, cut into quarters, and break those apart into petals, scattering them into the pan and adding an extra splash of oil, if needed. Cook for 15 minutes, or until soft and sticky, stirring occasionally. Stir in the mango chutney, then season to perfection.

Turn the heat up to high. Push the onion mixture to one side, then place the eggplants cut-side down in the pan for 5 minutes. Scatter in the tomatoes, pour over the coconut milk, then transfer to the oven for 30 minutes, or until nice and gnarly. Taste and tweak the seasoning, if needed. Meanwhile, cook the rice in a pan of boiling salted water according to the package instructions, then drain. One-by-one, puff up the dry pappadams in the microwave for around 30 seconds each.

Divide up the rice, then place half an eggplant proudly in each bowl, spooning over the sauce. Scatter with Bombay mix and cilantro leaves, and serve with the pappadams, more mango chutney, if you like, and a cooling dollop of yogurt.

| CALORIES | FAT | SAT FAT | PROTEIN | CARBS | SUGARS | SALT | FIBER |
|---|---|---|---|---|---|---|---|
| 635kcal | 24.6g | 9.6g | 16.8g | 93.8g | 20.1g | 1.5g | 5.4g |

# The wonderful world of
# POTATOES

# BEST ROAST POTATOES

## CRISPY, FLUFFY, SQUASHED SPUDS WITH GOOSE FAT, GARLIC, & SAGE

Simple as roast potatoes are, there's a handful of tiny, but important, details—picked up throughout my cooking career—that when combined give you this ultimate recipe, which I believe creates the perfect roast potato. What a luxury.

SERVES 10 AS A SIDE

2 HOURS

5 lbs medium Yukon Gold potatoes

¼ cup goose fat (see page 40) or unsalted butter

olive oil

1 bulb of garlic

½ a bunch of fresh sage (½ oz)

### GET AHEAD

Parboil your potatoes and dress them with the fat, garlic, and seasoning a day in advance. Simply cover and keep in a cool place until you're ready to roast.

Preheat the oven to 350°F. Peel the potatoes, keeping them whole, and ideally all about the same size (3 inches). Parboil them in a pan of boiling salted water for 15 minutes—this will ensure that the insides become really fluffy. Drain in a colander and leave to steam dry for 2 minutes—this will help the fat to stick to the potatoes. Give the colander a few light shakes to chuff up the edges of the potatoes, giving you maximum surface area for a crispy exterior as they roast.

Place the goose fat or butter and 1 tablespoon of oil in your largest roasting pan. Tip in the potatoes, add a good pinch of sea salt and black pepper, then toss to coat, and spread out in one fairly snug, even layer but with small gaps between them. Squash the garlic bulb, then lightly crush each unpeeled clove and add to the pan—this gives you sweet, caramelized garlic and adds a gentle perfume to the potatoes. Roast for 1 hour, or until the potatoes are crisp and golden all over.

Remove the pan from the oven. We're nearly there, but we've got one last application of love and care, which is the game-changer. Gently half-squash each potato with a slotted spatula or masher so they kind of push into each other and fill the pan. Pick the sage leaves and—importantly—toss with a little oil (this will transmit the flavor and make them deliciously crisp). Sprinkle the sage over the potatoes and roast for a further 20 to 25 minutes, or until golden and amazing. Heaven—you could even serve these on their own in a restaurant, they're so good.

| CALORIES | FAT | SAT FAT | PROTEIN | CARBS | SUGARS | SALT | FIBER |
|---|---|---|---|---|---|---|---|
| 216kcal | 7.6g | 2g | 4.2g | 35.4g | 2.8g | 0.2g | 4.2g |

# HASSELBACKS

## TURKEY DRIPPING, BLUE CHEESE, & CRUSHED HAZELNUT CRUMB

These sexy little beauties are super-fun to make, look amazing, loads of people will never have seen or enjoyed them before, and the flavor combination here just cooks into the potatoes so, so well. People. Will. Talk. About. These.

SERVES 10 AS A SIDE

1 HOUR 15 MINUTES

5 lbs Yukon Gold potatoes
(choose the smallest ones)

½ a bunch of fresh thyme (½ oz)

¼ cup turkey dripping
or olive oil

1¾ oz stale bread

1½ oz hazelnuts

3½ oz blue cheese

### GET AHEAD

You can cook these in advance up to the point where they're roasted and sprinkled with the toppings, then just finish them off when you're ready, ensuring that they're hot and crisp before serving.

Preheat the oven to 350°F. The fun and unique part of this side dish is that you need to slice multiple times through the potatoes, but—importantly—without going all the way through, giving you a kind of concertina-style potato. This looks beautiful but also makes them wonderfully absorbent of flavor and amplifies their crispiness. Try to choose small potatoes, give them a wash, and if you have any larger ones, cut them in half and use the flat side as a base.

To make this process as simple as possible, place a potato on a board between the handles of two wooden spoons, so that when you slice down into the potato the spoons stop the blade from going all the way through. Carefully slice at just under ¼-inch intervals all the way along. Repeat with all the potatoes, placing them in a large roasting pan as you go. Pick half the thyme leaves into a pestle and mortar and pound with the turkey dripping or oil. Spoon over the potatoes, making sure the fat gets down into the cuts you've made, then season with sea salt and black pepper. Roast for 1 hour, or until the potatoes are golden and tender.

Meanwhile, tear the bread into a baking dish, add the hazelnuts, and toast in the oven for 10 minutes. Remove and allow to cool, then tip into a food processor, strip in most of the remaining thyme leaves, add a pinch of sea salt and black pepper and half the cheese, and pulse into coarse crumbs.

When the hour is up, sprinkle the crumbs over the potatoes, then finely crumble a little bit of the remaining blue cheese onto each one. Dress the rest of the thyme sprigs with a tiny bit of oil and sprinkle randomly on top. Return to the oven for a final 10 minutes, or until the cheese starts to melt, then serve.

| CALORIES | FAT | SAT FAT | PROTEIN | CARBS | SUGARS | SALT | FIBER |
|---|---|---|---|---|---|---|---|
| 297kcal | 11.6g | 3.3g | 7.7g | 43.2g | 3.6g | 0.5g | 5.2g |

# POTATO AL FORNO

## COMFORTING CREAMY FENNEL, ONIONS, GARLIC, & PARMESAN

This is one of my favorite side dishes and, frankly, it's so good I sometimes just have it for lunch with a big fresh salad to provide a bit of contrast. It's easy to put together, and always delivers big on flavor, whatever you serve it with.

SERVES 8–10 AS A SIDE
1 HOUR 50 MINUTES

2 lbs Yukon Gold potatoes

2 onions

2 bulbs of fennel, with herby fronds attached

2½ cups whole milk

1⅔ cups heavy cream

6 anchovy fillets in oil

8 cloves of garlic

½ a bunch of fresh rosemary (½ oz)

6 fresh bay leaves

1 whole nutmeg, for grating

1¾ oz Parmesan cheese

Peel the potatoes and onions and trim the fennel bulbs, reserving any herby fennel tops for later. Finely slice the potatoes, onions, and fennel just under ¼ inch thick, with patient knife skills or, ideally, on a mandolin (use the guard!).

Preheat the oven to 350°F. Pour the milk and cream into a pan. Tear in the anchovies, crush in the unpeeled garlic through a garlic crusher, add the rosemary sprigs and bay leaves, and finely grate in half the nutmeg. Bring to a light boil on a medium heat, then immediately turn the heat off and leave to infuse for a few minutes. Fish out and discard the herbs, finely grate and whisk in most of the Parmesan, then taste and season to perfection.

In a 12- x 10-inch baking dish, layer up the slices of potato, onion, and fennel. Pour over the cream mixture and finely grate over the remaining Parmesan. Cover with aluminum foil and bake for 30 minutes, then remove the foil and bake for another 45 minutes, or until tender and nicely golden. Remove from the oven, tear and scatter over any reserved fennel tops, and serve.

### MIX IT UP

Feel free to swap out the fennel and hero other seasonal veg in this recipe, such as slices of celery root or tender celery heart.

| CALORIES | FAT | SAT FAT | PROTEIN | CARBS | SUGARS | SALT | FIBER |
|----------|-----|---------|---------|-------|--------|------|-------|
| 378kcal | 26.1g | 15.9g | 9.2g | 28.4g | 8.1g | 1.1g | 3.1g |

# CHAMP PIE

### LEEKS, WATERCRESS, CHEDDAR, & SUPER-CRISPY POTATO SKINS

Champ is a classic Irish potato dish. I've evolved that wonderful recipe here to utilize the potato skins, too. They get super-crisp and savoury, and once filled with the creamy smashed potatoes and baked are absolutely amazing.

SERVES 10 AS A SIDE
2 HOURS 15 MINUTES

10 large Yukon Gold potatoes
   (8 oz each)

6 medium leeks

2 tablespoons unsalted butter

olive oil

2 fresh bay leaves

1 bunch of fresh thyme (1 oz)

¾ cup + 5 teaspoons reduced-fat
   (2%) milk

3½ oz watercress

5 oz mature Cheddar cheese

1 whole nutmeg, for grating

3 large eggs

½ cup bread crumbs

### GET AHEAD

Make this the day before
and keep cool right up
until the point where
you're ready to bake it.

Preheat the oven to 350°F. Scrub the potatoes clean, then place them in a large roasting pan and prick each one a few times with a fork. Bake for 1 hour 15 minutes, or until golden and crisp, but still fluffy in the middle. Leave until cool enough to handle, then halve, scoop the insides into a bowl, and mash well, putting the skins aside for later.

Meanwhile, wash, trim, and finely slice the leeks. Place a large pan on a medium heat with the butter, 1 tablespoon of oil, and the bay, then strip in half the thyme leaves. Stir for 1 minute, then add the leeks. Stir and cook for 5 minutes, or until just softened, then pour in the milk. Pick in the watercress, then simmer gently on a low heat for 10 minutes, to infuse all the flavors. Turn the heat off, fish out and discard the bay leaves. Add the mashed spuds, grate over half the cheese, finely grate over half the nutmeg, beat and add the eggs, mix, and season to perfection.

Toss the reserved potato skins with 1 tablespoon of oil, most of the remaining thyme leaves, and a pinch of sea salt and black pepper. Reserving 2 potato skins for later, tear and squash the rest of the skins into a 8-inch loose-bottomed cake pan, crispy-side out, overlapping them as you go and sitting them up the sides of the pan, too—think pastry case. Don't worry if they feel a bit wobbly—start packing the champ into the center, compacting it as you go, and spreading it out to the sides. Work fairly gently but firmly, and this will help keep the potato skins in place. Keep going, packing, spreading, and piling it up until all the mash is in.

Roughly slice up the remaining two potato skins, then toss with the bread crumbs, and the remaining grated cheese and thyme. Scatter this mixture over the top of the pie. Bake for 45 minutes, or until golden and crispy. Leave to sit for 5 minutes, then release from the pan. Delicious served with salad and Branston pickle.

| CALORIES | FAT | SAT FAT | PROTEIN | CARBS | SUGARS | SALT | FIBER |
|---|---|---|---|---|---|---|---|
| 318kcal | 13.2g | 5.8g | 12.4g | 40.4g | 3.6g | 0.9g | 4.2g |

# TUSCAN POTATOES

### GARLIC, ROSEMARY, & LEMON

These tasty potatoes are a brilliant alternative to the classic roast potato or chip. Super-crispy on the outside, fluffy in the middle, and perfumed with garlic, rosemary, and lemon, they're simple and just utterly gorgeous.

SERVES 10 AS A SIDE
1 HOUR 30 MINUTES

5 lbs Yukon Gold potatoes

extra virgin olive oil

½ oz lardo or unsalted butter

4 cloves of garlic

1 lemon

½ a bunch of fresh rosemary
  (½ oz)

Preheat the oven to 350°F. Peel the potatoes, chop them into 1¼-inch chunks and parboil in a large pan of boiling salted water for 5 minutes. Drain in a colander and leave to steam dry, then tip into a large roasting pan. Season from a height with sea salt and black pepper, drizzle with 1 tablespoon of oil, add the lardo or butter, and toss together well to dress the potatoes nice and evenly. Roast for 35 minutes, or until lightly golden.

Meanwhile, peel and finely slice the garlic, peel the lemon zest into strips, and pick the rosemary leaves. When the time's up, scatter the garlic, lemon zest, and rosemary all over the potatoes, drizzle everything with 2 more tablespoons of oil, toss together, and roast for another 30 to 35 minutes, or until beautifully golden and crisp. Simple as that.

### MIX IT UP

Other veg will work a treat here, too. Feel free to chuck parsnips, carrots, celery root, or sweet potatoes into the mix, chopping them the same size as the spuds.

| CALORIES | FAT | SAT FAT | PROTEIN | CARBS | SUGARS | SALT | FIBER |
|----------|------|---------|---------|-------|--------|------|-------|
| 192kcal | 5.1g | 1.3g | 3.9g | 34.7g | 2.9g | 0.2g | 3.9g |

# BAKED MASH

## CRUSHED YUKON GOLDS & OOZY RED LEICESTER CHEESE

This delicious mash can be made in advance to make your life easier when you're cooking for big parties. In doing so, you'll only enhance that crispy-edged, oozy, mashed potato heaven with yummy bombs of Red Leicester. Amazing.

SERVES 10 AS A SIDE
1 HOUR 10 MINUTES

5 lbs Yukon Gold potatoes

½ cup unsalted butter
(at room temperature)

¾ cup + 5 teaspoons reduced-fat
(2%) milk

1 whole nutmeg, for grating

7 oz Red Leicester cheese

olive oil

Preheat the oven to 350°F. Peel the potatoes, cutting up any larger ones so they're all a similar size, then cook in a large pan of boiling salted water for 15 to 20 minutes, or until cooked through. Drain in a colander and leave to steam dry, then return to the pan and mash well. Mix in ¼ cup of butter and the milk, finely grate in half the nutmeg, then taste and season to absolute perfection.

Get yourself an appropriately sized dish and lightly grease it with a little of the remaining butter. Coarsely grate in enough cheese so you can pat it all around the dish. Spoon in the mash, randomly adding little bombs of the remaining cheese as you go, which will melt as it bakes, giving your lucky guests a nice surprise! Dot over the remaining butter, drizzle lightly with oil, then cook right away, or pop into the fridge ready to bake later. Bake for 35 minutes, or until golden and crispy.

| CALORIES | FAT | SAT FAT | PROTEIN | CARBS | SUGARS | SALT | FIBER |
|---|---|---|---|---|---|---|---|
| 375kcal | 16.3g | 9.9g | 10.5g | 50g | 3.3g | 0.4g | 5g |

# BALSAMIC POTATOES

## SWEET RED ONIONS, THYME, GARLIC, ARUGULA, & A LITTLE FAITH

These spuds really are a phenomenon. They look dark and gnarly, and they're beautiful yet kind of charmingly ugly at the same time. The volume of balsamic used here requires you to have faith. Trust me—incredible things will happen.

SERVES 10 AS A SIDE
2 HOURS 20 MINUTES

5 lbs Yukon Gold potatoes

extra virgin olive oil

4 red onions

4 cloves of garlic

¾ cup + 5 teaspoons cheap
  balsamic vinegar

¼ cup unsalted butter

½ a bunch of fresh thyme (½ oz)

1¼ oz arugula

Preheat the oven to 350°F. Peel the potatoes, cut them into even-sized chunky wedges, and parboil in a large pan of boiling salted water for 10 minutes. Drain in a colander, leave to steam dry completely, then divide the wedges between two large roasting pans. Drizzle 2 tablespoons of oil into each pan, and season with sea salt and black pepper. Toss together and spread out into a single layer. Roast for 45 minutes, or until lightly golden, tossing gently halfway.

Meanwhile, peel and slice the onions and garlic. When the time's up on the potatoes, scatter over the onions and garlic, then pour over the balsamic. Roast for 50 minutes to 1 hour, using a slotted spatula to carefully turn the potatoes in all the sticky balsamic yumminess a few times during cooking, and adding the butter and thyme leaves to the party for the last 10 minutes. In the spirit of this bonkers but genius dish, if you're in any doubt when you turn them that it's doing the right thing, just be brave and add an extra drizzle of balsamic, then return to the oven until gnarly and roasted. Serve on a platter sprinkled with the arugula.

This is amazing served as a side dish with any roasted or grilled meat, but is also brilliant as part of a Boxing Day buffet spread with cold cuts of meat. I've even enjoyed it as a lovely lunch with a big old salad. Delicious.

| CALORIES | FAT | SAT FAT | PROTEIN | CARBS | SUGARS | SALT | FIBER |
|---|---|---|---|---|---|---|---|
| 307kcal | 7.2g | 2.8g | 6.4g | 56.4g | 12.6g | 0.3g | 4.2g |

# MY POMMES ANNA

### FINELY SLICED POTATOES, ROSEMARY, THYME, & HORSERADISH

This is my take on the classic French potato cake—it's beautiful, elegant, and I've fired it up with the hum of delicious fresh horseradish and some herbs. For an extra-special finish, take a bit of time and care layering up your potatoes.

SERVES 8–10 AS A SIDE
1 HOUR 40 MINUTES

3⅓ lbs Yukon Gold potatoes

½ a bunch of fresh rosemary (½ oz)

½ a bunch of fresh thyme (½ oz)

½ cup unsalted butter

1 fresh horseradish root, for grating (or 3 teaspoons jarred grated horseradish)

Preheat the oven to 350°F. Peel the potatoes and finely slice ⅛ inch thick, ideally on a mandolin (use the guard!), or with patient knife skills. Pick and finely chop the rosemary leaves, and strip the thyme leaves into a little pile.

Melt the butter in a small pan, then generously brush it all over the inside of a 10-inch non-stick ovenproof frying pan. Take a bit of pride in beautifully arranging enough potato slices in the pan to cover the base, slightly overlapping them as you go. Brush with butter, sprinkle with a little rosemary, thyme, sea salt, and black pepper, then finely grate over some horseradish. Keep repeating the layers in this fashion until you've used up all the potatoes, keeping the last layer simple with just a coating of butter. Place on the stove over a medium heat for 10 minutes to start crisping up the base, jiggling the pan occasionally, then transfer to the oven. Roast for 30 minutes, then remove from the oven and use the flat base of a smaller pan to carefully press and compact it all down. Return to the oven for another 20 to 30 minutes, or until golden and cooked through.

When done, slide out or bang upside down onto a board or platter—both sides are so beautiful I can't pick my favorite way to serve it! Slice up and enjoy.

### GET AHEAD

Assemble up to the point when you place it on the stove, then cover and keep in the fridge until you're ready to cook, or simply make it in advance and reheat.

| CALORIES | FAT | SAT FAT | PROTEIN | CARBS | SUGARS | SALT | FIBER |
|----------|-----|---------|---------|-------|--------|------|-------|
| 199kcal | 8.8g | 5g | 3.4g | 28.2g | 1g | 0.2g | 2.2g |

# Scrumptious

# VEGETABLES

# CREAMED SPINACH

## WITH A CHEDDAR & OAT CRUMBLE TOPPING

This is a massive favorite at my restaurant Barbecoa, and it's hard to resist. Frozen spinach is not only cheap and convenient, it seems to work much better than fresh in this dish. A savoury crumble topping takes it to the next level.

**SERVES 10 AS A SIDE**
**1 HOUR 20 MINUTES**

2 onions

2 cloves of garlic

olive oil

2 teaspoons dried oregano

1 whole nutmeg, for grating

2 lbs frozen chopped spinach

½ cup unsalted butter (cold)

3½ oz Cheddar cheese

⅔ cup all-purpose flour

1 cup rolled oats

1 cup crème fraîche

Preheat the oven to 350°F. Peel and finely chop the onions and garlic, then place in a large frying pan on a low heat with 2 tablespoons of oil and the oregano. Finely grate in half the nutmeg and fry gently for 10 minutes, or until soft but not colored, stirring regularly. Add the spinach, turn the heat up to medium and cook down for 15 to 20 minutes, or until any liquid has evaporated.

Meanwhile, roughly chop the cold butter, grate the cheese, and place in a food processor with the flour, oats, and a pinch of sea salt and black pepper. Pulse into a nice crumble texture, then remove to a plate.

Put the cooked spinach mixture into the processor (there's no need to clean it), then add the crème fraîche and blitz for 1 minute. Taste and season to perfection, then tip evenly into a baking dish (12 x 8 inches). Sprinkle over the crumble and bake for around 45 minutes, or until golden and bubbling.

### GET AHEAD

Put this together a few days in advance, then simply keep it in the fridge until you're ready to bake it.

### LOVE YOUR LEFTOVERS

On the rare occasion that you have leftovers of this dish, it's amazing dotted on pizza, or blobbed into an omelet or frittata.

| CALORIES | FAT | SAT FAT | PROTEIN | CARBS | SUGARS | SALT | FIBER |
|----------|------|---------|---------|-------|--------|------|-------|
| 347kcal | 26.4g | 14.6g | 8.8g | 18g | 3.4g | 0.5g | 4g |

# ROASTED PARSNIPS

## SQUASHED WITH BAY, THYME, GARLIC, HONEY, & GROUND ALMONDS

These are the most insanely delicious parsnips. Squashing them creates the crispiest outsides and helps them to absorb all these wonderful flavors, while still maintaining super-fluffy middles. For the best results, don't peel them.

**SERVES 10 AS A SIDE**

**1 HOUR 20 MINUTES**

3 lbs medium parsnips

extra virgin olive oil

4 fresh bay leaves

1 clove of garlic

2 tablespoons red wine vinegar

2 tablespoons liquid honey

1 bunch of fresh thyme (1 oz)

2 heaping tablespoons ground almonds

Preheat the oven to 350°F. Scrub the parsnips clean, then blanch them whole in a large pan of boiling salted water for 5 minutes. Drain in a colander and leave to steam dry. Place in a single layer in a large roasting pan, drizzle with 3 tablespoons of oil, and sprinkle with a pinch of sea salt and black pepper. Toss together, then roast for 40 minutes.

Meanwhile, to make a game-changing bay glaze, rip away the bay leaf stalks, then bash the leaves hard with a pinch of sea salt and black pepper in a pestle and mortar until you have a paste. Peel the garlic and bash in until combined, then muddle in 1 tablespoon of oil, the vinegar, and honey.

Take the pan out of the oven, turn the parsnips over, then use a slotted spatula to press them all down so they almost squash into each other and completely fill out the pan. Use the thyme bunch as a brush to generously coat the parsnips with half the glaze, then separate and scatter over the thyme sprigs, along with the almonds. Return to the oven for another 30 minutes, or until really golden and crispy. To serve, loosen the edges with a slotted spatula, confidently bang the parsnips out onto a platter or board in one bold action, then drizzle with the remaining glaze.

### GET AHEAD

You can cook these in advance and simply reheat, or cook the parsnips for the first 40 minutes and make the bay glaze, then cool, cover, and pop them into the fridge until you're ready to finish cooking.

| CALORIES | FAT | SAT FAT | PROTEIN | CARBS | SUGARS | SALT | FIBER |
|---|---|---|---|---|---|---|---|
| 170kcal | 8g | 1.2g | 3.3g | 22.8g | 12g | 0.5g | 6.8g |

# RED ONION GRATIN

### GARLIC, THYME, WHITE WINE, CRÈME FRAÎCHE, GRUYÈRE, & PARMESAN

It's such a pleasure to celebrate sweet, tender red onions as vegetables in their own right and as the heroes of this dish. Serve up this gratin and it's bound to be the talk of the table, due to its ballsy flavor and incredible sweetness.

**SERVES 6 AS A SIDE**
**1 HOUR 30 MINUTES**

4 large red onions (7 oz each)

olive oil

4 cloves of garlic

4 sprigs of fresh thyme

6 tablespoons white wine

¼ cup crème fraîche

1½ oz Gruyère cheese

¾ oz Parmesan cheese

Preheat the oven to 350°F. Peel and quarter the onions, then break the quarters apart into petals. Place these in a roasting pan (12 x 10 inches) and drizzle with 1 tablespoon of oil and a pinch of sea salt and black pepper. Peel, finely slice, and add the garlic, strip over the thyme leaves, and toss it all together. Pour over the white wine, then cover with a tight double layer of aluminum foil and bake for 1 hour, removing the foil for the last 15 minutes.

When the time's up, your onions should be starting to lightly caramelize. Remove the pan from the oven and gently stir in the crème fraîche, then finely grate over the cheeses. Return to the oven to tick away for another 20 to 25 minutes, or until golden and gorgeous and the onions are starting to crisp up at the edges. Serve straight away, or cool it down, ready to flash under the broiler later to reheat.

### LOVE YOUR LEFTOVERS

Any leftovers will be gratefully received in a stew, a warm salad, or as a pizza topping.

| CALORIES | FAT | SAT FAT | PROTEIN | CARBS | SUGARS | SALT | FIBER |
|----------|-----|---------|---------|-------|--------|------|-------|
| 160kcal | 9.6g | 5.1g | 4.9g | 11.7g | 8.7g | 0.5g | 3.1g |

# GLAZED CARROTS

## THYME, CARAMELIZED GARLIC, CLEMENTINE, & HONEY

I love doing carrots like this, as the simple flavor combination teamed with the clever cooking technique gives you something that makes you go, "Wow!" Carrots are sometimes seen as everyday, but not here—these bad boys are special.

SERVES 8 AS A SIDE

30 MINUTES

2 lbs small mixed-color carrots, heirloom if you can get them

¼ cup unsalted butter

optional: 1 tablespoon dripping

6 cloves of garlic

8 sprigs of fresh thyme

2 clementines

2 tablespoons liquid honey

2 fresh bay leaves

Trim and wash the carrots, leaving a little of the green tops on so they look pretty. Melt the butter and the dripping, if you've got it, in a large frying pan over a medium heat. Crush the unpeeled garlic cloves with the flat side of your knife, then add to the pan, turning after 1 minute. Sprinkle in the thyme sprigs (they'll crackle a bit), squeeze in the clementine juice, and add the honey, bay, and a splash of water. Add the carrots, sprinkle with a good pinch of sea salt and black pepper, then jiggle the pan to coat them in all that flavor. Cover, reduce the heat to medium-low, and cook for 10 to 15 minutes, or until the carrots are tender.

When the time's up, uncover the pan and, being very vigilant, simply reduce the moisture away until you get a beautiful clementine glaze and the carrots start to catch and caramelize in a lovely way, turning often. Once you think they look great, simply serve straight away, or you can remove them from the heat and crack on with your other jobs, reheating them when needed. Delicious.

| CALORIES | FAT | SAT FAT | PROTEIN | CARBS | SUGARS | SALT | FIBER |
|---|---|---|---|---|---|---|---|
| 115kcal | 5.9g | 3.2g | 1.2g | 15.6g | 13.9g | 0.4g | 5.2g |

# BRUSSELS SPROUTS

ALL SERVE 6–8 AS A SIDE

## SQUASHED BRUSSELS
### ROASTED WITH CHORIZO & CHESTNUTS

Preheat the oven to 350ºF. Wash and trim **2 lbs of Brussels sprouts**, clicking off any tatty outer leaves. Cook for 8 minutes in a pan of boiling salted water, then drain well. Squeeze **5 oz of raw chorizo** out of its skin, crumbling it into a roasting pan with **1 tablespoon of olive oil**. On the stove, fry over a medium heat for 6 minutes, until you have ruby oil, then crumble in **3½ oz of vac-packed chestnuts**, strip in the leaves from **2 sprigs of fresh rosemary**, and shake about. Tip in the sprouts and toss in **1 tablespoon of sherry vinegar**. Squash and flatten the sprouts with a potato masher so they suck up more flavor. Roast for 25 minutes, or until starting to color. Season to perfection, bang out, and serve.

## MUSTARD BRUSSELS TOPS
### BUTTER & SILVERSKIN PICKLED ONIONS

Wash and trim **2 lbs of mixed Brussels sprouts and tops**, clicking off any tatty outer leaves from the sprouts. Cook the sprouts for 8 minutes in a pan of boiling salted water, adding the tops for just the last 2 minutes. Meanwhile, finely slice **6 silverskin pickled onions**, then place in a pan on a medium-low heat with **2 tablespoons of unsalted butter** and **1 heaping teaspoon of English mustard** until melted and combined. Spoon in a ladleful of the greens cooking water to emulsify it into a nice sauce. Drain the Brussels and tops, toss into the sauce until evenly coated, then season to perfection and serve.

## BRUSSELS IN A HUSTLE
### SHREDDED WITH GARLIC & SAGE

Peel and quarter **1 red onion**, push it through the fine slicing attachment of your food processor, and tip into a large pan on a medium heat with **¼ cup of unsalted butter**. Pick, finely slice, and add the leaves from **4 sprigs of fresh sage**, then fry for 4 minutes, or until soft, stirring occasionally. Meanwhile, wash and trim **2 lbs of Brussels sprouts**, clicking off any tatty outer leaves. In batches, push them through the same fine slicer. Add them to the pan, turn the heat up, cover, and fry for 10 minutes, or until soft, adding a splash of water, if needed. Toss in **¼ cup of Worcestershire sauce**, then turn the heat off and gun in **1 clove of unpeeled garlic** through a garlic crusher. Stir well, season to perfection, and serve.

## BRAISED BRUSSELS
### CRISPY BACON BITS, BAY, & SHALLOTS

Wash and trim **2 lbs of Brussels sprouts**, clicking off any tatty outer leaves. Cook for 4 minutes in a pan of boiling salted water, then drain well. Finely chop **3 rashers of smoked bacon** and place in a large frying pan on a medium heat with **1 tablespoon of olive oil**. Stir-fry until crispy while you peel and finely chop **3 shallots**. Stir into the pan with **2 fresh bay leaves** and **1 tablespoon of white wine vinegar**, and cook for 4 minutes, or until softened. Halve and add the Brussels and cook for 10 more minutes, or until nicely golden, stirring regularly. Season to perfection and serve.

| CALORIES | FAT | SAT FAT | PROTEIN | CARBS | SUGARS | SALT | FIBER |
|----------|-----|---------|---------|-------|--------|------|-------|
| 115kcal | 6.5g | 2.4g | 6g | 8.6g | 5.3g | 0.5g | 0.5g |

THESE VALUES ARE AN AVERAGE OF THE FOUR RECIPES ABOVE

# Nature's bounty

As well as all the wonderful seasonal fare on offer on the food front, our hedgerows, trees, and gardens will be heaving with bounty, too. Get out into your garden, take your clippers, and collect bits of foliage for decorating your fireplace, your table, your presents—you could even make a lovely natural wreath for your front door.

# CLAPSHOT

### SMASHED CARROT & RUTABAGA, MARMALADE, & LOADSA CHIVES

"Clapshot" is an old term that describes the ball-bearings in a shotgun cartridge, which are represented here by the chopped chives peppered throughout this delicious smashed veg purée. It's simple, but always a complete joy to eat.

SERVES 10–12 AS A SIDE
40 MINUTES

3 lbs carrots

1 large rutabaga (1¾ lbs)

1 bunch of fresh chives (1 oz)

¼ cup unsalted butter

1 tablespoon quality bitter
orange marmalade

extra virgin olive oil

Peel the carrots and rutabaga, then chop into 1¼-inch chunks. Cook them in a deep pan of boiling salted water for 25 to 30 minutes, or until tender.

Drain the veg well in a colander and leave to steam dry for a couple of minutes, then return to the pan and mash to the consistency of your liking. Finely chop the chives and stir most of them through the mash with most of the butter and all of the marmalade, then taste and season to perfection. Pile into a serving dish and use a palette knife to shape it into a little mountain, then rotate and indent it with your knife so it looks impressive. Put your last knob of butter on top, sprinkle with the remaining chives, and drizzle with a little oil, then serve.

### GET AHEAD

You can make this in advance—to reheat, put it in a heatproof bowl, cover with aluminum foil, and place over a pan of very gently simmering water until hot through.

| CALORIES | FAT | SAT FAT | PROTEIN | CARBS | SUGARS | SALT | FIBER |
|---|---|---|---|---|---|---|---|
| 104kcal | 5g | 2.4g | 1.2g | 14.6g | 13.9g | 0.3g | 6.2g |

# ROASTED BEETS

### GARLIC, THYME, & STICKY BALSAMIC

By roasting these beets you get the most unbelievable concentration of flavor. Coupled with the gentle sweet-and-sour acidity of the balsamic, and the fragrance of fresh thyme and garlic, whether served hot or cold they're a total treat.

**SERVES 8 AS A SIDE**
**1 HOUR 30 MINUTES**

3 lbs mixed-color baby beets

olive oil

¼ cup balsamic vinegar

1 bulb of garlic

½ a bunch of fresh thyme (½ oz)

Preheat the oven to 350°F. Wash and trim the beets, then cook in a large pan of boiling salted water for 25 to 30 minutes, or until just cooked (depending on their size). Drain, and as soon as they're cool enough to handle, peel away the skin (you might want to wear gloves!), chopping up any larger beets.

Place the beets in a roasting pan, then drizzle with 1 tablespoon of oil and the balsamic. Crush and break apart the bulb of garlic, then throw the unpeeled cloves into the pan. Add a good pinch of sea salt and black pepper and toss it all together. Dress the sprigs of thyme with a little oil, then sprinkle most of them over the beets—these will pass on their flavor in a beautiful way. Roast the beets for 50 minutes to 1 hour, or until gnarly and gorgeous-looking, adding the remaining thyme sprigs for the last few minutes so they retain their vibrancy.

If enjoying as part of a big roast dinner, I like to serve these on a bed of Horseradish sauce (see page 160) so you get that wonderful ripple of color as the beets bleed into the creamy sauce. Absolutely delicious.

| CALORIES | FAT | SAT FAT | PROTEIN | CARBS | SUGARS | SALT | FIBER |
|----------|------|---------|---------|-------|--------|------|-------|
| 103kcal | 2.4g | 0.3g | 3.9g | 17.4g | 14.9g | 0.6g | 3.9g |

# CAULIFLOWER CHEESE

## CREAMY CHEDDAR & BROCCOLI SAUCE, ALMOND BREAD CRUMB TOPPING

This is a big favorite in the Oliver household. With broccoli mushed into the white sauce and the beautiful crunch of almonds and bread crumbs on top—it's an epic combo! Remember, the better the cheese, the better the dish.

**SERVES 8 AS A SIDE**
**1 HOUR 35 MINUTES**

2 cloves of garlic

¼ cup unsalted butter

⅓ cup all-purpose flour

2½ cups reduced-fat (2%) milk

1 lb broccoli

2½ oz mature Cheddar cheese

2 lbs cauliflower

2 slices of ciabatta or stale bread

2 sprigs of fresh thyme

olive oil

1 oz flaked almonds

Preheat the oven to 350°F. To make the sauce, peel and finely slice the garlic and put it into a pan on a medium heat with the butter. When the butter has melted, stir in the flour for 1 minute to make a paste, then gradually add the milk, whisking as you go, until smooth and starting to thicken. Roughly chop and add the broccoli to the pan and simmer for around 20 minutes, then mash or blitz with an immersion blender until fairly smooth. Grate in half the Cheddar, mix well, taste, and season to perfection.

Snap off and wash the cauliflower leaves, discarding any tatty ones, then cut the center into florets, slicing up the stalk. Arrange it all in an appropriately sized baking dish, letting any leaves hang beautifully over the edge. Pour over the broccoli sauce and grate over the remaining Cheddar. In a food processor, blitz the bread and thyme leaves into rough crumbs with 1 tablespoon of oil and a pinch of sea salt and black pepper, then pulse in the almonds so they retain a nice bit of texture. Scatter the topping evenly over the cauliflower cheese and bake for 50 minutes to 1 hour, or until golden and cooked through, then enjoy!

### MIX IT UP

It's good fun to play around with different cheeses in this dish and see how they taste and melt, so this is a great one for using up any leftovers from your Christmas cheeseboard. It's also nice to try different veg instead of cauliflower—for instance, ¾- to 1¼-inch chunks of celery root, squash, potatoes, or leeks would all work a treat. Just remember, some veg might take longer to cook than others, so test with a knife to check they're cooked through before serving.

| CALORIES | FAT | SAT FAT | PROTEIN | CARBS | SUGARS | SALT | FIBER |
|---|---|---|---|---|---|---|---|
| 270kcal | 15.4g | 6.8g | 14.6g | 19.4g | 8.2g | 0.6g | 4.4g |

# RED CABBAGE

## CRISPY SMOKED BACON & ROSEMARY, APPLE, FENNEL SEEDS, & BALSAMIC

◇◇◇◇◇◇◇◇◇◇◇◇◇◇◇◇◇◇◇◇◇◇◇◇◇◇◇◇◇◇◇◇◇◇◇◇◇◇◇◇◇◇◇◇◇◇◇◇◇◇◇◇◇◇◇◇◇

Celebrating one of the most affordable veg out there—the humble red cabbage—this is a really delicious, classic veg dish. Wonderful as it is hot, I also love it cold, almost like a salad, with meat and cheese, so embrace those leftovers.

SERVES 8–10 AS A SIDE
35 MINUTES

1 red cabbage (2 lbs)

4 rashers of smoked bacon

olive oil

2 eating apples

2 sprigs of fresh rosemary

1 heaping teaspoon fennel seeds

3½ oz dried prunes

1 clementine

6 tablespoons balsamic vinegar

Click away any tatty outer leaves from your cabbage, trim off the base, cut the cabbage into wedges, then finely slice it and put aside. Finely slice the bacon and place in a large casserole pan on a medium heat with 1 tablespoon of oil. Leave it to crisp up while you peel, core, and dice the apples.

When the bacon is crispy, strip the rosemary leaves into the pan, stir for 1 minute, then use a slotted spoon to remove the bacon and rosemary to a plate, leaving the smoky bacon fat behind. Add the fennel seeds and diced apples to the pan, then tear in the prunes, removing any pits. Stir and fry for 2 minutes, then finely grate in the clementine zest and squeeze in the juice. Add the vinegar, cabbage, and a pinch of sea salt and black pepper. Cook with the lid ajar on a low heat for 20 to 25 minutes, or until cooked through and a pleasure to eat, stirring well every 5 minutes to help intensify and mix up the flavors. Serve sprinkled with the crispy bacon and rosemary leaves.

### GET AHEAD

Make this the day before and simply reheat it in a pan—it'll taste great, but if you do this I'd recommend stirring the bacon and rosemary through it rather than serving them on top as a garnish.

| CALORIES | FAT | SAT FAT | PROTEIN | CARBS | SUGARS | SALT | FIBER |
|----------|-----|---------|---------|-------|--------|------|-------|
| 96kcal | 2.6g | 0.4g | 2.4g | 16.2g | 15.6g | 0.4g | 3g |

# PUMPKIN PURÉE

## MARSHMALLOWS, MAPLE SYRUP, SPICES, & THYME

Pumpkin and marshmallows is a North American Thanksgiving classic. It might sound like a crazy combo, but it's delicious. I'm using sweet squash here, and I've stripped the mallows back so you can taste all the wonderful flavors.

2 butternut squash (2½ lbs each)

1 teaspoon coriander seeds

1 teaspoon fennel seeds

½ teaspoon sweet paprika

2 pinches of ground cinnamon

2 tablespoons unsalted butter

2 tablespoons maple syrup

3½ oz marshmallows

6 sprigs of fresh thyme

olive oil

Preheat the oven to 350°F. Place both whole squash in a roasting pan and bake them for 1 hour 30 minutes, or until soft and cooked through, then remove and leave until cool enough to handle.

In a pestle and mortar, pound up the coriander and fennel seeds, the paprika, cinnamon, and a good pinch of sea salt and black pepper until fine. Toast the spices in a large frying pan on a medium heat for 30 seconds, then add the butter and maple syrup and let it very gently bubble away while you halve each squash lengthways, scoop out and discard the seeds, then spoon the flesh off the skin, keeping it nice and chunky. Gently fold the squash flesh into the pan (discarding the skin), trying not to break it up too much so you get a range of textures. Reduce to a low heat and leave it to tick away for 5 minutes, stirring occasionally.

Transfer the mixture to an appropriately sized baking dish, then randomly poke the marshmallows into the top. Pick the thyme leaves, toss lightly with oil, and sprinkle over the dish from a height. Pop into the oven for 30 minutes, or until gorgeously golden and the marshmallows have melted. Yum.

| CALORIES | FAT | SAT FAT | PROTEIN | CARBS | SUGARS | SALT | FIBER |
|---|---|---|---|---|---|---|---|
| 107kcal | 3g | 1.4g | 1.8g | 19.7g | 13.2g | 0.1g | 2.1g |

# GRAVY, SAUCES,
## & all the trimmings

# DARK BONE GRAVY

## RED WINE, MARMITE, ENGLISH MUSTARD, & REDCURRANT JELLY

This is a serious gravy for serious gravy lovers. It's very easy, but it does require a little investment of time, which in turn allows you to harness incredible depth of flavor from roasted beef bones and all our favorite condiments.

**MAKES 6 CUPS**
**4 HOURS 30 MINUTES**

4½ lbs beef bones (ask your butcher to cut them up for you)

2 onions

2 stalks of celery

2 heaping tablespoons all-purpose flour

8 cups quality beef stock

2 cups Bordeaux

2 teaspoons Marmite

2 tablespoons Worcestershire sauce

2 tablespoons redcurrant jelly

2 teaspoons English mustard

Preheat the oven to 350°F. Place the beef bones in your largest deep roasting pan. Roughly chop the unpeeled onions with the celery and add to the pan. Sprinkle over the flour, toss to coat, and roast for 2 hours. Give everything a shake halfway through, also adding a splash of water.

Remove the pan from the oven and use tongs to transfer all the bones to a big pot, then pour over the stock and place on a low heat. Place the roasting pan over a medium heat on the stove. Skim away most of the fat from the surface into a jar, cool, and place in the fridge for tasty cooking another day. Pour the wine into the pan, bring to a boil, scraping up all the sticky goodness from the base, then pour the contents of the pan into the stockpot and add all the remaining ingredients. Leave it to bubble and reduce on a medium heat for around 2 hours, or until the gravy is the consistency of your liking, skimming the surface occasionally.

Carefully remove the bigger bones, then strain the gravy through a coarse sieve into another pan, season to perfection, then either keep warm on the lowest heat until needed, or cool and pop into the fridge to reheat another day, discarding any fat that settles on the top before reheating.

| CALORIES | FAT | SAT FAT | PROTEIN | CARBS | SUGARS | SALT | FIBER |
|---|---|---|---|---|---|---|---|
| 155kcal | 7.2g | 3.2g | 13.8g | 4.2g | 2g | 0.3g | 0.6g |

# GET-AHEAD GRAVY

## PERFECT FOR YOUR BIG-DAY TURKEY

Good gravy has the power to transform, or even save, a meal. This year, open your mind to a slightly radical idea: make your gravy a few days, or even weeks, in advance, simply reheating it in your turkey pan on the big day. Stress saved.

MAKES 4 CUPS
2 HOURS
PLUS COOLING
& DEFROSTING

2 onions

2 carrots

2 stalks of celery

2 rashers of smoked bacon

2 fresh bay leaves

2 sprigs of fresh sage

2 sprigs of fresh rosemary

2 star anise

10 chicken wings

olive oil

optional: ¼ cup sherry or port

¼ cup all-purpose flour

2 tablespoons Cranberry sauce
(see page 158)

Preheat the oven to 350°F. Peel the onions, wash the carrots, then roughly chop with the celery and bacon. Put the veg, bay leaves, sage, rosemary, and star anise into a sturdy high-sided roasting pan, then scatter the chopped bacon on top. Break the chicken wings open, bash with a rolling pin to help release extra flavor as they cook, then add to the pan. Drizzle with oil, season with sea salt and black pepper, toss, then cook for 1 hour, or until tender.

Remove the pan from the oven and transfer to a low heat on the stove. Really grind and mash everything with a potato masher, scraping up all the goodness from the base of the pan (the longer you let it fry, the darker your gravy will be). If you want to add sherry or port, now's the time to do so; just leave it to cook away for a few minutes. Gradually stir in the flour, then pour in 8 cups of boiling kettle water. Simmer for 30 minutes, or until thickened and reduced, stirring occasionally.

When the gravy is the consistency of your liking, pour it through a coarse sieve into a large bowl, pushing all the goodness through with the back of a spoon. Taste and season to perfection, cool to room temperature, then pour into containers or bags and pop into the fridge or freezer, ready to finish off on Christmas Day.

If frozen, take the gravy out to defrost when your turkey goes into the oven. When the turkey's perfectly cooked, remove it to a platter to rest for up to 2 hours, covered with a double layer of aluminum foil and a clean kitchen towel. Skim away most of the fat from the pan, cool, and place into a jar in the fridge for tasty cooking another day. Pour your Get-ahead gravy into the pan with the rest of the turkey juices. Bring to a boil over the stove and scrape up all those sticky bits from the base. Have a taste, then stir in the Cranberry sauce to balance the flavors.

Once your gravy is piping hot, carefully strain through a coarse sieve into a pan, then leave it on the lowest heat until you're ready to serve. Skim away any fat that rises to the top, and add any extra resting juices from the turkey before serving.

| CALORIES | FAT | SAT FAT | PROTEIN | CARBS | SUGARS | SALT | FIBER |
|---|---|---|---|---|---|---|---|
| 231kcal | 12.1g | 3.2g | 19.3g | 12.1g | 5g | 0.6g | 1.8g |

# VEGAN GRAVY

## RICH, DELICIOUS, SILKY, & SMOOTH

Achieving big flavor by slowly frying veg with dried porcini for added depth, we're drawing on our favorite pantry condiments and port here to ensure we deliver an epic gravy for our veggie and vegan friends.

MAKES APPROX. 3⅓ CUPS
1 HOUR

2 onions

2 carrots

2 stalks of celery

1 oz dried porcini mushrooms

olive oil

2 fresh bay leaves

2 sprigs of fresh thyme

2 tablespoons port

2 teaspoons quality
   blackcurrant jam

2 tablespoons all-purpose flour

2 teaspoons Marmite

2 tablespoons tomato paste

2 tablespoons red wine vinegar

6 cups veg stock

Peel the onions, wash the carrots, then roughly chop with the celery and porcini, and place in a large pan on a medium heat with 1 tablespoon of oil, the bay, and thyme. Fry for around 25 minutes, or until turning golden, stirring occasionally.

Add the port and jam to the pan and, once reduced, stir in the flour, followed by the Marmite, tomato paste, and vinegar. Pour in the stock, bring to a boil, then reduce to a simmer for around 10 minutes, or until thickened and reduced to the consistency of your liking.

Pass the gravy through a coarse sieve into another pan, pushing all the goodness through with the back of a spoon. Taste and season to perfection, then serve right away or keep warm over the lowest heat until needed.

### GET AHEAD

Make this in advance and simply keep in the fridge
for up to 5 days, ready to reheat when needed,
loosening with a splash more stock, if required.

| CALORIES | FAT | SAT FAT | PROTEIN | CARBS | SUGARS | SALT | FIBER |
|---|---|---|---|---|---|---|---|
| 105kcal | 2.7g | 0.3g | 4g | 16.3g | 11g | 0.2g | 2g |

# BAKED BREAD SAUCE

## SWEET TENDER ONIONS, ENGLISH MUSTARD, CLOVES, BUTTER, & BAY

Well, who would have thought bread sauce could be so extraordinary? Gone are the days of regular bread sauce—this recipe is more like an awesome savoury bread and butter pudding, with sweet onions and the gentle heat of mustard.

SERVES 8

1 HOUR 10 MINUTES

2 onions

6 cups reduced-fat (2%) milk

3 teaspoons English mustard

3 cloves

3 fresh bay leaves

1 whole nutmeg, for grating

2 tablespoons unsalted butter

1 rustic loaf of white bread
   (14 oz)

Preheat the oven to 350°F. Peel and finely slice the onions. Place them in a large pan with the milk, mustard, cloves, and bay. Simmer on a low heat for 20 minutes, so the flavors infuse and the onions soften, stirring occasionally.

Scoop out and discard the cloves, then season the milk mixture with sea salt and black pepper, finely grate in half the nutmeg, and stir in the butter. Tear the bread into 1-inch chunks and stir into the pan, then transfer it all to a baking dish (12 x 8 inches). Press it down into the dish and bake for around 40 minutes, or until golden and crispy at the edges but smooth and silky in the middle.

Serve hot or warm. It's the ultimate accompaniment to your roast turkey on Christmas Day, of course, but it also goes really well with roasted chicken and all game birds, and, to be honest, pretty much anything else you care to pair it with!

### GET AHEAD

This can be put together on Christmas Eve, ready to bake on the big day.

| CALORIES | FAT | SAT FAT | PROTEIN | CARBS | SUGARS | SALT | FIBER |
|---|---|---|---|---|---|---|---|
| 241kcal | 7g | 3.4g | 11g | 36.6g | 12g | 1.3g | 1.4g |

# CRANBERRY SAUCE

BURNT BUTTER, MAPLE SYRUP, APPLE, THYME, & SPICED RUM

Cranberry sauce is a great thing to make at this time of year. It's not only good with roasted meats but can be used in gravies, stews, or even a sweet dessert, like my Frangipane tart on page 244—leftovers need never go to waste!

SERVES 8–10

20 MINUTES

4 eating apples

⅓ cup unsalted butter

2 tablespoons maple syrup

4 sprigs of fresh thyme

10 oz fresh or frozen cranberries

3 tablespoons quality spiced rum

Peel and core the apples, then roughly chop and put aside. Melt the butter in a large pan on a medium heat until golden and bubbling. Stir in the maple syrup and when it's just beginning to lightly caramelize, strip in the thyme leaves and add the apples, cranberries, and spiced rum. Leave to cook and reduce with the lid on for around 15 minutes, or until the apples have softened and the sauce is nice and thick. Keep an eye on it and stir occasionally, adding a splash of water to loosen or removing the lid for the last few minutes to let it thicken up—it's your responsibility to get it to the consistency of your liking.

Have a little taste—I like the balance between natural sweetness and acidity, as it really helps to cut through the richness of the meat you're serving it with, but add a touch more maple syrup, if you want to. Transfer it to a serving bowl, let it cool to room temperature, then cover and chill in the fridge, until needed.

### GET GIFTING

Cranberry sauce makes a great gift—feel free to double or triple the recipe, decant while hot into sterilized jars (see page 312), and give to family and friends. It's delicious and will save them a job, too. It keeps happily in the fridge for a good few weeks.

| CALORIES | FAT | SAT FAT | PROTEIN | CARBS | SUGARS | SALT | FIBER |
|----------|-----|---------|---------|-------|--------|------|-------|
| 81kcal | 4.3g | 2.5g | 0.4g | 8.1g | 7.9g | 0g | 1.8g |

# HORSERADISH SAUCE

FIERY FRESH HORSERADISH, VINEGAR, & CRÈME FRAÎCHE

SERVES 12
10 MINUTES

Finely grate **3½ oz of fresh horseradish** onto a plate. Add **7 oz of half-fat crème fraîche**.
Season really well with sea salt, add a splash of **red wine vinegar**, and mix together well.
Taste, adjust the seasoning and the fieriness, then spoon across the plate to cover. Finely
grate over a little more fresh horseradish, drizzle with good **extra virgin olive oil**, and serve.

# MINT SAUCE

FRAGRANT FRESH MINT, RED WINE VINEGAR, SALT, & SUGAR

SERVES 12
10 MINUTES

Pick the leaves from **3 bunches of fresh mint (1 oz each)** into a blender. Add 2 good pinches of sea salt and **2 teaspoons of superfine sugar**, pour over 6 tablespoons of boiling kettle water, and leave for 1 minute. Add 3 **tablespoons of red wine vinegar**, then blitz to the consistency of your liking. Taste and season to perfection, adding good **extra virgin olive oil** to taste.

# PIGS IN BLANKETS

## GONE CRAZY . . .

Pigs in blankets are genius, but lots of clever combos, when wrapped in bacon, are equally delicious. Why don't you mix it up this year and get people talking? I've given you lots of ideas here, so pick your favorites and have fun with them.

EACH COMBO MAKES
1 PARCEL
30 MINUTES

Lay **1 rasher of smoked bacon**—and it must be smoked—on a board and run the side of your knife along it to flatten it out, meaning you can chop it in the middle and use half a rasher for each blanket. Place your filling on top, then roll and wrap it up, lining them up in an oiled roasting pan as you go. Cook in a preheated oven at 350°F for around 20 minutes, or until golden and cooked through, then serve.

TEAM ½ A RASHER OF BACON WITH . . .

- 1 knob of Brie-style cheese—1 shelled walnut half—1 fresh thyme tip

- ½ a cleaned chicken liver—1 fresh sage leaf—½ a dried apricot

- 1 freshly shucked oyster—1 slice of pickled onion—1 pinch of dried red chili flakes

- 1 pitted dried prune—a crumbling of blue cheese—2 chopped fresh rosemary leaves

- 1 fresh sage leaf—1 small slice of black pudding

- 1 fresh sage leaf—1 cocktail sausage

- 1 cube of crustless bread—2 fresh rosemary leaves

- 1 pitted date—2 crumbled blanched hazelnuts—1 drizzle of liquid honey

- 1 piece of torn ricotta or firm goat's cheese—slices of fresh red chile

- 1 wedge of ripe pear—a few dried cranberries—1 fresh thyme tip

- ½ a torn ripe fig stuffed with pine nuts—1 drizzle of liquid honey

- 1 little quenelle or ball of stuffing—2 scrapings of nutmeg

# MEAT STUFFING

## SWEET ONIONS, LEEKS, SAGE, SMOKY BACON, CHESTNUTS, & PORK SHOULDER

Everyone loves a good stuffing. The flavor from free-range pork shoulder is far more delicious than sausage meat—any good butcher will be able to grind this up for you—and with the slow-cooked onions and leeks, it's a total joy to eat.

**SERVES 10**
**1 HOUR 15 MINUTES**
**PLUS COOLING**

2 onions

2 leeks

1 bunch of fresh sage (1 oz)

olive oil

¼ cup unsalted butter

4 rashers of smoked bacon

1 whole nutmeg, for grating

14 oz stale bread

7 oz vac-packed chestnuts

2 lbs ground pork shoulder

1 x 15-oz can of peaches, in juice

1 clementine

Peel the onions, wash and trim the leeks, then finely chop them (saving the green leek tops for soup or stew). Pick the sage leaves, keep 2 nice big ones aside, then finely slice the rest. Place a large frying pan on a medium heat with 1 tablespoon of oil and the butter. Finely slice and add the bacon, fry until lightly golden, then stir in the sliced sage, followed by the onions and leeks. Finely grate in half the nutmeg, add a good pinch of sea salt and black pepper, and cook for 15 minutes, or until soft, stirring occasionally. Leave to cool.

Toast the bread, then whiz it to crumbs in a food processor with the chestnuts and tip into a large bowl. Add the cooled onion mixture, the ground pork shoulder, and drained peaches. Using your hands, really squash and squidge everything until well mixed. Put 8 oz of the stuffing mixture aside to stuff the neck of your turkey (see page 54), then pack the rest into an appropriately sized oiled baking dish. Flatten it down and use your hands to almost tuck the stuffing into the dish, so it mounds up in the middle. Halve the clementine, then push the halves into the top of the stuffing, cut-side up, placing 1 reserved sage leaf on each half. Drizzle with 1 more tablespoon of oil and, when needed, bake in a preheated oven at 350°F for 50 minutes, or until golden, gnarly, and cooked through.

### MIX IT UP

Feel free to add some ground game to this story, or even a handful of chopped chicken livers, for a nice variation.

### LOVE YOUR LEFTOVERS

Use them in my epic Toad in the hole (see page 176), or slice almost like a terrine and serve with cheese, bread, and pickles.

| CALORIES | FAT | SAT FAT | PROTEIN | CARBS | SUGARS | SALT | FIBER |
| --- | --- | --- | --- | --- | --- | --- | --- |
| 429kcal | 19.5g | 7.2g | 25.2g | 40.7g | 9.9g | 0.9g | 3.7g |

# VEGGIE STUFFING

## CARAMELIZED SQUASH, RED ONIONS, SAGE, CRANBERRIES, & PISTACHIOS

I love baking this beautiful veggie stuffing in a pudding bowl—it looks amazing and will get everyone really excited when you bring it to the table. It's open to the introduction of different nuts and dried fruits, so feel free to mix it up.

SERVES 8

2 HOURS
PLUS COOLING

1 small butternut squash (2 lbs)

2 red onions

olive oil

1 pinch of ground cinnamon

1 teaspoon ground coriander

1 whole nutmeg, for grating

1 bunch of fresh sage (1 oz)

1¾ oz unsweetened dried
  cranberries

1¾ oz unsalted shelled pistachios

1 lb stale bread

1¼ cups reduced-fat (2%) milk

Preheat the oven to 350°F. Wash the squash, then carefully quarter it lengthways and remove the seeds, placing the squash in a roasting pan, skin-side down. Peel, quarter, and scatter over the onions, drizzle with 1 tablespoon of oil, add the cinnamon, ground coriander, and a pinch of sea salt and black pepper, finely grate over half the nutmeg, then toss together. Roast for 40 minutes, then remove from the oven. Pick and roughly chop the sage leaves with the cranberries and pistachios, toss with a light drizzle of oil, then scatter over the squash and onions. Roast for another 5 minutes, then remove and leave to cool.

Tear the bread into a bowl, pour over the milk, and leave to soak for a few minutes. Squeeze out any excess milk, then pinch and tear the bread into the pan of cooled veg. Using your hands, really squash and squidge everything together with another pinch of sea salt and black pepper until well mixed.

Line a 6-cup pudding bowl with a scrunched-up sheet of wet, oiled parchment paper (or you can use a baking dish to give you a greater surface area for a crispy top, if you prefer). Pack in the stuffing and drizzle with 1 more tablespoon of oil, then cover with parchment paper, tying it in place with string. Bake for 1 hour to 1 hour 10 minutes, or until golden and gnarly. Use the parchment paper to help you lift it out of the bowl, then confidently flip it onto a plate and serve.

### GET AHEAD

Make this in advance up to the stage where it's ready to bake. You can use 8 oz of this stuffing in your turkey, should you so wish.

| CALORIES | FAT | SAT FAT | PROTEIN | CARBS | SUGARS | SALT | FIBER |
|---|---|---|---|---|---|---|---|
| 295kcal | 14.5g | 4.7g | 14.8g | 27.8g | 5.5g | 1.6g | 1.8g |

# YORKSHIRE PUDS

LIGHT, CRISPY, FLUFFY, AIRY PILLOWS OF JOY

I love making Yorkshire puddings—they're fantastic with any roast dinner, especially good stuffed with smoked salmon, watercress, and horseradish sauce, and you can even serve them with jam as a fun breakfast element or a naughty treat.

MAKES 12

30 MINUTES
PLUS RESTING

⅔ cup all-purpose flour

3 large eggs

1 cup reduced-fat (2%) milk

sunflower oil

Put the flour into a large bowl with a good pinch of sea salt. Crack and beat in the eggs, then gradually whisk in the milk until smooth. I find Yorkshire puds work well if you let the batter sit a little before cooking, so pour the mixture into a pitcher to make your life easier later, and put aside for up to 2 hours. You can even leave the batter covered in the fridge overnight—just whisk it up well before you use it.

Preheat the oven to full whack (475°F). Pour just under ½ inch of sunflower oil into each compartment of a 12-cup muffin pan—this may seem like a lot of oil, but you'll leave most of it behind after cooking; this volume is essential to ensure you get a good rise. Pop the pan on a baking sheet to catch any overspill later, then place in the oven for 10 minutes to heat up.

Carefully pull the baking sheet out of the oven with one oven-gloved hand, then, quickly and confidently, pour the batter into the muffin pan compartments—try to avoid dribbling batter between the compartments, as this will only hinder the rise. Slide the baking sheet back into the oven and cook for 16 minutes, or until the puds are dark golden and beautifully risen. Whatever you do, do not open the oven door. Once cooked, drain on paper towel for a moment, then serve right away.

GET AHEAD

Cook these in advance and they'll sit really well. If it's the big-day meal, just after your turkey comes out and before your spuds go in is the best time to cook them, then simply pop the whole baking sheet back into the oven for a couple of minutes to reheat just before serving.

| CALORIES | FAT | SAT FAT | PROTEIN | CARBS | SUGARS | SALT | FIBER |
|---|---|---|---|---|---|---|---|
| 175kcal | 14.8g | 2.1g | 3.5g | 7.5g | 1.2g | 0.2g | 0.3g |

# Incredible
## LEFTOVERS

# TURKEY RISOTTO

### SWEET LEEKS, PARMESAN, PROSECCO, CRISPY TURKEY SKIN, & GRAVY

Ladies and gentlemen, let me introduce you to one of the very nicest risottos on planet earth—it's oozy, delicate, and super-comforting, with wafer-thin crispy turkey skin, and a well in the middle for your steaming leftover gravy. Amen.

SERVES 4
OR 8 AS A STARTER
35 MINUTES

leftover cooked turkey skin

8 sprigs of fresh thyme

1 onion

1 leek

2 stalks of celery

olive oil

6 cups chicken or veg stock

1½ cups Arborio risotto rice

½ cup Prosecco

10 oz leftover cooked white turkey meat

6 tablespoons leftover turkey gravy

1¾ oz Parmesan cheese

2 tablespoons unsalted butter

1 tablespoon mascarpone cheese

optional: new season's extra virgin olive oil

I like to place any leftover turkey skin from the bottom of the carcass into a cold casserole pan, then put it on a medium heat so the fat naturally renders out and it becomes super-crisp, like crackling, turning halfway. When it's golden, strip in the thyme leaves to crisp up for just 10 seconds, then scoop the crispy skin and thyme onto a plate, keeping the pan of flavorsome fat to one side.

Peel the onion, wash the leek and trim with the celery, then finely chop it all. Return the pan of fat to a medium heat, then add the veg and fry for 10 minutes, or until soft but not colored, stirring occasionally, and adding a splash of oil, if needed. Pour the stock into a separate pan and bring to a simmer on a low heat. Stir the rice into the veg for a couple of minutes, then pour in the Prosecco. Let it cook away, then start adding the stock, a ladleful at a time, letting each one cook away before adding more. Keep a close eye on it and stir constantly for 17 minutes, or until the rice is cooked but still retains its shape. Meanwhile, finely chop the turkey meat, stirring it into the pan halfway through the 17 minutes. Reheat your gravy, then sieve it into a prewarmed pitcher ready to pour at the table.

When the risotto is done, add enough extra stock to make it oozy, then remove from the heat. Finely grate over most of the Parmesan and beat it in with the butter and mascarpone, then taste and season to perfection. Put the lid on and take to the table. Divide between your hot plates, make a well in the middle of each portion, and flamboyantly pour in the hot gravy, then crack and crumble the crispy skin and thyme over the top. Finish with a tiny extra grating of Parmesan, and a thimble of new season's extra virgin olive oil, if you've got it.

| CALORIES | FAT | SAT FAT | PROTEIN | CARBS | SUGARS | SALT | FIBER |
|----------|------|---------|---------|-------|--------|------|-------|
| 815kcal | 23.5g | 9.9g | 50.1g | 94.6g | 8.5g | 0.8g | 3.1g |

# TOAD IN THE HOLE

## YORKSHIRE PUDDING FILLED WITH LEFTOVERS & DIRTY GRAVY

What's not to love about this bad boy—all the best bits of the Christmas Day meal, wrapped up in crispy fluffy Yorkshire pudding like an extra present! You can pretty much use whatever leftovers you have in this epic creation—enjoy.

SERVES 4

45 MINUTES

2 rashers of smoked bacon

4 chipolata or small pork sausages

4 fresh sage leaves

4 leftover roast potatoes

¼ cup leftover stuffing

8 leftover Brussels sprouts

2 sprigs of fresh rosemary

6 tablespoons sunflower oil

YORKSHIRE BATTER

3 large eggs

⅔ cup all-purpose flour

1 cup reduced-fat (2%) milk

DIRTY GRAVY

1 leek

2 tablespoons unsalted butter
  or turkey dripping

3 oz leftover cooked turkey meat

1 heaping tablespoon all-purpose
  flour

1 tablespoon Cranberry sauce
  (see page 158)

2⅔ cups chicken stock

So, guys, to make this incredible treat obviously requires you to have leftovers, which will differ for all of us. I've given you the recipe for the pigs in blankets and the batter, and everything else is based on what you've got—just don't overload it.

Start by moving your oven shelves around so you have plenty of space in the middle of the oven for your Yorkshire to grow. Preheat the oven to 425°F. For the Yorkshire, beat the eggs into the flour with a pinch of sea salt, then gradually whisk in the milk to give you a smooth batter, and pour into a pitcher.

Wrap half a rasher of bacon around each sausage, poking in a sage leaf, too. Pop onto a baking sheet with the potatoes (roughly chop, if you like), balls or pinches of stuffing, and the sprouts. Pick over the rosemary leaves and place in the top of the oven for 10 minutes. Pour the sunflower oil into a baking dish (12 x 10 inches) and place in the oven on the shelf underneath, to preheat the oil properly.

Meanwhile, for the gravy, wash, trim, and finely slice the leek, then put it into a frying pan on a medium heat with the butter or dripping. Cook for 10 minutes, or until soft, stirring occasionally. Shred in the turkey meat and stir in the flour and cranberry sauce, followed by the stock. Simmer for 15 to 20 minutes, or until thick, then taste and season to perfection.

For the next bit, you need to be cool, calm, and safe, as you're working with hot oil, and you want to retain the heat from the oven. Have your pitcher of batter ready and two oven gloves or kitchen towels. Keep the pan of oil in the oven and carefully pull the shelf out a little. Holding it steady, pour in the batter, then gently transfer everything from the pan above into the center. Push the shelf back in and keep the door shut for 20 to 25 minutes, or until the Yorkshire is puffed up and golden.

Serve the Christmas toad in the hole with the dirty gravy, any extra cranberry sauce, and with a nice fresh Winter slaw (see page 320) on the side.

| CALORIES | FAT | SAT FAT | PROTEIN | CARBS | SUGARS | SALT | FIBER |
|---|---|---|---|---|---|---|---|
| 965kcal | 58.7g | 13.6g | 33.7g | 80.1g | 10.2g | 1.9g | 6.5g |

# CARBONARA CAKE

## SPAGHETTI, SMOKED HAM, & LOTSA LOVELY CHEESE

This is a delightfully simple, luxurious, yet slightly trashy leftover meal that is sure to wow everyone. It gives you classic carbonara flavors, but with a crisp exterior to contrast with that creamy interior. Total comfort heaven.

**SERVES 6**

**1 HOUR**

10 oz dried spaghetti

olive oil

3½ oz leftover hard cheese, such as Parmesan, Cheddar, Gruyère

3 large eggs

1 cup heavy cream

8 oz leftover cooked smoked or Jerk ham (see page 44)

3 sprigs of fresh rosemary

Preheat the oven to 350°F. Cook the spaghetti in a pan of boiling salted water according to the package instructions, then drain and leave to steam dry and cool in the colander. Meanwhile, rub the inside of an 8-inch loose-bottomed cake pan with oil, then finely grate a thin layer of cheese all over the base, shaking it up the sides.

Once the spaghetti is cool, transfer it to a large bowl, gently pulling it apart, then beat and add the eggs, along with the cream and a generous pinch of black pepper. Chop and add the ham, finely grate in the rest of your cheese, and pick, chop, and add the rosemary leaves. Toss together well, then pack into the cake pan and place on a baking sheet. Bake for 35 minutes, or until golden, crisp, and cooked through.

Leave the carbonara cake to sit for 3 minutes in the pan, then carefully and confidently run a knife around the rim and release it proudly onto a board. Serve with a fresh, zingy lemon-dressed salad on the side.

---

### MIX IT UP

This is a great base recipe that's able to embrace all sorts of seasonal loveliness at different times of the year—from spring peas and asparagus to autumn mushrooms or chunks of roasted winter squash.

| CALORIES | FAT | SAT FAT | PROTEIN | CARBS | SUGARS | SALT | FIBER |
|---|---|---|---|---|---|---|---|
| 545kcal | 19.1g | 10.3g | 22.2g | 38.4g | 2.8g | 1.4g | 1.9g |

# THAI GREEN CURRY

## ROASTED SQUASH, LEFTOVER GREENS, TOFU, & PEANUTS

The first time I ever had Thai green curry I was sixteen years old and it blew my mind! This green curry paste is so quick to make, yet the flavors are really complex, refreshing, and delicious. With Christmas leftovers, it's a dream. Boom.

**SERVES 8**
**1 HOUR 15 MINUTES**

1 butternut squash (2½ lbs)

peanut oil

2 x 14-oz cans of light coconut milk

14 oz leftover cooked greens, such as Brussels sprouts, Brussels tops, kale, cabbage, broccoli

12 oz firm silken tofu

2½ oz unsalted peanuts

sesame oil

1 fresh red chile

2 limes

**CURRY PASTE**

1 teaspoon cumin seeds

2 cloves of garlic

2 shallots

2-inch piece of fresh gingerroot

4 kaffir lime leaves

2 tablespoons fish sauce

4 fresh green chiles

2 tablespoons unsweetened desiccated coconut

1 bunch of fresh cilantro (1 oz)

1 stalk of lemongrass

1 lime

Preheat the oven to 350°F. Wash the squash, carefully cut it in half lengthways and remove the seeds, then cut into wedges. In a roasting pan, toss with 1 tablespoon of peanut oil and a pinch of sea salt and black pepper, then roast for around 1 hour, or until tender and golden.

For the paste, toast the cumin seeds in a dry frying pan for 2 minutes, then tip into a food processor. Peel, roughly chop, and add the garlic, shallots, and ginger, along with the kaffir lime leaves, 2 tablespoons of peanut oil, the fish sauce, chiles (pull off the stalks), coconut, and most of the cilantro (stalks and all). Bash the lemongrass, remove and discard the outer layer, then snap into the processor, squeeze in the lime juice, and blitz into a paste, scraping down the sides halfway.

Put 1 tablespoon of peanut oil into a large casserole pan on a medium heat with the curry paste and fry for 5 minutes to get the flavors going, stirring regularly. Tip in the coconut milk and half a can's worth of water, then simmer and thicken on a low heat for 5 minutes. Stir in the roasted squash, roughly chop and add the leftover greens, and leave to tick away on the lowest heat, then taste and season to perfection. Meanwhile, cube the tofu and fry in a pan on a medium-high heat with 1 tablespoon of peanut oil for 2 minutes, or until golden. Crush the peanuts in a pestle and mortar and toast in the tofu pan until lightly golden.

Serve the curry topped with the golden tofu and peanuts, drizzled with a little sesame oil. Slice the chile and sprinkle over with the reserved cilantro leaves. Serve with lime wedges, for squeezing over. Great with sticky rice.

### MIX IT UP

Veggies win in this beautiful recipe, but, of course, if you wanted to tear in some leftover cooked turkey or chicken meat, that would work a treat, too.

| CALORIES | FAT | SAT FAT | PROTEIN | CARBS | SUGARS | SALT | FIBER |
|----------|-----|---------|---------|-------|--------|------|-------|
| 324kcal | 24g | 9.7g | 10.2g | 18.2g | 10.3g | 0.5g | 3.7g |

# TURKEY PIE

## SWEET CREAMY LEEKS, SMOKY BACON, & CHESTNUT PUFF PASTRY

This amazingly comforting pie has to be one of my favorite ways, and one of the easiest, to use up leftover turkey and stuffing. The simple addition of crumbled chestnuts to the puff pastry means it's a total game-changer.

**SERVES 8**
**2 HOURS**

4 rashers of smoked bacon

2 tablespoons unsalted butter

olive oil

½ a bunch of fresh thyme (½ oz)

3 lbs leeks

1 lb leftover cooked turkey meat

optional: leftover stuffing

2 heaping tablespoons
  all-purpose flour,
  plus extra for dusting

4 cups turkey, chicken or
  veg stock

2 tablespoons crème fraîche

optional: leftover turkey gravy

8 oz all-butter puff pastry
  (cold)

6 vac-packed chestnuts

1 large egg

Preheat the oven to 400°F. Chop the bacon and place in a large pan on a medium heat with the butter and 1 tablespoon of oil. Strip in the thyme leaves and fry for 5 minutes while you wash, trim, and finely slice the leeks (it seems like a lot, but they'll cook down nicely). Toss the leeks into the pan with a good pinch of sea salt and black pepper, then cover and cook gently on a low heat for 40 minutes, or until soft and sweet, stirring regularly.

Tear up the turkey meat and stir it into the leeks, adding some stuffing too, if you've got it. Stir in the flour, followed by the stock and crème fraîche—any leftover turkey gravy will add great bonus flavor here, too. Simmer gently for 20 minutes, then taste, season to perfection, and turn the heat off. Quickly pour the mixture through a sieve over another large empty pan so most of the awesome gravy drips into the pan, then tip the filling into a 10-inch pie dish—you want your filling to still be a little bit saucy, so don't drain it completely.

Roll out the pastry, crumble the chestnuts over one half of it, then fold the other half over and roll out again, crushing the chestnuts into it. Brush the edges of your pie dish with beaten egg, then loosely roll the pastry around your rolling pin and unroll it over the pie dish. Trim off any excess, then pinch and crimp the edges to seal. Brush the top with beaten egg, and don't worry if the pastry tears, just use any pastry trimmings to patch up the cracks. You can also cut out little shapes to decorate the top of the pie, sticking them down with eggwash however you like. Bake for 30 minutes, or until the pastry is puffed up and golden. Reheat your gravy to serve on the side, reducing it, if needed, and everyone's happy! Good with steamed greens and peas.

| CALORIES | FAT | SAT FAT | PROTEIN | CARBS | SUGARS | SALT | FIBER |
|---|---|---|---|---|---|---|---|
| 512kcal | 28.2g | 12.6g | 28.8g | 37.7g | 6.4g | 1.6g | 2.9g |

# TURKEY FALAFEL

SHREDDED CABBAGE, PICKLED RED ONION & CHILES, HUMMUS, & WRAPS

I love this dish because the flavors couldn't be more different from traditional Christmas dinner. It makes a brilliant brunch or lunch, and with the bright colors and soft and crunchy textures it will add a bit of freshness to your table.

SERVES 4

35 MINUTES

3 red onions

olive oil

1 x 15-oz can of chickpeas

10 oz leftover cooked turkey meat

1 fresh green chile

½ a bunch of fresh cilantro (½ oz)

1 level teaspoon ground turmeric

1 level teaspoon smoked paprika

1¾ oz feta cheese

1 heaping teaspoon cumin seeds

extra virgin olive oil

2 lemons

½ a red cabbage (1 lb)

1 pinch of ground cloves

½ a bunch of mixed fresh Italian parsley and chervil (½ oz)

½ a tub of quality store-bought hummus

4 whole-wheat wraps

4 pickled chiles

Peel and finely chop 1 onion and place in a pan on a medium-low heat with 1 tablespoon of olive oil. Fry for 15 minutes, stirring occasionally. Meanwhile, drain the chickpeas and put them into a bowl, mashing half with a potato masher, then finely chop and add the turkey. Finely chop the chile and the top leafy half of the cilantro and add to the bowl with the turmeric and paprika. Crumble in the feta, add the cooked onions, and mix well. Divide into eight equal-sized portions, then shape and squash together into patties. Place on a pan, sprinkle over and evenly pat on the cumin seeds, then place in the fridge to firm up.

Meanwhile, peel and finely slice the remaining onions. Either dry fry or grill them on a medium heat to reduce the raw edge, then scrunch with 1 tablespoon of extra virgin olive oil and the juice of half a lemon in a little bowl to make them a vibrant pink. Trim and finely shred the cabbage, then toss with the cloves, a good pinch of sea salt, 1 tablespoon of extra virgin olive oil, the juice of half a lemon, and a few torn parsley and chervil leaves. Loosen the hummus with the juice of half a lemon and a little water to give you a nice drizzling consistency.

Drizzle the falafel with a little olive oil. Place a large non-stick frying pan on a medium-high heat and cook them for 3 to 4 minutes on each side, or until golden and cooked through. Lightly warm the wraps through for a few seconds, then lay out, sprinkle over some cabbage and pickled onion, and divide your falafel on top, busting them open and drizzling them with hummus. Squeeze over the remaining lemon juice, pick over the remaining herb leaves, add a pickled chile to each wrap, then grab, roll up, and enjoy!

| CALORIES | FAT | SAT FAT | PROTEIN | CARBS | SUGARS | SALT | FIBER |
|----------|-----|---------|---------|-------|--------|------|-------|
| 677kcal | 31.4g | 7.1g | 40.6g | 56.4g | 13.2g | 2.3g | 15.2g |

# KEDGEREE

## SMOKED HADDOCK, WINTER GREENS, FRAGRANT RICE, LIGHT SPICE, & EGGS

Kedgeree is one of my favorite things. I do have a bit of a problem in that I can't stop eating it when I make it because I find it so damn delicious. And it's also very comforting—perfect for breakfast, brunch, lunch, or a hangover.

**SERVES 6**

**45 MINUTES**

1½ cups brown rice

16 oz undyed smoked haddock fillets

2 red onions

1 fresh red chile

½ a bunch of fresh cilantro (½ oz)

2 cloves of garlic

2-inch piece of fresh gingerroot

olive oil

2 tablespoons unsalted butter

1 heaping teaspoon fennel seeds

1 heaping teaspoon curry powder

7 oz leftover cooked greens, such as Brussels sprouts, Brussels tops, kale, cabbage, broccoli

7 oz frozen peas

1 lemon

6 large eggs

Cook the rice in a pan of boiling salted water according to the package instructions, then drain and refresh under cold water, leaving it in the colander. At the same time, poach the fish in a large pan of simmering salted water on a medium heat for 10 minutes, then carefully remove with a slotted spoon. Turn the heat up under the poaching water and bring back to a good simmer.

Meanwhile, peel the onions and finely slice with the red chile (seed if you like) and cilantro stalks. Peel and finely chop the garlic and ginger. Place it all in a large frying pan on a medium heat with 1 tablespoon of oil and the butter and cook for 10 minutes, or until soft but not colored, stirring occasionally. Crush the fennel seeds in a pestle and mortar, and stir into the pan with the curry powder.

Slice and add the leftover greens, along with the frozen peas, then gently fold in the rice with two spoons so it stays nice and fluffy. Flake in the poached fish, gently fold again, season to perfection with sea salt, black pepper, and lemon juice, then keep on a low heat for just 3 or 4 minutes while you poach the eggs to your liking in the simmering water. Place the eggs on top of the kedgeree, scatter over the cilantro leaves, and a little extra chile, if you fancy, then tuck in. Delicious served with mango chutney, or dollops of lemon-spiked yogurt.

| CALORIES | FAT | SAT FAT | PROTEIN | CARBS | SUGARS | SALT | FIBER |
|---|---|---|---|---|---|---|---|
| 421kcal | 13.3g | 4.4g | 30.1g | 48.6g | 7.1g | 1.6g | 5.4g |

# ROYAL PASTA DOUGH

## FOR SILKY, VELVETY PASTA

This is my ultimate pasta dough recipe, hence the name. And the best bit is, it's still cheap for the volume it gives you. Enjoy this rolled or cut into a hundred different shapes, and feel the pride in making pasta yourself from scratch.

SERVES 8

30 MINUTES
PLUS RESTING

3 cups quality Tipo 00 flour,
    plus extra for dusting

½ cup fine semolina

12 large eggs

extra virgin olive oil

### CRACKING RECIPES

As well as helping you to celebrate your festive leftovers with my Lasagne (see page 196) and Cannelloni (see page 194), use this to hero seasonal veg in my Cracker ravioli (see page 96).

**THE DOUGH** Pile the flour and semolina into a large bowl and make a well in the middle. Separate the eggs and add the yolks to the well, putting the egg whites into a sandwich bag and popping into the freezer for making meringue another day (see page 222). Add 2 tablespoons of oil and ¼ cup of cold water to the well, then use a fork to whip up with the eggs until smooth, gradually bringing the flour in from the outside. When it becomes too hard to mix, get your clean floured hands in there and bring it together into a ball of dough. Knead on a clean flour-dusted surface for around 4 minutes, or until smooth and elastic (eggs can vary in size and flour can vary in humidity; this dough shouldn't be too wet or dry, but tweak it with a touch more water or flour if you need to—use your instincts). Wrap in plastic wrap and leave to relax for 30 minutes.

**ROLLING OUT** Traditionally, Italians would have used a very large rolling pin, and you can do that, too, if you like—it just requires a large flat surface and a bit of elbow grease. I think it's fun and advisable to use a pasta machine. Attach it firmly to a nice clean table and divide your pasta dough into four pieces, covering everything with a damp clean kitchen towel to stop it drying out as you go.

**STAGE 1** One at a time, flatten each piece of dough by hand and run it through the thickest setting, then take the rollers down two settings and run the dough through again to make it thinner. Importantly, fold it in half and run it back through the thickest setting again—I repeat this a few times because it makes the dough super-smooth and means it fills out the pasta machine properly.

**STAGE 2** Start rolling the sheet down through each setting, dusting with flour as you go. Turn the crank with one hand while the other maintains just a little tension to avoid any kinks, folds, or ripples. Take it right down to your desired thickness, and there you have it—your own pasta, made from scratch.

| CALORIES | FAT | SAT FAT | PROTEIN | CARBS | SUGARS | SALT | FIBER |
|---|---|---|---|---|---|---|---|
| 346kcal | 14.3g | 3.6g | 12.3g | 42.4g | 0.7g | 0.1g | 1.7g |

# WINTER RAGÙ

## LOVELY LEFTOVER MEAT IN A SWEET TOMATO & RED WINE SAUCE

Simple and delicious, this ragù makes the most of all your lovely leftover meat from the festive season, also giving you lots of further meal options. If you can, embrace a mixture of meats, and any gravy will be delicious in the mix, too.

**MAKES 6 PORTIONS**
**2 HOURS**

1 red onion

1 clove of garlic

1 carrot

1 leek

1 stalk of celery

1 sprig of fresh rosemary

olive oil

1 fresh bay leaf

¾ cup + 5 teaspoons Chianti

2 x 14-oz cans of plum tomatoes

14 oz leftover cooked meat

extra virgin olive oil

Peel the onion, garlic, and carrot, wash the leek and trim with the celery, and pick the rosemary leaves. Finely chop it all, adding it as you go to a large casserole pan on a medium-low heat with 1 tablespoon of olive oil and the bay. Cook for 20 minutes, or until the veg have softened, stirring occasionally.

Turn the heat up to high, pour in the wine and let it cook away for a few minutes, then tip in the tomatoes. Half-fill each empty can with water and swirl around, then pour into the pan. Roughly chop or tear in the leftover meat, stir well, and bring to a boil, breaking up the tomatoes with a wooden spoon. Reduce to a low heat and simmer for 1 hour to 1 hour 30 minutes, or until thick and delicious. Taste, season to perfection, then stir in a little extra virgin olive oil, to finish.

Serve the ragù with fresh pasta, fluffy rice, oozy polenta, jacket potatoes, or hunks of crusty bread for dipping. Or use it as a filling for my delicious Lasagne (see page 196), Cannelloni (see page 194), or Baked buns (see page 354).

| CALORIES | FAT | SAT FAT | PROTEIN | CARBS | SUGARS | SALT | FIBER |
|---|---|---|---|---|---|---|---|
| 192kcal | 8.9g | 2.4g | 13.1g | 9.4g | 8.4g | 0.5g | 1.8g |

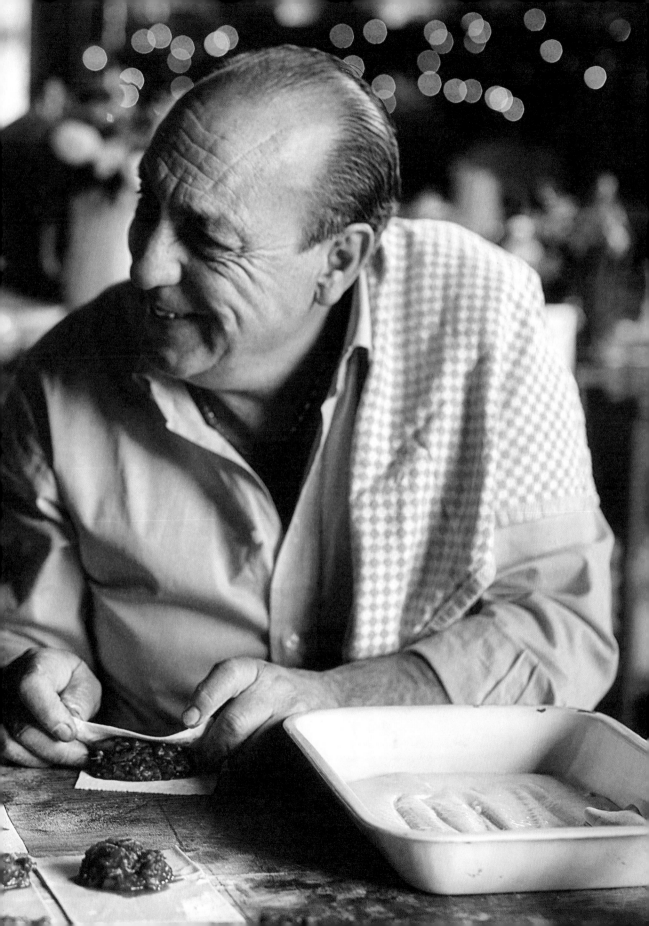

# CANNELLONI

### CRISPY TURKEY SKIN & CHESTNUT PANGRATTATO, WINTER RAGÙ

This is one of those beautiful recipes that's a lovely ritual to follow when you've got a batch of my Winter ragù in the fridge or freezer ready to go. Using leftover turkey skin and chestnuts to add crunch and contrast on the top is genius.

**SERVES 8**

**2 HOURS**

1 x Royal pasta dough
(see page 188)

1¾ lbs Winter ragù
(see page 190)

1 large onion

2 cloves of garlic

¼ cup unsalted butter

1 fresh bay leaf

2 tablespoons all-purpose flour

2½ cups reduced-fat (2%) milk

1¾ oz Parmesan cheese

1 whole nutmeg, for grating

7 oz vac-packed chestnuts

1¾ oz leftover cooked turkey skin

Make your Royal pasta dough (see page 188) and Winter ragù (see page 190).

For the white sauce, peel and finely slice the onion and garlic. Melt the butter in a large pan over a medium heat, add the onion, garlic, and bay leaf and cook for 25 minutes, or until soft and lightly golden, stirring occasionally and adding a splash of water, if needed. Stir in the flour, then, splash-by-splash, stir in the milk. Keep stirring over the heat until your sauce is smooth and thick, then finely grate in the Parmesan and mix well. Discard the bay leaf, then taste the sauce and season to perfection with sea salt, black pepper, and a fine grating of nutmeg.

Meanwhile, blitz the chestnuts and leftover turkey skin in a food processor, then cook in a dry frying pan on a medium heat until light golden and crispy.

Preheat the oven to 350°F. To make the cannelloni tubes, roll out the pasta dough into ¹⁄₁₆-inch-thick sheets, then cut them into 4-inch squares. Dot 1 heaping tablespoon of Winter ragù across the middle of each square, then roll each one up into a tube. Repeat until you've used up all the pasta and ragù.

To build the cannelloni, cover the base of a 12- x 10-inch baking dish with a layer of white sauce, then arrange the filled pasta tubes on top in two layers. Cover with the remaining sauce and scatter the crispy turkey skin and chestnut pangrattato over the top. Bake at the bottom of the oven for around 45 minutes, or until golden and bubbling, then serve. Great with a simple salad on the side.

| CALORIES | FAT | SAT FAT | PROTEIN | CARBS | SUGARS | SALT | FIBER |
|----------|-----|---------|---------|-------|--------|------|-------|
| 636kcal | 28.8g | 10.5g | 24.2g | 70.6g | 11.9g | 0.7g | 4.9g |

# LASAGNE

## FENNEL, CAVOLO NERO, & MOZZARELLA SAUCE, WINTER RAGÙ

A vivid bright green sauce made from cavolo nero and fennel is my gorgeous twist on a traditional lasagne. I like to make it with fresh pasta so you can layer the sheets up the sides, creating more of a lasagne parcel, which looks incredible.

SERVES 8

2 HOURS 30 MINUTES
PLUS RESTING

1 x Royal pasta dough
  (see page 188)

1 x Winter ragù
  (see page 190)

1 onion

1 bulb of fennel

¼ cup unsalted butter

1 fresh bay leaf

1 pinch of ground cloves

⅓ cup all-purpose flour

2½ cups reduced-fat (2%) milk

7 oz cavolo nero

1¾ oz Parmesan cheese

1 whole nutmeg, for grating

olive oil

1 x 4½-oz ball of mozzarella
  cheese

1¾ oz mascarpone cheese

6 sprigs of fresh thyme

extra virgin olive oil

Make your Royal pasta dough (see page 188) and Winter ragù (see page 190).

For the green sauce, peel and finely slice the onion, then trim and finely slice the fennel. Melt the butter in a large pan over a medium heat, then add the onion, fennel, and bay leaf and cook for 25 minutes, or until the veg are soft and lightly golden, stirring occasionally and adding a splash of water, if needed. Stir in the cloves and flour, then, splash-by-splash, stir in the milk. Strip the cavolo nero leaves off the stalks, then roughly chop the leaves and stir them into the pan. Cook and stir for 5 minutes, then pour the whole lot into a blender, discarding the bay leaf. Finely grate in most of the Parmesan and blitz until smooth. Taste, and season to perfection with sea salt, black pepper, and a fine grating of nutmeg.

Preheat the oven to 350°F. To build your lasagne, start by rolling out the pasta dough into thin sheets. Cover the base of a lightly oiled baking dish (12 x 10 inches) with a single layer of pasta, leaving a decent overhang. Spoon in a layer of Winter ragù, top with pasta and a layer of green sauce, randomly interspersing the layers with little bombs of mozzarella and mascarpone. Repeat twice more, folding in the overhanging pasta to create the top, then finish with a final layer of green sauce and any leftover mozzarella and mascarpone. Finely grate over the remaining Parmesan, then lightly dress the thyme sprigs with extra virgin olive oil and scatter over the top. Bake at the bottom of the oven for around 45 minutes, or until golden and bubbling. Leave to rest for 10 minutes, then serve, making sure everyone gets some of that incredible crispy edge. Yum.

| CALORIES | FAT | SAT FAT | PROTEIN | CARBS | SUGARS | SALT | FIBER |
|---|---|---|---|---|---|---|---|
| 727kcal | 37.7g | 15g | 32.4g | 62g | 13.7g | 0.8g | 4.2g |

# BUBBLE & SQUEAK

## THE ULTIMATE LEFTOVER VEG FLAVOR PARTY

I've always liked making this, since I was a kid. We'd have the pan going for well over an hour, slowly turning those precious leftovers into an incredible pile of gnarly, starchy, veggie gorgeousness. Good bubble & squeak is hard to beat.

SERVES 4

30 MINUTES

olive oil

2 tablespoons unsalted butter

4 sprigs of fresh woody herbs,
    such as rosemary, sage, thyme

1¼ lbs leftover roast potatoes

1¼ lbs leftover cooked veg, such
    as carrots, rutabaga, turnips,
    parsnips, Brussels sprouts, kale

optional: leftover vac-packed
    chestnuts

Put an 11-inch non-stick frying pan on a medium heat with 1 tablespoon of oil and the butter (or, even better, any leftover dripping you have in the fridge). Pick in the fresh herb leaves and let them crisp up for a minute, then add the potatoes, veg, and any leftover chestnuts you've got. There's no need to chop anything first, as now we're going to mash it all up with a potato masher into a nice, flat, even layer. Season well with sea salt and black pepper, and cook for 3 to 4 minutes, or until a lovely golden crust starts forming on the bottom.

Now we get into the rhythm of the secret to good bubble & squeak. Use a slotted spatula to fold those lovely crispy bits back into the mash, then pat and flatten everything down again. Let it crisp up again, then repeat the process, and—importantly—keep repeating it over a period of about 20 minutes, until it's golden, super-crispy, and delicious. About halfway through, nick a bit, taste it, and correct the seasoning if you need to. When it's looking good, you can serve it right away, or you can leave it on the lowest heat for a while—the flavor will only improve.

You can serve this any which way you like—let's be honest, it's going to be amazing whatever you have it with. I like mine with fried eggs, a little lemon-dressed watercress, and a few bombs of Piccalilli (see page 310). Slices of leftover Jerk ham (see page 44) are always going to go down a treat, too.

| CALORIES | FAT | SAT FAT | PROTEIN | CARBS | SUGARS | SALT | FIBER |
|----------|-----|---------|---------|-------|--------|------|-------|
| 376kcal | 18.4g | 4.6g | 6.9g | 48.5g | 8.1g | 0.6g | 6.3g |

# CHILI CON CARNE

## PULLED TURKEY, SWEET PEPPERS, & POPPED BUTTER BEANS

There's nothing easier and more sociable than a good, hearty pot of chili to feed your friends or family. Celebrating a whole rainbow of veggies, and making brilliant use of those lovely turkey leftovers, this version is sure to please.

**SERVES 8**

**2 HOURS 20 MINUTES**

1 butternut squash (2½ lbs)

olive oil

2 heaping teaspoons ground cumin

2 heaping teaspoons smoked paprika

2 red onions

2 carrots

2 mixed-color peppers

1 bunch of fresh cilantro (1 oz)

2 cloves of garlic

2 fresh red chiles

1 tablespoon liquid honey

2 tablespoons Worcestershire sauce

2 teaspoons chipotle Tabasco sauce

1 lb leftover cooked turkey meat

2 x 14-oz cans of plum tomatoes

1 x 15-oz can of butter beans

2 limes

Preheat the oven to 350°F. Wash the squash, carefully cut it in half lengthways and remove the seeds, then chop into chunky wedges. Place in a roasting pan, drizzle lightly with oil, sprinkle over 1 heaping teaspoon each of cumin and paprika, and season with sea salt and black pepper. Roast for 1 hour 15 minutes, or until golden and cooked through, then remove. Meanwhile, peel the onions and carrots, seed the peppers, then roughly chop and place in a large ovenproof casserole pan on a medium-low heat with 2 tablespoons of oil. Pick the cilantro leaves into a bowl of cold water for later. Peel the garlic and finely chop with the cilantro stalks and chiles, then stir into the pan with the remaining cumin and paprika. Cook for 15 to 20 minutes, or until soft, stirring occasionally.

Stir the honey, Worcestershire, and Tabasco into the pan for 2 minutes, then tear in the turkey meat and cook for 5 minutes, or until sticky and gnarly, adding any leftover juices or gravy, if you've got them. Add a good pinch of salt and pepper, then stir in the tomatoes, breaking them up with a wooden spoon, as well as 2 cans' worth of water. Transfer the pan to the oven to cook for 1 hour 20 minutes, stirring halfway through and loosening with a splash of water, if needed.

Meanwhile, drain the butter beans and quickly pat dry with paper towel, then toast for a few minutes in a non-stick frying pan on a high heat with 1 tablespoon of oil, until crisp, gnarly, and bursting open. Season well and put to one side.

When the time's up, take the squash pan and the pan of chili out of the oven. Stir the beans into the chili and tear in the squash, loosening the chili with splashes of boiling water, if needed. Taste, season to perfection with salt, pepper, and squeezes of lime juice, then stir in most of the cilantro leaves. Serve with steamed rice, jacket potatoes or tortillas, yogurt, guacamole, hot chili sauce, and a simple salad. Scatter over the remaining cilantro leaves and some extra finely sliced fresh chile, if you fancy, then tuck in.

| CALORIES | FAT | SAT FAT | PROTEIN | CARBS | SUGARS | SALT | FIBER |
|----------|-----|---------|---------|-------|--------|------|-------|
| 299kcal | 8.8g | 1.8g | 25.8g | 31.4g | 19.8g | 0.4g | 8g |

# TURKEY SLOPPY JOES

## TASTY SLAW WITH GHERKINS & CHILE, HOMEMADE BBQ SAUCE

The sloppy Joe is so much more than a sandwich or a burger, and giving it the Christmas treatment means we're taking that bun filled with delicious pulled meat and exciting crunchy veg, served with gravy for dunking, to the next level.

SERVES 4

20 MINUTES

7 oz leftover cooked turkey meat

1 cup leftover turkey gravy

1 carrot

1 apple

½ a red onion

2 sprigs of fresh mint

2 gherkins

1 fresh red chile

4 whole-grain buns with seeds

BBQ SAUCE

2 tablespoons tomato ketchup

1 tablespoon HP sauce

1 teaspoon English mustard

½ teaspoon chipotle Tabasco
sauce

1 splash of Worcestershire sauce

Shred and pull apart your leftover turkey meat and place in a small pan with a splash of water and ¼ cup of gravy. Pop a lid on and place on the lowest heat for 10 minutes to warm through. Warm the rest of the gravy in a separate pan on a low heat, ready to use it for dunking later.

Meanwhile, peel and finely shred the carrot, matchstick the apple, peel and finely slice the red onion, and pick and slice the mint leaves. Place it all in a bowl with 1 tablespoon of pickling liquor from your gherkin jar. Finely slice the gherkins, using a crinkle-cut knife if you've got one, and the chile, add to the bowl, mix well, lightly season, and put aside. Mix all the BBQ sauce ingredients together.

Split and toast your buns, then spread the BBQ sauce inside them, top and bottom. Pile your pulled turkey on the bun bases, drizzle with a little gravy, and top with some of that tasty slaw. Pop the bun lids on, and you're away. Serve the rest of the gravy on the side for a naughty dunk, along with any leftover slaw.

### DOUBLE UP

This is a great recipe for parties, as it's quick, and it's easy to double or even quadruple the quantities—let your guests build their own buns.

| CALORIES | FAT | SAT FAT | PROTEIN | CARBS | SUGARS | SALT | FIBER |
|----------|-----|---------|---------|-------|--------|------|-------|
| 639kcal | 29.4g | 6.8g | 39.7g | 52.7g | 12.6g | 2.1g | 14.1g |

# PEA SOUP

### ROASTED HAM, STILTON, HONEY, & APPLE TOASTS

This spectacular soup brings a bit of optimism into wintertime. Heroing delicious roasted ham and cheeseboard leftovers, it also celebrates humble frozen peas, showing how easy it is to draw on your freezer for awesome meals.

SERVES 6

40 MINUTES

SOUP

1 onion

2 cloves of garlic

1 leek

2 stalks of celery

olive oil

6 cups frozen peas

7 cups chicken or veg stock

6 sprigs of fresh mint

extra virgin olive oil

optional: plain yogurt or crème fraîche

TOASTS

6 slices of whole-grain bread with seeds

5½ oz leftover cooked smoked or Jerk ham (see page 44)

1 crunchy eating apple

1¾ oz Stilton cheese

¾ oz mature Cheddar cheese

1 tablespoon liquid honey

4 sprigs of fresh rosemary

Preheat the oven to 350°F. Peel the onion and garlic, then wash the leek and trim with the celery. Roughly chop it all and place in a large pan on a medium-low heat with 1 tablespoon of olive oil. Cook for 10 to 15 minutes, or until softened but not colored, stirring occasionally. Stir in the frozen peas, then pour in the stock and bring to a boil. Add a pinch of sea salt and black pepper, then simmer on a medium heat for 10 minutes.

Meanwhile, lay out your bread slices side-by-side on a large roasting pan. Shred the ham into a bowl, matchstick and add the apple, crumble in the Stilton, and mix together, then divide between the bread slices. Finely grate over the Cheddar, drizzle with a tiny bit of olive oil and the honey, pick and lightly oil the rosemary leaves and sprinkle them over the top. Pop into the oven for 10 minutes, or until golden, then place one piece of loaded toast in each of your warm soup bowls.

Pick the mint leaves into the soup, then blitz it with an immersion blender or tip into a blender until super-smooth, adding a splash of water, if needed, to get it to the consistency of your liking. Have a taste, and season to perfection. Ladle the soup into your bowls around the toasts, drizzle with a little extra virgin olive oil, and serve with a dollop of yogurt or crème fraîche, if you fancy.

❖

#### GET AHEAD

Make the soup in advance, and simply reheat it when needed, even getting your bread topped and ready to toast ahead of time, too.

| CALORIES | FAT | SAT FAT | PROTEIN | CARBS | SUGARS | SALT | FIBER |
| --- | --- | --- | --- | --- | --- | --- | --- |
| 358kcal | 11.6g | 4g | 24.5g | 41.3g | 13g | 2.1g | 12g |

# TURKEY STEW

## SWEET LEEK & SMOKY BACON BISCUIT DUMPLINGS

This is a super-easy, old-school dish that uses leftover turkey or chicken in a brilliant way. As a kid I made it with dumplings, but when I was in the USA they would top stews with these lovely biscuits, so this is my hybrid of the two.

SERVES 6
1 HOUR
PLUS COOLING

**DUMPLINGS**

2 rashers of smoked bacon

2 small leeks

olive oil

heaping ¾ cup all-purpose flour

2 tablespoons maize flour
 or polenta

1½ teaspoons baking powder

½ teaspoon baking soda

2 tablespoons unsalted
 butter (cold)

½ cup buttermilk

1 large egg

**STEW**

3 onions

3 stalks of celery

2 sprigs of fresh rosemary

3 sprigs of fresh thyme

3 fresh bay leaves

2 teaspoons English mustard

2 tablespoons all-purpose flour

6 cups veg stock

5 oz leftover stuffing

1 lb leftover cooked turkey
 or chicken meat

To start the dumplings, roughly chop the bacon and place in a large frying pan on a medium-low heat to crisp up while you wash, trim, and finely slice the leeks. Stir them into the pan with 1 tablespoon of oil, then cook for 15 minutes, or until soft and sweet, stirring occasionally. Remove from the heat and leave to cool.

Meanwhile, for the stew, peel the onions, trim the celery, then roughly chop both and place in a large, wide casserole pan on a medium heat with 2 tablespoons of oil (or even better, use turkey dripping to intensify the flavors). Add the herb sprigs and bay, and cook for 15 minutes, or until soft but not colored, stirring regularly. Stir in the mustard and flour for 2 minutes, then gradually stir in the stock to make a nice thick sauce. Crumble in the leftover stuffing and turn the heat off. Scoop out and discard the herb sprigs and bay leaves, then shred the turkey or chicken meat, stir it into your stew, taste, and season to perfection.

Preheat the oven to 400°F. Place the flours, baking powder, and baking soda in a large bowl. Dice and add the butter, then use your thumbs and forefingers to rub the butter into the flour until it resembles bread crumbs. Make a well in the middle, pour in the buttermilk, then gradually mix into the crumbs, bringing them in from the outside. Stir in the cooled leeks and bacon until just combined, but don't overwork it—we want the dough as light as possible. Gently roll it out on a clean flour-dusted surface until ¾ inch thick, then use a 2-inch fluted cutter to stamp out as many round dumplings as you can, rerolling and using up any offcuts—you should get at least 12 from this amount.

Brush the dumplings with beaten egg, then sit them on top of the stew. Bake for 25 to 30 minutes, or until the dumplings are risen and golden and the stew is blipping and bubbling away nicely. Delicious with simple steamed greens.

| CALORIES | FAT | SAT FAT | PROTEIN | CARBS | SUGARS | SALT | FIBER |
|----------|-----|---------|---------|-------|--------|------|-------|
| 490kcal | 19.7g | 6.2g | 38.1g | 42g | 10.7g | 1.9g | 4g |

# TURKEY CHOWDER

### SWEETCORN, SWEET POTATOES, CRISPY SMOKED BACON, & MATZO CRACKERS

There's always turkey or chicken leftovers come Chrimbo, and a good chowder is a very comforting way to use them up. Also bigging up handy frozen corn and lovely sweet potatoes, this is guaranteed to be a satisfying, hearty bowlful.

SERVES 6–8
1 HOUR 25 MINUTES

1 leftover turkey carcass,
plus up to 10 oz leftover
cooked turkey meat

2 onions

2 carrots

2 large sweet potatoes
(12 oz)

½ a bunch of fresh Italian
parsley (½ oz)

8 rashers of smoked bacon

optional: turkey dripping

3 cups frozen sweetcorn

6 tablespoons heavy cream

cayenne pepper

1 handful of matzo or cream
crackers

Start by getting a stock on the go. Strip all the meat you can find off the turkey carcass, shred, and put aside. Fill your largest pan with the bones, smashing them with a rolling pin to help get them in. Cover with 12 cups of water, bring to a boil, then simmer for 1 hour, skimming away any scum from the surface.

With 30 minutes to go, peel the onions, carrots, and sweet potatoes and cut into ½-inch dice. Finely slice the parsley stalks, then the bacon (any leftover cooked turkey skin will be delicious here, too). Fry the bacon and any turkey skin in a large pan on a medium-low heat with a little turkey dripping, if you've got it, until golden and crispy, then remove with a slotted spoon and put aside, leaving the pan on the heat. Add the onions, carrots, sweet potatoes, and parsley stalks to the pan and cook for around 25 minutes, or until soft, stirring regularly.

Carefully pour the stock through a sieve into the veg pan. Add the frozen corn and shredded turkey meat, then simmer for 15 minutes. You can leave the soup coarse and chunky, or you can use an immersion blender to whiz up about a quarter of the soup until smooth, then stir it back through, leaving the rest fairly chunky to create a nice range of textures. Remove from the heat and stir in the cream, then taste and season to perfection with sea salt and cayenne. Crumble over the crispy bacon and the crackers, add a sprinkling of parsley leaves, and serve.

| CALORIES | FAT | SAT FAT | PROTEIN | CARBS | SUGARS | SALT | FIBER |
|---|---|---|---|---|---|---|---|
| 275kcal | 9.5g | 3.7g | 20.9g | 28.4g | 11g | 0.8g | 1.2g |

# BÁNH MÌ

## CRISPY SESAME TURKEY, SILKY PÂTÉ, & PICKLED VEG BAGUETTES

◇◇◇◇◇◇◇◇◇◇◇◇◇◇◇◇◇◇◇◇◇◇◇◇◇◇◇◇◇◇◇◇◇◇◇◇◇◇◇◇◇◇◇◇◇◇◇◇◇◇◇◇◇◇◇◇◇◇◇◇◇◇◇◇◇◇◇◇◇◇◇◇◇◇◇◇◇◇◇◇◇◇◇

I've given this French Vietnamese classic a festive spank with traditional Christmas flavors. It's a joy to eat, fantastic for using up those turkey leftovers, and creates a wonderful epic sarnie that everyone will just love tucking into!

**SERVES 8**

**30 MINUTES**

olive oil

14 oz leftover cooked turkey meat

optional: leftover cooked turkey skin

2 tablespoons raw sesame seeds

2 tablespoons chili jam

2 French baguettes

10 oz leftover Silky pâté (see page 32) or quality store-bought chicken liver pâté

½ a bunch of fresh cilantro (½ oz)

**QUICK PICKLED VEG**

1 small red onion

2 carrots

1½-inch piece of fresh gingerroot

¼ of a white cabbage (8 oz)

½ an English cucumber

1 tablespoon liquid honey

3 tablespoons white wine vinegar

For the pickled veg, peel the red onion, carrots, and ginger, click off any tatty outer leaves from the cabbage, halve the cucumber lengthways and scrape away the watery core. Using the finest blade on your food processor or a mandolin (use the guard!), finely slice the onion, then place in a large bowl. Finely slice and add the cabbage and cucumber. Switch to a julienne or fine grating cutter and shred the carrots and ginger, scattering them into the bowl as you go. Add the honey, vinegar, and a good pinch of sea salt, and scrunch well to lightly pickle the veg.

Place a large pan on a medium-high heat with 1 tablespoon of oil. Shred and add the turkey (the brown meat is best in this dish), plus any bits of crispy skin you've got left over. Toss for a couple of minutes until lightly golden, then add most of the sesame seeds for 1 minute, followed by the chili jam. Cook for another 5 minutes, or until gnarly, sticky, and glazed, tossing regularly.

Meanwhile, warm your baguettes through in a low oven, then halve them lengthways and spread the pâté inside. Spoon in the crispy turkey, then squeeze out any excess liquid from the pickled veg and pile into the baguettes. Sprinkle over the remaining sesame seeds, pick over some cilantro leaves, pop on the tops of the baguettes, press together, slice, and serve. Good served with extra chili jam, hot chili sauce, or a bit of hoisin sauce, for dunking.

| CALORIES | FAT | SAT FAT | PROTEIN | CARBS | SUGARS | SALT | FIBER |
|---|---|---|---|---|---|---|---|
| 565kcal | 20.6g | 6.5g | 29.6g | 69.1g | 14.8g | 2.5g | 5.1g |

# Spectacular festive
# DESSERTS

# CHRISTMAS PUDDING

## DRIED FRUIT, PECANS, GINGER, ROSEMARY, BOURBON, & GOLDEN SYRUP

This is based on my dear Nan's beautiful pudding recipe, which gives you a much lighter result than a traditional Christmas pud. It has more dynamic flavors, and is super-easy to make—this is exactly the way I like it best. Enjoy!

**SERVES 8**

**4 HOURS 30 MINUTES**

unsalted butter, for greasing

5 oz Medjool dates

5 oz dried apricots

5 oz pecan nuts

2½ oz crystallized ginger

1 small sprig of fresh rosemary

5 oz unsweetened dried
 cranberries

5 oz raisins

5 oz suet

1 cup all-purpose flour

heaping ½ cup fresh bread
 crumbs

¾ cup + 5 teaspoons reduced-fat
 (2%) milk

1 large egg

1 clementine

golden syrup

barrel-aged Bourbon

Grease a 6-cup pudding bowl with butter. Pit your dates, then, by hand or in a food processor, finely chop the flesh with the apricots, pecans, ginger, and rosemary leaves. Place it all in a mixing bowl with the cranberries, raisins, suet, flour, bread crumbs, and milk. Crack in the egg, finely grate in the clementine zest, squeeze in the juice, and mix it all together really well.

Tip the mixture into the greased bowl and cover with a single layer of parchment paper and a double layer of aluminum foil. Tie a piece of string around the bowl to secure them in place and make it watertight, then sit it in a large, deep saucepan and pour in enough water to come halfway up the sides of the bowl. Bring the water to a boil, cover the pan with a tight-fitting lid, and reduce to a simmer for 4 hours. Check the water regularly, and keep topping it up with boiling water, if needed.

When the time's up, lift out the bowl, remove the foil and paper, then carefully turn the pudding out onto a plate ready to serve, or leave to cool and reheat just before you need it. You can either drizzle it with golden syrup and a swig of Bourbon—gorgeous—or be a bit more flamboyant and gently heat a good few swigs of Bourbon just to warm it, then strike a match to the pan (stand back!), let it flame, and carefully pour it over your pudding. Present it to your guests and sing some Christmassy songs, then when the flame subsides drizzle with golden syrup. Serve with cream, custard, or even ice cream.

**LOVE YOUR LEFTOVERS**

Cold leftovers are delicious with a slice
of British cheese, such as Lancashire, or
in a Christmas sundae (see page 252).

| CALORIES | FAT | SAT FAT | PROTEIN | CARBS | SUGARS | SALT | FIBER |
|----------|------|---------|---------|-------|--------|------|-------|
| 627kcal | 33.8g | 11.4g | 7.8g | 74g | 49.6g | 0.3g | 5g |

# RETRO TRIFLE

## MY MUM'S ULTIMATE PARTY PUD

Mum first enjoyed trifle like this as a postwar treat, hence the use of pantry ingredients. Of course, if you can make your own jelly and blancmange rather than using packaged versions, that's always going to up the quality of your pud.

SERVES 20

30 MINUTES
PLUS SETTING STAGES

10 trifle sponges or 1 large
   Swiss roll

1¼ lbs ripe strawberries

6 tablespoons Cointreau

3-oz (85g) package of strawberry
   jelly powder

2½ cups reduced-fat (2%) milk

2 teaspoons superfine sugar

1-oz (35g) package of strawberry
   blancmange

1 x 16-oz can of mandarin
   segments, in juice

3-oz (85g) package of orange jelly
   powder

2 cups + 6 tablespoons
   Bird's custard

2 cups + 6 tablespoons
   heavy cream

1 orange

quality dark chocolate (70%)

Use the sponges to line the base of a large glass bowl, slicing the Swiss roll first (if using). Hull, slice, and layer in two-thirds of the strawberries, then drizzle over the Cointreau. Tear the strawberry jelly package into a pitcher and cover with 1¼ cups of boiling kettle water. Stir until dissolved, then top up with 1¼ cups of cold water. Pour the jelly into the bowl over the strawberries, and pop into the fridge to set.

Pour a little milk into a bowl with the sugar and the blancmange and stir to dissolve. Bring the remaining milk just up to a boil, then whisk in the blancmange mixture, continuing to whisk as you bring it back up to a boil. Remove the pan from the heat and allow to cool, whisking occasionally, then pour the blancmange over the set red jelly and return to the fridge so it can set.

Drain the mandarin segments well (reserving the juice), and arrange nicely over the set blancmange. Make the orange jelly, following the instructions above (using the mandarin juice in place of some of the cold water), leave the mix to cool a bit, then pour over the mandarin layer and, again, pop into the fridge to set.

Pour over the custard, then pop it back into the fridge so that can set, too. Whip the heavy cream into soft peaks, then spread it over the set custard. Slice and arrange the remaining strawberries on top, as delicately or randomly as you wish—it's nice to take a bit of pride in this, like Mum has in the picture. Finely grate over the orange zest and a little chocolate, and enjoy!

| CALORIES | FAT | SAT FAT | PROTEIN | CARBS | SUGARS | SALT | FIBER |
|---|---|---|---|---|---|---|---|
| 317kcal | 20.7g | 12.3g | 4.1g | 26.9g | 21.8g | 0.3g | 1.3g |

# CHOCOLATE POTS

## CLEMENTINE SYRUP & CRÈME FRAÎCHE

Crispy on the top, but super-gooey in the middle, rich and an utterly mind-blowing chocolate experience, these pots are an honest and delicious expression of chocolate—they really celebrate the quality of the chocolate you choose.

**SERVES 12**

**1 HOUR 10 MINUTES**
**PLUS COOLING**

10 oz quality dark chocolate (70%)

14 tablespoons unsalted butter

300g superfine sugar

5 large eggs

**SYRUP & TOPPING**

8 clementines

2 tablespoons superfine sugar

12 teaspoons crème fraîche

Preheat the oven to 325°F. Snap the chocolate into a heatproof bowl, add the butter and a pinch of sea salt, and place over a pan of gently simmering water until smooth and melted, stirring occasionally. Remove from the heat and leave to cool for 15 minutes. In a separate bowl, whisk the sugar and eggs together until thick and fluffy. Whisking constantly, pour the chocolate mixture into the eggs, until combined. Divide between 12 small ovenproof teacups or ramekins, then place them in a large, deep roasting pan. Place the pan in the oven, then carefully pour enough boiling kettle water into the pan to come halfway up the side of the cups. Bake for 25 minutes, then carefully remove the cups from the pan and leave them to sit for at least 15 minutes before serving.

Meanwhile, to make the syrup, squeeze all the clementine juice through a sieve into a small pan. Add the sugar and bring to a boil, then reduce to a gentle simmer for 15 minutes, or until starting to thicken and coat the back of a spoon. Remove from the heat and leave to cool to room temperature.

For maximum pleasure, enjoy the chocolate pots at room temperature—if they're hot, they'll be too runny, and if they even touch the fridge, they become too firm. Serve with a spoonful of crème fraîche and a drizzle of the syrup. Heaven.

| CALORIES | FAT | SAT FAT | PROTEIN | CARBS | SUGARS | SALT | FIBER |
|---|---|---|---|---|---|---|---|
| 441kcal | 30.3g | 17.8g | 5g | 38g | 37g | 0.3g | 2.5g |

# PAVLOVA

## RUBY POACHED PEARS, CHOCOLATE, MULLED WINE JELLY, & CREAM

◇◇◇◇◇◇◇◇◇◇◇◇◇◇◇◇◇◇◇◇◇◇◇◇◇◇◇◇◇◇◇◇◇◇◇◇◇◇◇◇◇◇◇◇◇◇◇◇◇◇◇◇◇◇◇◇◇◇◇◇◇◇◇◇◇◇◇◇◇◇◇◇◇◇

A good pavlova like this is really easy for a dinner party, as you can make all the elements ahead and simply assemble it at the last minute, ready to wow your guests. Feel free to vary the toppings, but this is my favorite festive combo.

SERVES 10

3 HOURS
PLUS COOLING & SETTING

### MERINGUE

4 large egg whites

1 cup superfine sugar

### PEARS & JELLY

1 bottle of fruity red wine

½ teaspoon ground allspice

¼ cup liquid honey

1 clementine

6 small just-ripe pears

6 sheets of gelatin

### CREAM

¾ cup + 5 teaspoons
 heavy cream

1 teaspoon vanilla bean paste

1 tablespoon superfine sugar

½ cup Greek yogurt

### TOPPING

2 tablespoons blanched
 hazelnuts or pecan nuts

1¾ oz quality dark chocolate
 (70%)

1 clementine

Preheat the oven to 250°F. Whisk the egg whites with a pinch of sea salt in a free-standing electric mixer until they form stiff peaks, then, with the mixer still running, very gradually add the sugar. Turn to the highest setting and leave to mix for 8 minutes, or until the sugar has fully dissolved (rub a pinch of the mixture between your thumb and forefinger—if it feels smooth you're good to go). Line a large baking sheet with parchment paper, dollop the mixture in the center, then spread it out into a circle 10 inches in diameter, using the back of the spoon to flick up peaks and make troughs. Bake for 1 hour 20 minutes, then turn the oven off and leave the meringue in there until the oven is cool, even overnight.

To poach your pears, pour the wine into a pan on a medium-low heat and add the allspice and honey. Finely grate in the clementine zest and squeeze in the juice. Bring up to a good simmer while you neatly peel the pears, using a vegetable peeler. Place the pears in the wine, cover with a damp piece of scrunched-up parchment paper, and simmer on a low heat for 25 to 30 minutes, or until the pears are tender, turning halfway. Gently remove them, then pour the wine into a jelly mold. Soak the gelatin sheets in cold water for a few minutes, then drain, squeeze out the excess liquid, and stir into the wine until dissolved. Cool, then set in the fridge.

To make a Chantilly-style cream, pour the cream into a bowl, add the vanilla bean paste and sugar, whisk by hand until it forms soft peaks, then fold in the yogurt. For the topping, toast the nuts in a pan on a medium heat until golden, then smash up in a pestle and mortar. Snap the chocolate and melt in a heatproof bowl over a pan of gently simmering water until smooth and glossy.

To assemble, gently dollop the cream over the meringue, then add spoonfuls of the jelly (you only need about half, so save the rest for another time, or serve alongside). Halve the pears, removing the cores, then slice into fans, leaving them attached at the top, and arrange delicately over the jelly. Finely grate over the clementine zest, scatter over the nuts, drizzle with melted chocolate, and serve.

| CALORIES | FAT | SAT FAT | PROTEIN | CARBS | SUGARS | SALT | FIBER |
|---|---|---|---|---|---|---|---|
| 365kcal | 14.9g | 8.9g | 4.1g | 41.6g | 41.1g | 0.3g | 2.7g |

# APPLE PIE

## SOUR CRANBERRIES, BLOOD ORANGE, VANILLA, & CINNAMON

I love cooking a nice apple pie, and this is my super-solid, go-to, classic recipe. Of course you can embrace other seasonal fruit, such as pears and quince, but it's really good to always keep in the sour cranberries to contrast the fresh fruit.

SERVES 8–10
2 HOURS 20 MINUTES
PLUS CHILLING & RESTING

### PASTRY

1 cup + 1 tablespoon unsalted
   butter (cold), plus extra
   for greasing

2½ cups all-purpose flour,
   plus extra for dusting

1 tablespoon superfine sugar

### FILLING

3 lbs apples (I like a mixture of
   Bramley, Russet, Braeburn, Cox,
   and good old Granny Smith)

1 blood or regular orange

1 vanilla bean

3½ oz unsweetened dried
   cranberries

½ cup light muscovado or light
   brown sugar

1 good pinch of ground cinnamon

1 tablespoon cornstarch

2 tablespoons unsalted butter

### TOPPING

1 large egg

1 tablespoon demerara or
   raw sugar

To make the pastry, chop the butter into ½-inch cubes and pop into the freezer until super-cold. Put the flour, a good pinch of sea salt, the superfine sugar, and cold butter into a food processor and pulse until just combined but still a little chunky. Pour in 6 tablespoons + 2 teaspoons of ice-cold water and pulse again until it just forms a rough dough. Use clean hands to bring the dough together into two equal flat rounds, wrap them in plastic wrap and pop into the fridge to rest for at least 1 hour.

Meanwhile, for the filling, peel and core the apples, then cut 3 apples into eight wedges and the rest into ¾-inch chunks so you end up with a range of textures. In a large pan, toss them with the orange juice, then cook on a medium heat for 10 minutes, or until slightly softened, and remove from the heat. Halve the vanilla bean lengthways and scrape out the seeds, then add to the pan with the cranberries, muscovado sugar, cinnamon, and cornstarch. Chop and add the butter, then stir until the apples are evenly coated.

Preheat the oven to 350°F. On a clean flour-dusted surface, roll out one piece of pastry, turning and dusting with flour as you go, until it's around ⅛ inch thick. Grease a 10-inch pie dish with butter, then loosely roll the pastry around your rolling pin and unroll it over the top. Gently ease the pastry into the shape of the dish and trim the edges neatly, then pile in the dressed warm apples.

Now it's time to get creative! Roll out the remaining piece of pastry. You can either simply cover the pie with it in one piece, crimping the edges and cutting a cross in the center, or you can cut enough ¾-inch-wide strips to lattice the top of the pie, weaving and criss-crossing as you go, or have a bit of fun with cutters and shapes and do a mixture, like me and Anna did in the picture. Trim off any excess, then press the edges to seal. Brush the top of the pie with beaten egg, also using it to help you stick on any pastry decorations you've cut out. Scatter over the demerara sugar, then bake at the bottom of the oven for 50 minutes to 1 hour, or until golden and the apples are soft and delicious. Leave to stand for 30 minutes, then serve with lashings of custard or cream.

| CALORIES | FAT | SAT FAT | PROTEIN | CARBS | SUGARS | SALT | FIBER |
| --- | --- | --- | --- | --- | --- | --- | --- |
| 500kcal | 25.9g | 15.8g | 4.8g | 65.4g | 33.9g | 0.3g | 4.6g |

# TIRAMISÙ

## CHOCOLATE, ORANGE, VIN SANTO, MASCARPONE, & SILKY RICOTTA

This is my Christmas take on the undeniably decadent yet simple, classic Italian dessert of tiramisù. Jools prefers this version, as it doesn't contain raw eggs, and I've lightened it up by pairing mascarpone with glorious ricotta cheese.

SERVES 12
40 MINUTES
PLUS SETTING

¾ cup + 5 teaspoons heavy cream

3½ oz quality dark chocolate (70%), plus extra to serve

3½ oz sponge fingers

⅔ cup good hot strong sweetened coffee

¼ cup Vin Santo or sweet sherry

1 lb ricotta cheese

8 oz mascarpone cheese

1 teaspoon vanilla bean paste

3 tablespoons liquid honey

1 orange or clementine

To make a ganache, pour the cream into a pan and gently bring to a simmer over a medium heat. Add a pinch of sea salt, snap in the chocolate, and stir until melted, thickened, and smooth, then remove from the heat and leave to one side.

Line a dish (12 x 8 inches) with the sponge fingers (or Genoese sponge, if you've made it), carefully pour over the hot sweetened coffee, and drizzle over the Vin Santo or sweet sherry. Spread the chocolate ganache over the top in an even layer.

In a food processor, blitz the ricotta, mascarpone, vanilla bean paste, and honey until super-smooth. Spoon this creamy mixture evenly on top of your chocolate layer. Place in the fridge for at least 2 hours, to set. Serve with a good grating or shaving of chocolate and a fine grating of orange or clementine zest. Heaven.

### GET AHEAD

Make this delicious dessert a day or two in advance, or even freeze it and defrost it overnight in the fridge, when needed.

| CALORIES | FAT | SAT FAT | PROTEIN | CARBS | SUGARS | SALT | FIBER |
|----------|------|---------|---------|-------|--------|------|-------|
| 309kcal | 23.6g | 15.8g | 6.4g | 16.7g | 14.3g | 0.2g | 1g |

# WINTER BOMBE

## CHOCOLATE, CHERRIES, VIN SANTO, PANETTONE, & PISTACHIOS

Get-ahead desserts are great. I make this frozen classic every year without fail. It looks amazing, is crazy delicious, and is a clever assembly job. It's a sort of cross between a summer pud and an Arctic roll, and it's sure to wow.

SERVES 12

20 MINUTES
PLUS FREEZING

2 x 1-lb tubs of quality vanilla
   ice cream

2 lbs panettone

½ cup Vin Santo

3 heaping tablespoons quality
   raspberry jam

3½ oz canned cherries, in juice

2½ oz candied clementines
   (or other candied fruit)

1 clementine

1¾ oz unsalted shelled pistachios

10 oz quality dark chocolate
   (70%)

2 tablespoons unsalted butter

Get the ice cream out of the freezer so it can soften a little while you get things ready. Line an 8-cup pudding bowl with three layers of plastic wrap. Use a serrated knife to slice four ¾-inch-thick rounds off your panettone, then cut them in half. You'll have some panettone left over, so keep this for another day. Arrange six of your panettone slices in a single layer around the inside of the bowl, pushing them down if they overlap. Drizzle some of the Vin Santo onto the panettone so it soaks in, then use the back of a spoon to spread the jam all over it.

Drain the cherries, and thinly slice the candied clementines. Finely grate the fresh clementine zest and put aside, then peel and finely slice the clementine into rounds. Spoon one tub of ice cream into the bowl, spreading it around in a thick layer. Sprinkle in the pistachios, cherries, and candied fruit, then layer on the clementine slices. Add the other tub of ice cream. Spread it out, working quickly so the ice cream doesn't completely melt. Put the remaining two panettone slices on top of the ice cream, drizzle over the rest of the Vin Santo, then cover the bowl tightly with plastic wrap. Press a plate down on top to push and compact everything down, pop a weight on, then freeze overnight, or until needed.

Around 20 minutes before you want to serve it, unwrap your amazing winter bombe, carefully turn it out onto a beautiful serving dish, then leave to thaw slightly (I tend to transfer my bombe from the freezer to the fridge just before serving up the main to give it a head start). Snap up the chocolate, place in a heatproof bowl with the butter over a pan of gently simmering water on a low heat, and leave to melt. Once nicely melted, stir in the reserved clementine zest, then pour the chocolate over the pudding so it oozes down the sides and looks super-tempting and delicious. Serve up any extra sauce in a little pitcher.

| CALORIES | FAT | SAT FAT | PROTEIN | CARBS | SUGARS | SALT | FIBER |
|---|---|---|---|---|---|---|---|
| 648kcal | 31.9g | 15.2g | 11.3g | 78.1g | 48.7g | 0.5g | 5.8g |

# BREAD & BUTTER PUDDING

## CHOCOLATE, MARMALADE, CUSTARD, & PANETTONE GALORE

OK guys, we all know we love bread and butter pudding, but it's time for a change. This version is super-fun—ripping up a panettone, layering it with chocolate, marmalade, and custard, then baking it until golden and gorgeous in a tart pan.

**SERVES 12–14**
**1 HOUR**
**PLUS COOLING**

9 tablespoons unsalted butter, plus extra for greasing

¼ cup demerara sugar

1½ lbs plain panettone

1 vanilla bean

1¼ cups whole milk

1¼ cups heavy cream

5 large eggs

½ cup superfine sugar

2 oz quality dark chocolate (70%)

2 oz quality bitter orange marmalade

Preheat the oven to 350°F. Lightly grease an 11-inch loose-bottomed tart pan with butter. Bash 2 tablespoons of demerara sugar in a pestle and mortar until fine, then mix with the remaining demerara so you have a range of textures. Tip into the tart pan and shake around to coat. Tap gently, then tip any excess back into the mortar for later. Cut ½-inch slices off the edges of the panettone and use them to line the base and sides of the tart pan, pressing down hard to compact them and create a pastry-like shell.

To make a custard, halve the vanilla bean lengthways and scrape out the seeds, then put both bean and seeds into a pan on a medium heat, along with the milk, cream, and butter, and simmer for 5 minutes, or until the butter has melted. Meanwhile, in a large bowl, whisk the eggs and superfine sugar for 2 minutes, or until smooth. Whisking constantly, add the hot cream mixture to the bowl until combined, then discard the vanilla bean.

Pour one-third of the custard into the tart case. Tear up all the remaining panettone into rough chunks, soak them in the remaining custard for 2 minutes, then spoon the mixture into your case, interspersing the spoonfuls with chunks of chocolate and bombs of marmalade. Pour over any leftover custard, leaving it to soak in if necessary, then sprinkle with the last of the demerara sugar. Bake for around 25 minutes, or until golden and set. Allow to sit for 10 minutes in the pan, then release and serve with cream, custard, or ice cream.

| CALORIES | FAT | SAT FAT | PROTEIN | CARBS | SUGARS | SALT | FIBER |
|---|---|---|---|---|---|---|---|
| 455kcal | 28.9g | 15.1g | 7.1g | 42.7g | 24.3g | 0.3g | 2g |

# ICELANDIC RICE PUDDING

## CREAMY VANILLA RICE RIPPLED WITH TANGY BERRY JAM SAUCE

Us Brits are big rice pudding lovers, but it's also a really big dessert in Iceland. They like to serve it with a sharp fruit sauce, which cuts through the richness of the creamy sticky pudding beautifully—clever and absolutely delicious!

SERVES 6

45 MINUTES

### SAUCE & TOPPING

5 oz mixed dried fruit, such as cranberries, sour cherries, blueberries

¼ cup vodka

6 teaspoons crème fraîche

5 oz redcurrants or other berries

### PUDDING

1½ cups short-grain rice, such as pudding rice or arborio risotto rice

6 cups reduced-fat (2%) milk

2 cups heavy cream

3 tablespoons liquid honey

1 stick of cinnamon

1 vanilla bean

Put the dried fruit and vodka into a large pan and add just enough water to cover. Cook gently for 10 minutes on a medium heat, then tip into a blender with 5 tablespoons of cold water and blitz until smooth, to make your sauce.

Place the rice, milk, cream, honey, and cinnamon stick in a deep pan. Score the vanilla bean lengthways and scrape out the seeds, adding both bean and seeds to the pan. Gradually bring to a boil, then simmer very gently, stirring occasionally, for 35 to 40 minutes, or until the liquid has been absorbed, the rice is just cooked through, and it's lovely and oozy.

Spoon the rice pudding into a serving dish or across a large platter, ripple through the tangy fruit sauce, and top with crème fraîche. Scatter with fresh redcurrants or other berries and serve right away.

| CALORIES | FAT | SAT FAT | PROTEIN | CARBS | SUGARS | SALT | FIBER |
|----------|-----|---------|---------|-------|--------|------|-------|
| 604kcal | 22.5g | 14.2g | 16.6g | 85.2g | 43.6g | 0.4g | 1.6g |

# PANNACOTTA

### LIGHT, WOBBLY, CREAMY VANILLA HEAVEN

A good pannacotta should never be underestimated. Easy to make, these keep well in the fridge, look dramatic when you serve them, whether in or out of the mold, and they allow you to embrace all kinds of seasonal flavors on the side.

SERVES 10

25 MINUTES
PLUS SETTING

2 cups whole milk

2 cups heavy cream

⅔ cup superfine sugar

2 vanilla beans

5 sheets of gelatin

Pour the milk and cream into a pan and add the sugar. Halve the vanilla beans lengthways and scrape out the seeds, then add both beans and seeds to the pan. Place on a low heat for 20 minutes, stirring occasionally. Meanwhile, soak the gelatin sheets in cold water for a few minutes. Remove the pan from the heat, drain the gelatin, squeeze out the excess liquid, and stir into the cream until dissolved. Cool to room temperature, then strain through a fine sieve into a pitcher, discarding the vanilla beans. Whisk again to evenly distribute the vanilla seeds, then divide between 10 small pudding molds or ramekins. Place on a pan, cover, and set in the fridge for at least 3 hours, where they'll sit happily for up to 2 days.

To serve, simply half dip each mold into a bowl of hot water for 5 seconds, give the mold a little shake to ease the pannacotta away from the sides, and plop out onto your plate. Here are some of my favorite things to serve them with:

Mulled ruby fruits, 8 oz of sour dried fruit simmered in a little mulled wine until plump, served with a drizzle of the syrup and an almond biscotti on the side

A generous sprinkle of candied violets, half a shot of quality vodka, and a fine grating of lemon zest per pannacotta

Affogato style, with half a shot of espresso and 1 almond biscotti per pannacotta

Sweet poached rhubarb, 14 oz of sliced rhubarb, poached with 1 ball of stem ginger, ¾ cup + 5 teaspoons of Prosecco, 1 tablespoon of superfine sugar, and a fine grating of orange zest, served with baby mint leaves and crushed nuts or almond biscotti

A tangy tropical sauce, made from the liquidized ripe flesh from 1 big mango, 2 sieved wrinkly passion fruit, and a squeeze of lime juice

A simple chocolate sauce, made by melting 3½ oz of quality dark chocolate (70%) with 6 tablespoons of milk until super-smooth and glossy

| CALORIES | FAT | SAT FAT | PROTEIN | CARBS | SUGARS | SALT | FIBER |
|----------|-----|---------|---------|-------|--------|------|-------|
| 342kcal | 28.7g | 17.8g | 3.2g | 18.9g | 18.9g | 0.1g | 0g |

# BANOFFEE ALASKA

## ALMOND PASTRY, CARAMEL, BANANAS, & VANILLA ICE CREAM

I had this idea to marry off two of my favorite desserts—banoffee pie and baked Alaska, which means you get creamy cold vanilla ice cream in the middle of a delicious warm tart. And let me tell you, this marriage is blooming amazing!

SERVES 12

1 HOUR
PLUS COOLING & FREEZING

11 tablespoons unsalted butter (cold), plus extra for greasing

1 orange

1⅓ cups all-purpose flour, plus extra for dusting

¾ cup ground almonds

6 large eggs

1 pint quality vanilla ice cream

¼ cup dulce de leche or caramel sauce

1⅓ cups superfine sugar

2 large ripe bananas

1 lime

1 tablespoon Camp coffee syrup

Preheat the oven to 350°F. Lightly grease a deep, 10-inch loose-bottomed tart pan. To make the pastry, finely grate the orange zest into a food processor, add the cold butter, the flour, almonds, and 1 egg, then blitz until it comes together into a ball of dough, wrap in plastic wrap, and chill for 30 minutes. Roll out on a clean flour-dusted surface until just under ¼ inch thick, then loosely roll up around the rolling pin and unroll over the tart pan, easing it in and pushing it carefully into the sides. Trim off any excess, patch up any holes, then prick the base with a fork, cover, and chill in the fridge for 30 minutes (use any leftovers for mince pies). When the time's up, line the pastry case with quality plastic wrap (non-PVC), then fill with rice, making sure you pack it right out to the sides. Bake blind for 15 minutes, remove the plastic and rice, and bake for another 5 minutes, or until lightly golden, then leave to cool. Soften your ice cream in the fridge.

Once the pastry case is cool, spread the dulce de leche or caramel across the base, scoop over the ice cream, and freeze until frozen solid—you could get it up to this stage a day in advance. Turn the oven up to 425°F. To make your meringue topping, separate the remaining 5 eggs (keep the yolks for another day). In a stand mixer, whisk the egg whites with a pinch of sea salt until they form soft peaks. Place the sugar and ⅓ cup + 1 teaspoon of water in a pan on a high heat. Use a sugar thermometer to monitor it getting up to 230°F, then reduce the temperature to low. Let it gently bubble until it gets up to 250°F. Remove from the heat and let the bubbles settle for 30 seconds, then very gradually pour it into the egg whites, whisking constantly on a low speed. Leave it whisking for 10 minutes to cool and thicken the mixture. Meanwhile, peel and slice the bananas, finely grate over the lime zest, and squeeze over the juice, then toss together.

Get your tart out of the freezer, arrange the bananas over the ice cream, then pile on the meringue in nice peaks. Use a fork to ripple through drips of Camp coffee syrup. Bake on the bottom of the oven for just 4 minutes, or until the meringue is lightly golden, leaving the ice cream frozen inside. Remove from the pan, and serve.

| CALORIES | FAT | SAT FAT | PROTEIN | CARBS | SUGARS | SALT | FIBER |
|----------|-----|---------|---------|-------|--------|------|-------|
| 423kcal | 17.7g | 8.4g | 6.8g | 59.5g | 44.7g | 0.3g | 1.1g |

# ARCTIC ROLL

## BLACK FOREST STYLE WITH CHOCOLATE SPONGE, KIRSCH, & CHERRIES

Here's a wonderful Germanic nod to the classic Arctic roll of my childhood. It's easy to make, even weeks before you need it, always fun and dramatic to tuck into, and great for feeding a crowd. Stick a sparkler in it, and you're winning.

SERVES 10–12

1 HOUR 15 MINUTES
PLUS FREEZING

SPONGE

unsalted butter, for greasing

3 large eggs

½ cup superfine sugar,
    plus extra for dusting

½ cup all-purpose flour

¼ cup quality unsweetened cocoa
    powder, plus extra for dusting

FILLING & TOPPING

1 pint quality chocolate ice cream

1 clementine

kirsch

heaping ½ cup quality black
    cherry jam

1¾ oz blanched hazelnuts

6 tablespoons heavy cream

½ cup Greek yogurt

1 teaspoon vanilla bean paste

1 tablespoon confectioner's sugar

Preheat the oven to 350°F. For the sponge, grease a baking sheet (15 x 10 inches) with butter, line the bottom and sides with parchment paper, then lightly grease the paper. By hand or with an electric mixer, beat the eggs and superfine sugar until pale, thick, and creamy. Sift in half the flour and cocoa, very gently fold them in using a large metal spoon, then repeat with the rest. Pour the mixture into your prepared pan and spread out evenly. Bake for 10 minutes, or until springy to the touch. Meanwhile, soften your ice cream in the fridge.

Place a large sheet of parchment paper on top of a clean damp kitchen towel, and evenly sprinkle over a thin layer of superfine sugar from a height. While it's still hot and flexible, turn the sponge out onto the paper. Peel off and discard the baked piece of parchment. With one of the shortest sides in front of you, fold up the excess paper, then roll up the sponge with the paper inside (as it cools this will set the shape but prevent the sponge from cracking). Leave to cool.

For the fillings, finely grate the clementine zest into a bowl, squeeze in the juice, add a splash of kirsch and the jam, and mix well. Toast the hazelnuts in a dry pan until golden, then bash until fine. Whip the cream to soft peaks, then fold in the yogurt, vanilla bean paste, and sifted confectioner's sugar. To assemble, unroll the sponge so it's flat, removing the paper. Drizzle with kirsch, cover with a layer of cream, then dot over half the jam filling. Rustically spoon over the softened ice cream, leaving a 2-inch gap at one of the shorter ends, then dot over most of the remaining jam filling and most of the nuts. Carefully reroll—if the filling starts to slip out, just push it back in. Wrap well in parchment and freeze overnight, or until needed.

Get your Arctic roll out of the freezer and into the fridge 30 minutes before you're ready to serve. Carefully trim the ends to give you nice edges, then brush over the remaining jam filling, dust with cocoa, and scatter over the remaining nuts. I like to decorate it with shavings of dark chocolate, fresh cherries, and gold leaf, too!

| CALORIES | FAT | SAT FAT | PROTEIN | CARBS | SUGARS | SALT | FIBER |
|---|---|---|---|---|---|---|---|
| 290kcal | 15.2g | 7.5g | 5.4g | 33.7g | 28.2g | 0.0g | 0.7g |

# FRANGIPANE TART

## HAZELNUTS, ALMONDS, CHOCOLATE, & SOUR CRANBERRIES

A good frangipane tart is one of life's true joys and a staple dessert in my repertoire. Feel free to swap out the sauce for different seasonal jams to make your tart really of the moment, making it super-versatile. Here's my festive version.

**SERVES 12–14**

**2 HOURS 15 MINUTES
PLUS COOLING**

### PASTRY

11 tablespoons unsalted butter (cold), plus extra for greasing

1⅔ cups all-purpose flour, plus extra for dusting

½ cup superfine sugar

1 large egg

⅓ cup quality unsweetened cocoa powder

### SAUCE

10 oz unsweetened dried cranberries

4 oranges

### FRANGIPANE

3½ oz blanched hazelnuts

3½ oz blanched almonds

1 cup + 1 tablespoon unsalted butter (at room temperature)

1¼ cups superfine sugar

3 large eggs

heaping ⅓ cup all-purpose flour

### TOPPING

3½ oz quality dark chocolate (70%)

3½ oz blanched hazelnuts

Preheat the oven to 350°F. Lightly grease an 11-inch loose-bottomed tart pan. To make the pastry, place the cold butter, the flour, sugar, a pinch of sea salt, the egg, and cocoa in a food processor, then blitz until it comes together into a ball of dough, wrap in plastic wrap, and chill for 30 minutes. Roll out on a clean flour-dusted surface until just under ¼ inch thick, then loosely roll up around the rolling pin and unroll over the tart pan, easing it in and pushing it carefully into the sides. Trim off any excess, prick the base with a fork, cover, and chill in the fridge for 30 minutes. When the time's up, line the pastry case with quality plastic wrap (non-PVC), then fill with rice, making sure you pack it right out to the sides. Bake blind for 15 minutes, remove the plastic wrap and rice, and bake for another 7 minutes, or until crisp, then leave to cool.

Meanwhile, to make the sauce, place the cranberries in a small pan on a medium-low heat. Squeeze in all the orange juice to cover the cranberries, topping up with a little boiling kettle water, if needed. Cook for 15 minutes, or until thick and jammy, stirring occasionally and adding extra splashes of boiling water, if needed. I like the sauce chunky, but you can absolutely blitz up half of it and stir it back through the rest to make it more jammy, if you prefer. Remove and leave to cool. For the frangipane, blitz the hazelnuts and almonds in a food processor until fine, then add the butter, sugar, eggs, and flour, and pulse until combined.

Once the pastry case is cool, spread the cranberry sauce across the base, then place the tart pan on a baking sheet. Spoon the frangipane over the sauce, spreading it out evenly. Snap up the chocolate and randomly poke it into the top of the frangipane so it's almost submerged. Roughly crush the hazelnuts and sprinkle most of them over the top, poking them in, too. Bake for 45 to 50 minutes, or until golden, set, and cooked through. Serve scattered with the remaining crushed hazelnuts. Delicious with crème fraîche, honey, and some fresh figs or clementine slices.

| CALORIES | FAT | SAT FAT | PROTEIN | CARBS | SUGARS | SALT | FIBER |
|---|---|---|---|---|---|---|---|
| 614kcal | 42.5g | 18.3g | 9g | 51.7g | 33g | 0.2g | 2.7g |

# MONTE BIANCO

### SILKY CHESTNUT, VANILLA CREAM, CHOCOLATE, ALMOND BISCOTTI, & CLEMENTINES

◇◇◇◇◇◇◇◇◇◇◇◇◇◇◇◇◇◇◇◇◇◇◇◇◇◇◇◇◇◇◇◇◇◇◇◇◇◇◇◇◇◇◇◇◇◇◇◇◇◇◇◇◇◇◇◇◇◇◇◇◇◇◇◇◇◇◇◇◇◇◇◇◇◇

This is a super-delicious, quite fantastically unusual dessert. The balance of the silky chestnut flavor with the cream, the chocolate, and the crunch of the biscuits works together absolutely beautifully, and it's fun to put together, too.

**SERVES 10**
**1 HOUR 30 MINUTES**
**PLUS CHILLING**

3 cups reduced-fat (2%) milk

5 clementines

1 small sprig of fresh rosemary

¼ cup liquid honey

2 vanilla beans

1⅔ cups heavy cream

1¼ lbs vac-packed chestnuts

2 tablespoons confectioner's sugar

2 oz almond biscotti

3½ oz quality dark chocolate (70%)

Pour the milk into a large pan on a low heat. Use a vegetable peeler to add strips of zest from 1 clementine, then add the rosemary sprig and the honey. Halve the vanilla beans lengthways, scrape out the seeds, place in a bowl with the cream, and pop into the fridge, adding the empty beans to the milk pan. Bring to a gentle simmer, then add the chestnuts and simmer for 1 hour.

When the time's up, use a slotted spoon to scoop just the chestnuts into a food processor, and pulse a few times. Strain the milk, discarding the peel, vanilla beans and rosemary, then gradually pulse enough milk into the processor to give you a silky smooth paste, stopping to scrape down the sides and help it along. Spoon into a large piping or sandwich bag and pop into the fridge for at least 1 hour.

Meanwhile, sift the confectioner's sugar into the bowl of cream, then whisk to soft peaks. Spoon into another piping or sandwich bag and pop that into the fridge, too. Bash the biscuits to a fine dust. Peel the remaining clementines and slice into rounds.

To serve—and this is the fun bit—use a small sharp knife to stab little holes and slits into one corner of each piping or sandwich bag, then squeeze the cream into your serving dishes like wiggly worms. Shave over some chocolate, add a couple of slices of clementine, then sprinkle over the biscuit dust and tuck in!

### GET AHEAD

You can make all the elements of this delightful pud ahead of time, then simply assemble it at the last minute, or even at the table for a bit of theater—there's nothing else quite like it.

| CALORIES | FAT | SAT FAT | PROTEIN | CARBS | SUGARS | SALT | FIBER |
|----------|------|---------|---------|-------|--------|------|-------|
| 554kcal | 31.7g | 17.8g | 7.1g | 63.4g | 29.2g | 0.2g | 6.3g |

# GRANITA

## APPLE, MINT, CELERY, & ELDERFLOWER

◇◇◇◇◇◇◇◇◇◇◇◇◇◇◇◇◇◇◇◇◇◇◇◇◇◇◇◇◇◇◇◇◇◇◇◇◇◇◇◇◇◇◇◇◇◇◇◇◇◇◇◇◇◇◇◇◇◇◇◇◇◇

A fresh, zingy, refreshing pud is sometimes just the ticket to finish off a rich meal. You might think celery is an odd choice for a dessert, but, trust me, paired with sweet apples and elderflower, and creamy crème fraîche, it really works.

SERVES 10

15 MINUTES
PLUS CHILLING
& MACERATING

8 Granny Smith apples

4 sprigs of fresh mint

3 lemons

⅓ cup St-Germain elderflower
   liqueur

2 tablespoons maple syrup

4 stalks of celery

2 tablespoons superfine sugar

10 heaping teaspoons crème
   fraîche

Peel and core the apples and chuck into a blender. Pick in the mint leaves, squeeze in the juice of 2 lemons, add the elderflower liqueur and maple syrup, along with a splash of water, and blitz until super-smooth—you can do this in batches, if necessary. Pour the mixture through a fine sieve into a freezable container, really pushing everything through with the back of a spoon, then freeze until needed.

About half an hour before you're ready to serve, pop your serving glasses or bowls into the freezer to chill. Trim and finely slice the celery stalks at an angle, with patient knife skills or, ideally, on a mandolin (use the guard!). Place in a bowl, squeeze over the remaining lemon juice, stir in the sugar, mix and massage together, then leave to macerate for 30 minutes.

Get your granita out of the freezer and scratch it all up with a fork into ice crystals. Divide the granita between your chilled glasses or bowls, dollop with crème fraîche, and serve with the macerated celery for a bit of crunch and contrast.

MIX IT UP

Use half elderflower gin and half elderflower cordial
instead of St-Germain liqueur, if you prefer, or you can
opt for straight-up cordial, if you want to go booze-free.

| CALORIES | FAT | SAT FAT | PROTEIN | CARBS | SUGARS | SALT | FIBER |
|----------|-----|---------|---------|-------|--------|------|-------|
| 83kcal | 2.5g | 1.5g | 0.9g | 14.9g | 14.8g | 0.1g | 1.1g |

# APPLE CARPACCIO

## POMEGRANATE, MINT, GREEK YOGURT, & CANDIED PINE NUTS

◇◇◇◇◇◇◇◇◇◇◇◇◇◇◇◇◇◇◇◇◇◇◇◇◇◇◇◇◇◇◇◇◇◇◇◇◇◇◇◇◇◇◇◇◇◇◇◇◇◇◇◇◇◇◇◇◇◇◇◇◇◇◇◇◇◇◇◇◇◇◇◇◇◇

It's nice to have a lighter dessert in the mix, and this simple principle of carpaccio can embrace many other fruits, too, such as pears, pineapple, or even mango. On top of that, it's truly beautiful to look at, and to eat, of course!

**SERVES 4**

**20 MINUTES**

1¾ oz pine nuts

1 tablespoon confectioner's sugar

4 heaping tablespoons Greek yogurt

1 pomegranate

3 clementines

3 large crunchy eating apples

2 sprigs of fresh mint

liquid honey

Preheat the oven to 350°F. Rinse the pine nuts in cold water, then drain well and spread them out in a single layer on a small baking sheet. Sift over the confectioner's sugar and bake for 6 minutes, or until the nuts turn golden, then leave to cool. Crush 1 spoonful's worth in a pestle and mortar, then muddle in the yogurt.

Meanwhile, cut the pomegranate in half. Hold one half over a bowl, cut-side down in your fingers. Gently smack it with a wooden spoon so that the seeds tumble out into the bowl. Squeeze the other half through a sieve into a pan, squeeze in the clementine juice, and gently mix together. Slice the apples as thinly as you can (ideally on a mandolin—use the guard!). Place two-thirds of them in the pan of juice, then slice the rest the other way into matchsticks. Add those to the pan, too, toss together, and leave it all to soften a little.

It's nice to do a big platter of this—it looks quite grand and very pretty—or you can do individual portions. Arrange the apple slices, then divide up the apple matchsticks and pile in the center. Dollop over the yogurt, then scatter with the pomegranate seeds and the remaining sugared pine nuts, and pick over the baby mint leaves. Drizzle with a little honey and some extra juice from the pan, if you like, and serve right away.

| CALORIES | FAT | SAT FAT | PROTEIN | CARBS | SUGARS | SALT | FIBER |
|----------|-----|---------|---------|-------|--------|------|-------|
| 192kcal | 9.9g | 1.5g | 4.7g | 22.2g | 22.1g | 0g | 2.3g |

# CHRISTMAS SUNDAES

### LAYERS OF CHEEKY FESTIVE PUDDING JOY

◇◇◇◇◇◇◇◇◇◇◇◇◇◇◇◇◇◇◇◇◇◇◇◇◇◇◇◇◇◇◇◇◇◇◇◇◇◇◇◇◇◇◇◇◇◇◇◇◇◇◇◇◇◇◇◇◇◇◇◇◇◇◇◇◇◇◇◇◇◇◇◇◇◇◇◇◇◇◇◇◇◇

If you've got some leftover Christmas pudding, let me inspire you to create a fabulous, extravagant Christmas sundae in a glass, made up from all the things you're bound to have in your pantry at this wonderful time of year.

### 10 MINUTES

This is more of a principle than a recipe—you can make individual portions in cute little glasses, or you could even make a bigger version for everyone to share, kinda like a cheat's trifle. It really depends on how much Christmas pudding you've got left over, and what other lovely bits and bobs you can add to the story. Layer up your ingredients in whichever order you like and, of course, you don't have to use everything I've listed here, nor should you feel limited by it—if you've got your own seasonal favorites to throw into the mix, go for it! The more the merrier. A really great combo might include:

The only essential, crumbled Christmas pudding (see page 216), cold or warmed through, and I like to drizzle each piece with a few drips of Vin Santo or sweet sherry

Delicate slices or peeled segments of clementine, satsuma, or blood orange

Bombs of leftover Cranberry sauce (see page 158), cold or reheated

Toasted, crushed nuts, such as pecans, almonds, hazelnuts, Brazil nuts, or whatever you've got in your nut basket—as long as they're not salted, of course

Spoonfuls of custard, Greek or plain yogurt, a drizzle of cream, some whipped Chantilly, or the odd spoonful of quality vanilla or chocolate ice cream

A little crumbling of Badass brownies (see page 280) adds an extra dimension

Fine slices of stem or crystallized ginger add a lovely bit of warmth

Shavings of quality dark chocolate (70%) always finish it off nicely or, even better, use melted chocolate, which you can ripple through all the layers above

And there you have it, the perfect little Christmas sundae.

# Afternoon tea &

## SWEET TREATS

# CHOCOLATE LOG

### SWEET CHESTNUT PURÉE, HONEYED CREAM, & CRUSHED HONEYCOMB FILLING

This Yule log brings back loads of happy memories for me—it was one of the first desserts I ever made as a kid, at Christmastime, of course! This is my slightly more grown-up version, which is really good fun to make and decorate.

**SERVES 12–14**
**1 HOUR**
**PLUS COOLING**

### SPONGE

4 large eggs

½ cup confectioner's sugar, plus extra for dusting

½ cup self-rising flour

2 tablespoons quality unsweetened cocoa powder

2 teaspoons vanilla bean paste

2 tablespoons superfine sugar

### FILLING

8 oz sweetened chestnut purée

1 pinch of ground cinnamon

¾ cup + 5 teaspoons heavy cream

1 tablespoon liquid honey

1 Crunchie bar or 1½ oz Honeycomb (see page 302)

### BUTTERCREAM

5 oz quality dark chocolate (70%)

11 tablespoons unsalted butter (at room temperature)

1 heaping cup confectioner's sugar

Preheat the oven to 350°F. For the sponge, line a 12- x 10-inch baking sheet with parchment paper. Separate the eggs. In an electric mixer, whisk the egg whites to stiff peaks with a pinch of sea salt. Gradually whisk in the confectioner's sugar, then, one-by-one, whisk in the egg yolks until really pale and light. Sift in the flour and cocoa powder, add the vanilla bean paste, then fold everything together with a large metal spoon so you keep in as much air as possible. Spoon the mixture onto the lined baking sheet, gently and evenly spread it out, then bake for 8 to 10 minutes, or until just cooked through and springy to the touch.

Place a large sheet of parchment paper (18 x 14 inches) on a flat surface and evenly sprinkle over the superfine sugar from a height. While it's still hot and flexible, turn the sponge out onto the paper. Peel off and discard the baked piece of parchment paper. With one of the longest sides in front of you, fold up the excess paper, then roll up the sponge with the paper inside (as it cools, this will set the shape but prevent the sponge from cracking). Leave to cool.

For the filling, mix the chestnut purée and cinnamon together. In a separate bowl, whisk the cream to soft peaks, then fold in the honey. To assemble, unroll the sponge so it's flat, removing the paper. Spread all over with the chestnut purée, followed by the cream, then smash and sprinkle over the Crunchie bar or Honeycomb. Reroll and pop into the fridge. Meanwhile, make your buttercream. Melt the chocolate in a heatproof bowl over a pan of gently simmering water, then remove and leave to cool. Beat the butter in an electric mixer until pale, then, with the mixer still running, gradually add the confectioner's sugar and cooled melted chocolate.

Take the log out of the fridge, chop off a quarter at an angle—that's the branch—and position it on your serving board like in the picture, using a splodge of buttercream to keep it in place. Evenly cover the whole log with buttercream, then use a fork to decorate it. Dust with extra confectioner's sugar and a pinch of sea salt, shaved chocolate, sprinkles, plastic Bambi figures, whatever you like—go to town!

| CALORIES | FAT | SAT FAT | PROTEIN | CARBS | SUGARS | SALT | FIBER |
|---|---|---|---|---|---|---|---|
| 397kcal | 1 oz | 14.7g | 5.1g | 39.7g | 31.3g | 0.2g | 2.3g |

# MY VICTORIA SPONGE

## ORANGE BLOSSOM CHANTILLY CREAM, STRAWBERRY JAM, & SPRINKLES

Embracing orange blossom in the vanilla Chantilly cream and spiking our strawberry jam with just a little touch of fragrant rosewater creates a wonderful tutti-frutti-flavored evolution of the classic Victoria sponge—you'll love it!

SERVES 12

50 MINUTES
PLUS COOLING

### SPONGE

1 cup unsalted butter
(at room temperature),
plus extra for greasing

1 cup + 1½ tablespoons
superfine sugar

4 large eggs

1 orange

1½ cups self-rising flour

1 heaping teaspoon baking
powder

### FILLING & TOPPING

1 vanilla bean

1¼ cups heavy cream

2 tablespoons confectioner's
sugar

orange blossom water

rosewater

¼ cup quality strawberry jam

5 oz naturally colored hundreds
and thousands (nonpareils)

Preheat the oven to 350°F. Grease two 8-inch round cake pans and line the bases with parchment paper circles. For the sponge, by hand or with an electric mixer, beat the butter and sugar together until super-light and fluffy. One-by-one, beat in the eggs, then finely grate in the orange zest and fold in the flour and baking powder. Divide between the prepared pans and spread out evenly. Bake for 20 to 25 minutes, or until golden, risen, and an inserted skewer comes out clean. Cool a little in the pans, then transfer to a wire rack to cool completely.

For the Chantilly cream, halve the vanilla bean lengthways, scrape out the seeds, place them in a bowl with the cream, then sift in the confectioner's sugar. Whisk until you get soft peaks, then add just a few drips of orange blossom water, to taste. Mix just a few drips of rosewater into your strawberry jam.

Place your scruffiest sponge on a cake stand and spread the jam over the top, followed by a thin layer of cream. Place the other sponge on top, then, dipping a palette knife into a bowl of boiling kettle water as you go, spread the rest of the cream all over the top and sides of the cake, smoothing it out nice and evenly. Rotate the stand as you go to help you, but try not to overwork the cream.

Place the cake stand in a large roasting pan and sprinkle your hundreds and thousands on top, flicking and gently patting them up the sides of the cake until you have an even coating. Hopefully all the ones that miss will fall into the pan, allowing you to scoop them up and put them to good use, too. Decorate with candles, sparklers, or bunting, if you want, and serve with a good cup of tea.

| CALORIES | FAT | SAT FAT | PROTEIN | CARBS | SUGARS | SALT | FIBER |
|---|---|---|---|---|---|---|---|
| 520kcal | 32.7g | 19g | 4.6g | 54.7g | 38.4g | 0.4g | 0.6g |

# MY CHRISTMAS CAKE

### PACKED WITH DRIED FRUIT, COCOA, STOUT, & SPICE

If I'm completely honest, I've never been a massive Christmas cake fan, but my mum insisted I put one in the book, so I spent months developing this, which I do like! It's lighter than most—have fun decorating it, like I did with Buddy.

**SERVES 16–24**

**3 HOURS 30 MINUTES**
**PLUS COOLING &**
**DECORATING**

14 tablespoons unsalted butter
   (at room temperature),
   plus extra for greasing

5 oz mixed Medjool dates and
   prunes

1 lb mixed dried apricots,
   cranberries, peel, currants

1 apple

1 clementine

6 tablespoons + 2 teaspoons stout

1 cup + 2 tablespoons soft light
   brown sugar

4 large eggs

¾ cup + 5 teaspoons whole milk

2 cups all-purpose flour

1 level teaspoon baking powder

3 tablespoons quality
   unsweetened cocoa powder

1 teaspoon each ground ginger,
   pumpkin pie spice,
   ground cinnamon

Preheat the oven to 300°F. Grease an 8-inch square cake pan with butter and line the base and sides with parchment paper, lining the sides high.

Tear the pits out of the dates and prunes, then place all the dried fruit in a food processor and pulse until roughly chopped. Decant the mixture into a large bowl, coarsely grate in the apple, finely grate in the clementine zest and squeeze in the juice. Pour in the stout, mix well, and leave aside to soak for a few minutes.

Meanwhile, blitz the butter and sugar together in the processor until pale, smooth, and fluffy. With the processor still running, one-by-one crack in the eggs, then pour in the milk in a steady stream, blitzing until smooth. Scrape this mixture into the bowl of fruit and fold together with a spatula. Sift in the flour, baking powder, cocoa, and spices, then fold together again. Transfer to your prepared pan and bake for around 2 hours, or until cooked through and an inserted skewer comes out clean—if it needs a little longer, simply cover the top with parchment paper to prevent it from catching. Leave to cool for 30 minutes in the pan, then transfer to a wire rack to cool completely.

Now the fun bit, the decoration. You'll see from the following pages that my lovely mum likes to keep things traditional—she brushes her cake with warm apricot jam, covers it with marzipan, then uses fondant icing to finish it off nice and smoothly. I, on the other hand, prefer to go a bit more to town. I do brush my cake with warm jam, too, preferably a sour variety, then embracing my inner Mary Berry, I make proper royal icing, and all my old toys come out (for decoration only, of course, so watch those little hands) ... To make royal icing, whisk **3 large egg whites** in a large bowl until fluffy. Sift **5½ cups of confectioner's sugar** separately, then, a spoonful at a time, fold it into the egg whites. Once combined, stir in the juice of **½ a lemon** and **½ a teaspoon of glycerine**. Beat until it forms stiff peaks, then use it to decorate the cake.

| CALORIES | FAT | SAT FAT | PROTEIN | CARBS | SUGARS | SALT | FIBER |
|----------|-----|---------|---------|-------|--------|------|-------|
| 355kcal | 8.5g | 4.9g | 4g | 69.5g | 58.3g | 0.2g | 1.5g |

# CLASSIC MINCE PIES

### FLAKY PASTRY, MINCEMEAT, SWEET SQUASH, ALMONDS, & MAPLE SYRUP

I love all mince pies at Christmastime. This is my nod to the more traditional variety, but I think these are just a bit more interesting than usual, as the addition of delicious, sweet squash really lightens the classic mix.

MAKES 24

2 HOURS 15 MINUTES
PLUS COOLING

FILLING

1 butternut squash (2½ lbs)

3⅔ cups quality
   mincemeat

¼ cup maple syrup

3½ oz blanched almonds

PASTRY

2⅓ cups all-purpose flour,
   plus extra for dusting

¾ cup confectioner's sugar,
   plus extra for dusting

1 cup + 1 tablespoon unsalted
   butter (cold), plus extra
   for greasing

3 large eggs

1 tablespoon reduced-fat (2%)
   milk

GET AHEAD

I love making these in
advance. Stack them in the
freezer and you can cook
them directly from frozen,
with a light egg wash,
for 35 minutes.

Preheat the oven to 350°F. Roast the whole squash for 1 hour 30 minutes, or until cooked through. Once cool enough to handle, halve and seed, then scoop half the soft flesh into a bowl to cool (you only need half here, so keep the remaining roasted squash for another recipe, such as the one on page 146).

Meanwhile, to make the pastry, sift the flour and confectioner's sugar onto a clean work surface. Cube the cold butter, then use your thumbs and fingertips to rub it into the flour and sugar until you end up with a fine, crumbly mixture. Beat 2 eggs and the milk and add to the mixture, then gently work it together until you have a ball of dough—don't work it too much at this stage as you want to keep it crumbly and short. Flour your work surface, pat the dough into a flat round, flour it lightly, wrap in plastic wrap, and pop it into the fridge for at least half an hour.

Lightly grease two 12-cup muffin pans with butter. Add the mincemeat and maple syrup to the bowl of cooled squash, then chop and add the almonds and mix together. Roll out the pastry on a clean flour-dusted surface to ⅛ inch thick. Use a 4-inch pastry cutter to cut out 24 circles of dough, then ease and press them into your prepared cups. Equally divide up the filling, then cut out 3-inch circles from your leftover pastry to top the pies, crimping the edges together as you go. You can also add pastry shapes to decorate, depending on how many offcuts you have. Brush the tops of the pies with beaten eggs, also using it to help you stick on any pastry decorations you've cut out.

Bake for 25 to 30 minutes in the middle of the oven, or until golden. Leave to cool and firm up for 10 minutes in the pans, then carefully transfer to a wire cooling rack. Dust lightly from a height with confectioner's sugar and serve. Lovely hot with a drizzle of custard, or warm or cold with a cup of tea. You can also box them up for another day, and they're great as a gift, too.

| CALORIES | FAT | SAT FAT | PROTEIN | CARBS | SUGARS | SALT | FIBER |
|----------|-----|---------|---------|-------|--------|------|-------|
| 317kcal | 13.6g | 5.6g | 4.6g | 47.4g | 29.4g | 0.1g | 1.4g |

# PHYLLO MINCE PIES

## SOUR DRIED FRUIT, BRANDY, & MINCEMEAT PUFF-PASTRY SWIRLS

This tasty little number is my reinvention of the traditional mince pie, because it's always nice to have options. I'm using a combination of puff and phyllo pastry, both of which you can buy ready-made in the shops for extra convenience.

**MAKES 24**
**50 MINUTES**

4½ oz quality mincemeat

1 oz unsweetened dried cranberries or blueberries

2 clementines

1 splash of brandy

all-purpose flour, for dusting

8 oz all-butter puff pastry (cold)

¼ cup unsalted butter

6 sheets of phyllo pastry (8½ oz)

1 large egg

1 oz flaked almonds

confectioner's sugar, for dusting

Preheat the oven to 350°F. Put the mincemeat into a mixing bowl. Finely chop and add the dried berries, finely grate in the clementine zest, add the brandy, and mix well to make your filling.

Dust a clean work surface with flour and roll out the puff pastry into a rectangle about 16 x 8 inches and ⅛ inch thick. Thinly spread over the mincemeat mixture, leaving a ½-inch gap at the edges. Tightly roll up the pastry lengthways, like a Swiss roll, place it on a floured pan, and firm up in the fridge.

Melt the butter, then use a little to lightly grease each compartment of two 12-cup cupcake pans. Place one layer of phyllo pastry over the pan (you may need more than one sheet to cover it, depending on the size of the sheets) and ease the pastry into each hole. Brush all over with more melted butter, then cover with a second layer of phyllo pastry and brush again with butter.

Take the puff pastry roll out of the fridge and, with a sharp knife, cut it into 24 slices. Place each slice, with a swirl-side up, into a phyllo-lined hole. Brush all over with beaten egg and sprinkle a few flaked almonds on top of each little pie. Dust lightly with confectioner's sugar, then cook for about 30 minutes, or until cooked through, crispy, and golden. Leave to cool, then crack the individual pies out of the pans. Dust with a little more confectioner's sugar before serving.

### GET AHEAD

You can freeze these uncooked in the pans—just wrap the whole lot in plastic wrap. Simply unwrap and cook for 35 minutes in your hot oven, straight from the freezer. Or, once cooked and cooled, you can freeze leftover mince pies, ready to reheat from frozen when you need them—perfect for unexpected guests!

| CALORIES | FAT | SAT FAT | PROTEIN | CARBS | SUGARS | SALT | FIBER |
|----------|-----|---------|---------|-------|--------|------|-------|
| 121kcal | 5.4g | 2.4g | 2.3g | 17.2g | 4.7g | 0.2g | 0.5g |

# MINCE PIE STRUDELS

## APPLE, SWEET POTATO, MINCEMEAT, PECANS, HONEY, & WHISKY

Back when I was a teenager, I used to love making big strudels at Christmas. Inspired by that, I came up with these mini cigar-shaped ones, which are a perfect companion or replacement for an old-school classic puff-pastry mince pie.

**MAKES 12**

**1 HOUR**

1 eating apple

5 oz sweet potato

½ cup unsalted butter

1 teaspoon fennel seeds

2½ oz whisky

1 clementine

1¾ cups quality mincemeat

6 sheets of phyllo pastry (8½ oz)

1½ oz pecan nuts

1 tablespoon liquid honey

Peel and core the apple, peel the sweet potato, then chop both into ½-inch dice. Melt 1 knob of butter in a pan on a medium heat, add the fennel seeds for a couple of minutes, then add the apple, sweet potato, and whisky. Finely grate in the clementine zest and squeeze in the juice. Cook with the lid ajar for 15 minutes, or until softened, stirring occasionally and adding a splash of water, if needed. Leave to cool completely, then mix with the mincemeat.

Preheat the oven to 350°F. Melt the remaining butter and use some of it to brush the inside of a roasting pan (11 x 7 inches). Unroll the phyllo pastry and cut the sheets in half down the middle. Working one-by-one, brush the edges of each pastry sheet with butter, place 3 heaping teaspoons of filling in the center at one end, roll it over a couple of times, then fold in the sides and finish rolling it up into a mini strudel. Place each one in the buttered pan as you go, with the seal at the bottom, then brush the tops with more butter. Chop the pecans and toss with the remaining butter, then scatter over the pan of strudels.

Bake at the bottom of the oven for 30 minutes, or until golden and crispy. Drizzle all over with the honey and you're ready to go. Now, the only decision remains what to have on the side—a cup of tea, or more whisky...?

### GET AHEAD

Make these up to the point where you're ready to bake them, and place the whole pan in the freezer to get ahead. Cook directly from frozen for 40 minutes.

| CALORIES | FAT | SAT FAT | PROTEIN | CARBS | SUGARS | SALT | FIBER |
|----------|------|---------|---------|-------|--------|------|-------|
| 279kcal | 11.2g | 4.3g | 3g | 39.8g | 25.5g | 0.2g | 1.5g |

# THE JAFFA CAKE

## LAYERED SPONGE, DARK CHOCOLATE, & BITTER ORANGE MARMALADE

◇◇◇◇◇◇◇◇◇◇◇◇◇◇◇◇◇◇◇◇◇◇◇◇◇◇◇◇◇◇◇◇◇◇◇◇◇◇◇◇◇◇◇◇◇◇◇◇◇◇◇◇◇◇◇◇◇◇◇◇◇◇◇◇◇◇

Inspired by a fantastic German Christmas cake, but also embracing the old-school chocolate orange Jaffa Cakes that we enjoyed as kids, this is a really fun, satisfying cake to put together—there's real comfort in the making here.

**SERVES 16**

**1 HOUR 30 MINUTES**
**PLUS CHILLING**

1 cup unsalted butter
  (at room temperature),
  plus extra for greasing

10 oz golden marzipan

6 tablespoons + 2 teaspoons
  heavy cream

1 cup + 1½ tablespoons
  superfine sugar

10 large eggs

½ tablespoon vanilla bean paste

1 orange

1 cup self-rising flour

½ cup cornstarch

5 oz quality rindless bitter
  orange marmalade

5 teaspoons whisky

10 oz quality dark chocolate
  (70%), plus extra to serve

1½ oz candied orange peel

Preheat the broiler to medium-high. Grease a deep 9-inch loose-bottomed cake pan and line the base with a parchment paper circle. Roughly chop the marzipan and blitz in a food processor with a splash of cream, ¾ cup of butter, and the sugar until pale and creamy. Separate the eggs, then, one-by-one, beat in the yolks, followed by the vanilla bean paste, the rest of the cream, and the finely grated orange zest. Sift the flour and cornstarch, then use a large metal spoon to fold them into the cake batter. Whisk the egg whites with a pinch of sea salt till they form firm peaks, then gently fold into the batter using the same spoon.

Melt the marmalade in a small pan over a low heat, loosening it with the whisky, and keep warm. Smash up 3½ oz of the chocolate and melt with 2 tablespoons of butter in a heatproof bowl over a pan of gently simmering water. Keep both to one side.

To assemble the cake, use a ladle to spoon just enough batter into the prepared cake pan to cover the base in a thin layer. Spread it out evenly, then cook on the top shelf under the broiler for 3 to 4 minutes, or until set and golden all over—this is really important, otherwise your layers won't show. Ladle another thin layer of batter on top, and return to the broiler. Continue layering and broiling, mixing up the batter with thin layers of warm marmalade and melted chocolate as you go. Repeat until the batter is used up, then brush the top of the cake with a good layer of marmalade and run a knife around the outside. Leave to cool, then cover with plastic wrap and chill for a few hours.

A couple of hours before you're ready to serve, melt the remaining 6½ oz of chocolate and 2 tablespoons of butter in a heatproof bowl over a pan of gently simmering water. Once glossy, leave to cool for 5 minutes. Remove the cake from the pan and set it on a serving plate. Pour over the chocolate sauce and use a spatula to spread it evenly over the top, letting it drizzle down the sides, smoothing it out if you like. Leave it to set, avoiding the fridge, which can make the chocolate go dull, then top with strips of candied orange peel. Great with extra shavings of chocolate on top.

| CALORIES | FAT | SAT FAT | PROTEIN | CARBS | SUGARS | SALT | FIBER |
|---|---|---|---|---|---|---|---|
| 482kcal | 24.6g | 12.1g | 7.5g | 61g | 47.6g | 0.3g | 0.9g |

# CHURROS

## WARM, SPICED, FLUFFY MINI DOUGHNUTS

These are naughty and delicious. I don't make them very often, and that's partly why we all love them so much. Dipped in melted or hot chocolate, they're just a dream to eat—grubby hands and fingers guaranteed (and that's just the adults).

**MAKES 20–24**
**35 MINUTES**
**PLUS COOLING**

6 tablespoons whole milk

5 tablespoons unsalted butter

1 cup self-rising flour

1 teaspoon baking powder

1 large egg

4 cups vegetable oil

¼ cup superfine sugar

1 teaspoon ground cinnamon

Pour ⅔ cup of cold water into a medium pan and add the milk and butter. Bring just to a boil on a high heat, keeping a close eye on it, then remove and stir in the flour, baking powder, and a good pinch of sea salt, until you get a nice, smooth dough. Cool for 10 minutes, then beat in the egg until well combined.

Pour the vegetable oil into a large sturdy pan and place on a high heat. You want it to reach 350°F, so your best bet is to use a thermometer, but, if you don't have one, simply use a little piece of peeled potato as your guide. Drop it into the oil, and when it rises to the top and turns golden, you'll know the oil is hot enough. Now add a spoonful of batter and see how that reacts. Please make sure you are safe and pay attention, and don't have kids or pets running around.

You can either keep it simple and add little pieces of the batter, or you can mold it with your hands into fun shapes (about ½ inch thick). Working in batches, very carefully and gently add the shapes to the hot oil to fry for 3 to 4 minutes. Keep watching and turning them with a slotted spoon until they're golden and puffed up all over, then use the slotted spoon to move them to a pan lined with paper towel to drain. Make sure the oil is back up to temperature before adding more.

Place the sugar and cinnamon in a shallow bowl, and while they're still hot, toss in the drained churros until well coated. Best served warm with a little glass or mug of my Hot chocolate (see page 304), but equally delicious simply with melted quality dark chocolate (70%) for dunking. These are finger-lickingly good.

### SPICE IT UP

If you've made a batch of my Spiced Christmas sugar (see page 360), that would be delicious used here in place of the cinnamon sugar.

| CALORIES | FAT | SAT FAT | PROTEIN | CARBS | SUGARS | SALT | FIBER |
|----------|------|---------|---------|-------|--------|------|-------|
| 106kcal | 7.2g | 2.1g | 1.2g | 9.7g | 2.9g | 0.2g | 0.3g |

# CANNOLI BRANDY SNAPS

## FILLED WITH SILKY SWEET RICOTTA, CHOCOLATE CHIPS, & FRUIT

This is an outrageously delicious treat, with a crispy, crunchy outside and a gorgeous sweet filling. They're easy to make, a little bit messy to put together—but boy will you have fun doing it—and, of course, they're super-tasty to eat.

**MAKES 16**

**1 HOUR**

**BRANDY SNAPS**

5 tablespoons unsalted butter, plus extra for greasing

⅓ cup soft light brown sugar

2 tablespoons golden syrup

½ cup all-purpose flour

½ teaspoon ground ginger

½ an orange

1 tablespoon brandy

confectioner's sugar, for dusting

**FILLING**

2 tablespoons liquid honey

1 teaspoon vanilla bean paste

8 oz ricotta cheese

3½ oz quality dark chocolate (70%)

1¾ oz unsweetened dried cranberries

1¾ oz mixed peel

Preheat the oven to 350°F. Lightly grease a baking sheet and line it with parchment paper. To make the brandy snaps, dice the butter and place in a small pan on a low heat with the soft light brown sugar, golden syrup, and a good pinch of sea salt to gently melt, until you have a lovely golden caramel. Meanwhile, sift the flour and ground ginger into a large mixing bowl. Finely grate in the orange zest, then make a well in the middle. Pour in the buttery caramel, add the brandy, and beat everything together until smooth.

Using a teaspoon, dollop 4 heaping spoonfuls of the brandy snap mixture onto the lined baking sheet, as far away from each other as possible—they spread out a lot as they cook. Bake for around 7 minutes, or until golden brown—keep an eye on them. Leave to cool for exactly 1 minute on the pan, then carefully pry the brandy snaps off the baking sheet and gently bend each one around the handle of a wooden spoon to create a tube. Leave to cool on the spoons—you should get two on each one. Keep going with the mixture, patiently cooking the brandy snaps in batches, until all the mixture is used up.

To make the filling, beat the honey, vanilla bean paste, and ricotta cheese in a food processor until silky smooth, then very finely chop the chocolate, cranberries, and peel, and stir into the mixture. Spoon the filling into a piping bag, or a sandwich bag (then snip the corner off), and carefully pipe into the brandy snaps from both ends. You will get a little bit creeping through the holes but that all adds to the charm! Finish by sifting a little confectioner's sugar over the top, then serve.

### GET AHEAD

Store the cooled brandy snaps in an airtight container and keep the filling in the piping bag in the fridge, then simply assemble when you're ready to serve.

| CALORIES | FAT | SAT FAT | PROTEIN | CARBS | SUGARS | SALT | FIBER |
|----------|-----|---------|---------|-------|--------|------|-------|
| 163kcal | 8.5g | 5.3g | 2.1g | 19.5g | 14.7g | 0.1g | 1.2g |

# BILLIONAIRE'S SHORTBREAD

## GUINNESS CARAMEL, DARK CHOCOLATE, & SEA SALT

This one is hard to beat. Whether enjoyed as a gift, for afternoon tea, or even lightly warmed and served with ice cream for dessert—it's all good, and a wonderful twist on a simple classic. Shortbread, caramel, chocolate—what's not to love?

**MAKES 40 PIECES**
**1 HOUR**
**PLUS CHILLING & SETTING**

**SHORTBREAD**

12 tablespoons unsalted butter (cold), plus extra for greasing

2 cups all-purpose flour

¼ cup superfine sugar

**CARAMEL**

1½ cups soft light brown sugar

1 cup + 1 tablespoon unsalted butter

6 tablespoons Guinness

1¼ cups crème fraîche

**CHOCOLATE**

10 oz quality dark chocolate (70%)

2 tablespoons unsalted butter

Preheat the oven to 350°F. Grease a 12- x 8-inch baking pan with butter. For the shortbread, mix the flour and superfine sugar together in a mixing bowl, then rub in the butter with your thumb and forefingers until you have fine crumbs. Add a little water to bring the mixture together into a dough, then push it into your prepared pan in an even layer. Prick all over with a fork and bake for 20 minutes, or until cooked through and lightly golden. Leave to cool in the pan.

To make the caramel, place the soft light brown sugar, butter, Guinness, and ⅔ cup of water in a pan on a medium-high heat. Bring to a boil and reduce by half, stirring occasionally. Whisk in the crème fraîche, then reduce the heat to low and leave to gently bubble for 20 minutes, whisking often. When it's thick and fudgy, pour over the shortbread—don't try it, it'll be super-hot! Tilt the pan to help the caramel find its natural level, then chill in the fridge for 2 hours.

Snap your chocolate into a heatproof bowl over a pan of gently simmering water, add the butter, then leave to melt, stirring occasionally. Let it cool for a few minutes, then pour over the caramel—you don't want the caramel to melt. Sprinkle with a little sea salt and leave aside until set, then transfer to a board and slice smoothly into bite-sized chunks using a warm knife (dip it in a cup of hot water, for ease). They're good for a few days in an airtight container.

### JAZZ UP YOUR SLICE

Before the chocolate sets, sprinkle over chopped dried fruit and nuts, go mad with a scattering of toffee popcorn (I love how dramatic this looks), swirl through milk or white chocolate, add a pinch of dried red chili flakes, a scattering of seeds, smashed-up pretzels, or any Christmas chocolates. Use your imagination and have fun—this isn't for every day, so seize the opportunity to go all out!

| CALORIES | FAT | SAT FAT | PROTEIN | CARBS | SUGARS | SALT | FIBER |
| --- | --- | --- | --- | --- | --- | --- | --- |
| 235kcal | 18.4g | 11.7g | 1.5g | 16.3g | 9.9g | 0.1g | 1.1g |

# BADASS BROWNIES

## DOUBLE CHOCOLATE, MAPLE SYRUP, MACADAMIAS, & SOUR CHERRIES

Having a good, solid brownie recipe up your sleeve is no joke—every house deserves one. Here's mine, and it's pimped with festive flavors. These oozy, gooey, delicious, naughty treats are guaranteed to get you massive brownie points.

**MAKES 20**
**40 MINUTES**
**PLUS COOLING**

1⅓ cups unsalted butter,
  plus extra for greasing

3½ oz quality white chocolate

7 oz quality dark chocolate
  (70%)

¾ cup + 5 teaspoons
  maple syrup

4 large eggs

⅔ cup all-purpose flour

1 cup quality unsweetened cocoa
  powder, plus extra for dusting

1 teaspoon baking powder

3½ oz macadamia nuts

3½ oz dried sour/tart cherries

Preheat the oven to 325°F. Grease a 9-inch square baking pan and line the base with parchment paper. Chop up the white chocolate, place in the pan, and pop into the freezer while you make the brownie mix—freezing helps prevent the white chocolate from melting too much as the brownies bake.

In a large heatproof bowl over a pan of gently simmering water, melt the butter and dark chocolate, stirring until smooth. Remove from the heat and whisk in the maple syrup, then, one-by-one, beat in the eggs, whisking constantly. Sift in the flour, cocoa, and baking powder, then roughly chop the nuts and fold in with the cherries until just combined. Remove the pan from the freezer, quickly fold the frozen white chocolate through the brownie mix, then spoon it into the pan and spread out evenly. Sprinkle from a height with a pinch of sea salt, then bake for 17 minutes 30 seconds—you don't want to overcook it, and remember, butter and chocolate solidify as they cool, so have faith that after 1 hour of cooling the brownies will have a whole spectrum of amazing textures that will send you wild!

When the cooling time's up, transfer the brownies to a chopping board and slice, then pile up and dust with a little extra cocoa powder before serving. Keep them in an airtight container for up to 1 week (you'll be lucky if they last that long!).

| CALORIES | FAT | SAT FAT | PROTEIN | CARBS | SUGARS | SALT | FIBER |
|---|---|---|---|---|---|---|---|
| 300kcal | 20.5g | 10.7g | 4.5g | 21.5g | 16.1g | 0.1g | 1.7g |

# CUPCAKES

## WITH CHOCOLATE, CARDAMOM, & CRUSHED PISTACHIO TOPPING

There's nothing better than the smell of freshly baked chocolate cupcakes, and these are drizzled with top-quality glossy chocolate, then dunked in crushed pistachios, too. Perfect with a cup of tea or, even better, a little sweet tipple.

MAKES 12

35 MINUTES
PLUS COOLING

6 cardamom pods

14 tablespoons unsalted butter
(at room temperature)

1 cup soft light brown sugar

2 large eggs

1⅓ cups self-rising flour

1 level teaspoon baking powder

2½ tablespoons quality
unsweetened cocoa powder

7 oz quality dark chocolate
(70%)

5 oz shelled unsalted pistachios

6 tablespoons reduced-fat
(2%) milk

heaping ⅓ cup confectioner's
sugar

Preheat the oven to 350°F. Crack the cardamom pods in a pestle and mortar and pick just the inner seeds into the mortar, discarding the husks. Finely grind the seeds into a fine cardamom dust.

In a food processor, beat 11 tablespoons of butter and the soft light brown sugar together until light and fluffy. One-by-one, beat in the eggs until smooth and combined. Sift in the flour, baking powder, and cocoa, snap in half the chocolate, add half the pistachios and all of the cardamom dust, then pulse until just combined, adding enough of the milk to give you a nice spoonable consistency. Stop halfway and use a spatula to scrape down the sides and help it along.

Line a 12-cup cupcake pan with paper liners, then use two teaspoons to evenly divide the mixture between them. Bake for 20 minutes, or until cooked through and an inserted skewer comes out clean of cake mixture (don't worry if you hit some melted chocolate!). Transfer to a wire rack and leave to cool.

To make the topping, put the remaining 3 tablespoons of butter and 3½ oz of chocolate into a heatproof bowl, sift in the confectioner's sugar, then place over a pan of gently simmering water and stir until melted, combined, and all the sugar has dissolved, adding a tiny splash of water to loosen, if needed. Smash up the remaining pistachios until superfine in a pestle and mortar. Now, upside-down, dunk each cupcake in the chocolate topping, then dip into the pistachios for a nice even topping. Be careful not to drop one of them completely in the chocolate, but if you do—chef's treat! Store in an airtight container to keep them fresh.

| CALORIES | FAT | SAT FAT | PROTEIN | CARBS | SUGARS | SALT | FIBER |
|---|---|---|---|---|---|---|---|
| 385kcal | 24.7g | 14.4g | 5.3g | 36.3g | 22g | 0.3g | 2.6g |

# AMALFI CAKE

## ALMOND SPONGE LAYERS, LIMONCELLO LEMON CURD, & RASPBERRY SAUCE

Here we have four layers of the most delicious almond and lemon curd cake, inspired by my mentor, Gennaro Contaldo, who lives and breathes lemons in all that he does. Great as a tea cake, birthday treat, or beautiful dessert—enjoy!

SERVES 16–20

1 HOUR
PLUS COOLING

### SPONGE

1½ cups unsalted butter
   (at room temperature),
   plus extra for greasing

1½ cups superfine sugar

6 large eggs

3 lemons

2 cups self-rising flour

5 oz ground almonds

2 teaspoons baking powder

### FILLING & TOPPING

5 oz frozen raspberries

1 teaspoon liquid honey

½ a lemon

1 cup + 5 tablespoons unsalted
   butter (at room temperature)

4 cups confectioner's sugar

reduced-fat (2%) milk

limoncello, for drizzling

7 oz Lemon curd (see page 306)

Preheat the oven to 350°F. Grease two 8-inch springform cake pans and line the bases with parchment paper circles. For the sponge, by hand or with an electric mixer, beat the butter and sugar together until super-light and fluffy. One-by-one, beat in the eggs, then finely grate in the lemon zest and fold in the flour, ground almonds, baking powder, and a good pinch of sea salt. Divide between the prepared pans and spread out evenly. Bake for 40 to 45 minutes, or until golden, risen, and an inserted skewer comes out clean. Cool a little in the pans, then transfer to a wire rack to cool completely.

Mix the raspberries with the honey and lemon juice and leave to macerate for 30 minutes, mashing occasionally, then push through a sieve to make a smooth sauce. For the buttercream, beat the butter by hand or with an electric mixer until pale. Sift in half the confectioner's sugar and beat for 1 minute, then sift in the rest. Add a splash of milk and beat for 3 to 4 minutes, or until pale and creamy.

To assemble the cake, start by very carefully cutting each sponge in half so you end up with four rounds. Place one sponge on a cake stand, add a few drips of limoncello to the sponge, top with a thin, even layer of buttercream, then one of Lemon curd, and repeat until you've got all four sponges stacked on top of each other. Spread the rest of the buttercream all over the top and sides of the cake, smoothing it out nice and evenly. Rotate the stand as you go to help you, but try not to overwork the buttercream. Gently spoon the remaining lemon curd on top, letting it drizzle artfully down the sides. Serve the raspberry sauce in a little pitcher on the side, ready to drizzle over each slice at the table.

| CALORIES | FAT | SAT FAT | PROTEIN | CARBS | SUGARS | SALT | FIBER |
|---|---|---|---|---|---|---|---|
| 564kcal | 34.4g | 18.8g | 5.7g | 61.2g | 50.7g | 0.4g | 0.6g |

# GINGERBREAD

## VERY SPECIAL GIANT CRUMBLY PERSON (MAN OR WOMAN)

As the title suggests, this is a very special gingerbread recipe that I spent months and months trying to perfect, based on one of the most famous secret recipes in the UK. This is as close as I can get to the real deal, and it's incredibly good.

**SERVES 8**

**35 MINUTES**

14 oz quality shortbread

1 cup demerara sugar

3 level teaspoons ground ginger

½ cup all-purpose flour

1 pinch of baking powder

1½ oz mixed peel

1½ oz crystallized ginger

2 tablespoons golden syrup

2 tablespoons black treacle
  or golden syrup

5 tablespoons unsalted butter

Preheat the oven to 350°F. Line a shallow baking pan (14 x 8 inches) with parchment paper. Roughly crumble the shortbread into a food processor, then add the sugar and 2 teaspoons of the ground ginger and blitz into crumbs. Remove 3½ oz of the mixture and put aside, then add the remaining teaspoon of ginger, the flour, and baking powder to the processor. Chop the peel and crystallized ginger, add that to the processor, too, and blitz until well mixed.

Melt the golden syrup, treacle, and butter together in a large pan, then stir in the mixture from the processor until everything is thoroughly mixed. Tip into the pan and spread out evenly, compacting the mixture well with the back of a spoon.

Bake for 8 to 10 minutes, or until nicely golden, then remove from the oven and scatter over the reserved crumb mixture, pressing that in well with the back of a spoon. Carefully cut into the shape of a gingerbread man or woman with a sharp knife. Cut the surrounding gingerbread into bite-sized chunks, using little cutters to stamp in shapes where you've got more room. Leave to cool completely in the pan, then, to get your person out in one piece, carefully ease out all the little pieces around the edge first, allowing you a bit of space to carefully and proudly lift out your gingerbread person. Decorate as you wish, then serve in the middle of the tea table and let everyone snap off the bit they want most!

### LOVE YOUR LEFTOVERS

This is always best eaten on the day you make it, but any leftovers are good crumbled over vanilla ice cream with a shot of espresso—gingerbread affogato, here we go.

| CALORIES | FAT | SAT FAT | PROTEIN | CARBS | SUGARS | SALT | FIBER |
|----------|-----|---------|---------|-------|--------|------|-------|
| 498kcal | 22g | 13.1g | 3.8g | 75.6g | 44.2g | 0.6g | 1.9g |

Cute

# EDIBLE GIFTS

# FUDGE

## SPIKED WITH WHISKY & CLEMENTINE

Fudge is one of those simple pleasures in life, and learning how to make your own really is a joy. It allows you to accent the flavors however you like, and create the most unbelievable, chewy yet silky texture. Delicious!

2 x 14-oz cans of condensed milk

1½ cups soft light brown sugar

11 tablespoons unsalted butter

¼ cup whisky

2 clementines

Line a shallow pan (12 x 8 inches) with parchment paper. Put a large heavy-based non-stick pan on a medium heat. Pour in the condensed milk, and add the sugar, butter, and a pinch of sea salt. Stir until everything comes together and the sugar starts to dissolve, then add the whisky and finely grate in the zest of 1 clementine. Stir constantly to prevent the mixture from catching on the bottom of the pan. You need to use a candy thermometer here—heat the mixture to 240°F. Whatever you do, do NOT touch or taste the fudge, as it will burn you. It's best to keep kids and pets out of the room while you're making this.

When it reaches the right temperature, use a rubber spatula to help you carefully tip and pour the mixture into the lined pan. Gently tilt the pan a little from side to side to spread the mixture out into a fairly even layer, again being careful not to come into contact with the hot fudge. Finely grate over the zest of the remaining clementine, leave to set at room temperature for 30 minutes, then transfer the fudge to the fridge for at least 1 hour.

To portion up, use the paper to help you lift the fudge out of the pan and onto a chopping board, then slice into portions. You can eat the fudge straight away, or, if you prefer a more crumbly texture, store in an airtight container, where it'll keep happily for a couple of weeks, packaging up at the last minute for gifting.

### MIX IT UP

Swap out the whisky and clementines for 3½ oz of raisins soaked overnight in 6 tablespoons of Vin Santo until plump and juicy. Mix half the raisins into your base fudge mixture with 2 tablespoons of the Vin Santo, and sprinkle the rest of the raisins over the top before it sets.

### MIX IT UP — TAKE 2

Another option is to mash and add 7 oz of roasted, peeled pumpkin and whisk in ½ a teaspoon of ground cinnamon to your base fudge on the heat, then, once it's in the pan, scatter over 1¾ oz of chopped toasted pecan nuts before it sets.

| CALORIES | FAT | SAT FAT | PROTEIN | CARBS | SUGARS | SALT | FIBER |
|----------|-----|---------|---------|-------|--------|------|-------|
| 87kcal | 3.5g | 2.2g | 1.1g | 13.1g | 13g | 0g | 0g |

# TRUFFLES

## SPICED RUM, CRUSHED NUTS, & COCOA

Give tins of the truffle mix and nuts to lucky friends or family, or serve up the separate parts at a party so your guests can scoop up their own silky, shiny truffles, rolling them in whichever coating they prefer. Fun and super-cute.

**MAKES 30**
**20 MINUTES**
**PLUS SETTING**

3 tablespoons dark spiced rum

1¼ cups heavy cream

2 tablespoons unsalted butter

3 drips of orange blossom water

10 oz quality dark chocolate (70%)

1¾ oz mixed blanched almonds and hazelnuts

quality unsweetened cocoa powder

Pour the rum into a pan and heat gently on a medium heat, then set fire to it with a match (stand back!). As the flames begin to subside, add the cream and bring to a gentle simmer. Remove from the heat and stir in the butter and orange blossom water. Once the butter has melted, add a pinch of sea salt, then snap the chocolate and stir it in so it melts nice and slowly. If the mixture splits slightly, don't worry, you can bring it right by adding a splash of boiling kettle water.

Once completely smooth, pour your melted chocolate mixture into a nice little pan or bowl and pop it into the fridge for 2 hours to set. Toast the nuts in a pan on a medium heat until lightly golden and smelling delicious, then crush up in a pestle and mortar and either pour into a dish or wrap up ready to go.

I like to give this as a gift by packaging up the pan of truffle mixture and the crushed nuts with a nice spoon, so in effect you've created a DIY truffle set! These will keep for 5 days in an airtight container in the fridge. Just remind your friends that they should take the truffle mixture out of the fridge about 30 minutes before they need it, so it's at room temperature, then they can start scooping and dunking. You can give them a little pouch of cocoa powder as well as the nuts, to roll the truffles in, should they wish. If you're serving it yourself with a cup of tea or at a dinner party, remember to do the same. Enjoy!

### LEFTOVERS

Any leftovers can be divided up between espresso cups and sprinkled with the crushed nuts, to serve as little chocolate pots for pudding.

| CALORIES | FAT | SAT FAT | PROTEIN | CARBS | SUGARS | SALT | FIBER |
|---|---|---|---|---|---|---|---|
| 152kcal | 14g | 7.1g | 1.2g | 3.5 | 2.9g | 0.1g | 1.2g |

# BISCOTTI

## WITH DARK CHOCOLATE, ALMONDS, & HAZELNUTS

I like biscotti chewy, but I also like biscotti crunchy, so cooking them fresh puts you in control to go either way, or even better, do some of each. They're so much fun to make, and they can take on different flavors, so feel free to experiment.

**MAKES 40 PIECES**

**1 HOUR 15 MINUTES PLUS CHILLING**

1 cup + 1 tablespoon unsalted butter (at room temperature)

1½ cups soft light brown sugar

1 teaspoon vanilla bean paste

1 clementine

3 large eggs

4½ cups Tipo 00 flour

5 oz quality dark chocolate (70%)

2½ oz blanched almonds

2½ oz blanched hazelnuts

In a very large bowl, cream the butter, sugar, vanilla bean paste, and finely grated clementine zest together. Whip the eggs, then beat into the creamed mixture with a pinch of sea salt. Slowly stir in the flour, until combined. Roughly chop the chocolate and nuts, then use your hands to push and squash them into the mixture, distributing them as evenly as you can. Shape the dough into an 8½- x 11-inch rectangle, wrap it in plastic wrap, and pop in the fridge to chill for 30 minutes.

Preheat the oven to 350°F and line two large baking sheets with parchment paper. Unwrap the dough and cut it in half lengthways, reshaping each piece into a long rectangle. Place one in the center of each pan so they have room to spread. Bake for about 35 minutes, or until just starting to brown.

Let the biscotti logs cool for 5 minutes, then use a serrated knife to cut each one into slices just under ¾ inch thick. Lay the slices on their sides on the pans and return to the oven for another 8 to 10 minutes, or until they look gorgeous and lightly golden. You can either eat them straight away or, if you want them to last, leave them in the oven when you turn it off until the oven is cold, so that they dry out and get really crunchy. Store in an airtight container, where they'll keep happily for a good couple of weeks, packaging up at the last minute for gifting.

### BE PREPARED

To prepare for unexpected teatime guests, wrap and freeze the pans of sliced biscotti before the second bake so you've got them ready and raring to go. Bake for 10 minutes from frozen.

| CALORIES | FAT | SAT FAT | PROTEIN | CARBS | SUGARS | SALT | FIBER |
|----------|-----|---------|---------|-------|--------|------|-------|
| 172kcal | 9.7g | 4.6g | 3.6g | 17.8g | 7.7g | 0.1g | 0.9g |

# FLORENTINES

## CRANBERRIES, ALMONDS, CANDIED PEEL, SEEDS, & CHOCOLATE

Florentines are a joy to make and a joy to eat, and are really open to all kinds of festive flavors, so mix up the dried fruit, nuts, and seeds to embrace your favorites. They're the perfect gift, but are also good gifted to yourself with a cup of tea.

MAKES 30
50 MINUTES
PLUS COOLING

¼ cup unsalted butter,
  plus extra for greasing

2½ oz unsweetened dried
  cranberries

2½ oz mixed peel

⅔ cup superfine sugar

1 heaping tablespoon
  all-purpose flour

⅔ cup heavy cream

3½ oz flaked almonds

1½ oz raw sunflower seeds

1½ oz raw sesame seeds

7 oz quality dark chocolate
  (70%)

Preheat the oven to 350°F. Lightly grease two large baking sheets and line them with parchment paper. Chop the cranberries and slice the peel. Melt the butter and sugar in a small saucepan over a low heat, then whisk in the flour and cream until you get a light caramelly sauce. Remove from the heat and stir in the cranberries, peel, almonds, and all the seeds until well mixed.

Working in batches, place teaspoons of mixture on the lined pans, flattening them slightly with the back of the spoon. Make sure you leave at least 4 inches between the spoonfuls, as they spread a lot while they cook. Bake for 10 to 12 minutes, or until golden around the edges—keep an eye on them! Remove and leave to harden slightly on the pan, then lift up the paper and transfer to a cooling rack to cool completely, while you crack on with another batch. You can either leave the florentines as they are, with a bit of scruffy charm or, while they're still warm, you can trim them with a round cutter, like I've done to a few of mine in the picture. The benefit of the latter choice is you get to enjoy the offcuts as a chef's treat, and they're great crumbled over ice cream.

When done, melt the chocolate in a heatproof bowl over a pan of gently simmering water. Once the florentines have cooled, dunk them in the chocolate, put back on the sheets of paper to set, then portion up and get gifting. These will keep for up to 5 days in an airtight container—if you can resist them for that long!

| CALORIES | FAT | SAT FAT | PROTEIN | CARBS | SUGARS | SALT | FIBER |
|---|---|---|---|---|---|---|---|
| 144kcal | 10.5g | 4.9g | 1.8g | 10.4g | 8.8g | 0g | 0.9g |

# Get gifting

Not only are edible gifts super-fun to make and receive, they're fun to wrap up, too. Enjoy choosing your receptacles, remembering that often you'll need to sterilize a jar (see page 312), or use an airtight container, then decorate with ribbons, string, and lovely personalized tags, adding any instructions you might need. Your kids will love helping you with name tags. Just remember to store your gifts as suggested until right before it's time to give them out, and pass the same instructions on to the lucky recipient.

# ROCKY ROAD

## POPCORN, NUTS, CLEMENTINE, GINGER, SOUR FRUIT, & CHOCOLATE

Making your own rocky road, which is so utterly simple and fun to do, means you can use top-quality ingredients fit for the festive season, creating a brilliant megamix of your favorite Christmassy flavors that everyone is sure to enjoy.

MAKES 20 PIECES

35 MINUTES
PLUS COOLING

vegetable oil

1 small sprig of fresh rosemary

1 oz popcorn kernels

1¾ oz mixed unsalted nuts

¼ cup unsweetened desiccated coconut flakes

1 clementine

2 tablespoons stem ginger syrup

1¾ oz dried fruit, such as cranberries, sour/tart cherries, golden sultanas

2½ oz treats, such as Turkish delight, marshmallows, gingernut biscuits

14 oz quality dark chocolate (70%)

1¾ oz quality milk chocolate

1¾ oz quality white chocolate

Put a pan on a high heat with 1 tablespoon of vegetable oil and the rosemary sprig. Stir in the popcorn kernels until well coated. Put the lid on and, as the corn starts to pop, hold the lid firmly in place with a kitchen towel and give the pan a shake every few seconds to make sure all the kernels get popped. Turn the heat off, then remove any unpopped kernels with a spoon, along with the rosemary sprig.

Roughly chop the nuts and stir into the popcorn with the coconut, then finely grate in the clementine zest and return the pan to a low heat, stirring for 2 to 3 minutes, or until smelling incredible. Drizzle in the ginger syrup, add the dried fruit, and chop or crumble in the mixed treats, then turn the heat off. Remove a large spoonful of the mixture and put aside to decorate the rocky road later.

Snap the dark chocolate into a large heatproof bowl over a pan of gently simmering water and leave to melt, stirring occasionally. Once glossy and smooth, add the popcorn mixture and stir well. Grease and line a baking sheet (12 x 10 inches) with parchment paper, then pour over the mixture, spreading it out fairly evenly. Melt the milk and white chocolate in separate bowls and drizzle over the rocky road in whatever fashion you like, then scatter over the reserved handful of mixture, poking it into the chocolate. Leave to cool for a few hours so it hardens and sets. Break into random chunks, or slice up more delicately. Delicious bagged up and given as a gift, or with a cup of tea or coffee, or a glass of port or Vin Santo.

| CALORIES | FAT | SAT FAT | PROTEIN | CARBS | SUGARS | SALT | FIBER |
|---|---|---|---|---|---|---|---|
| 199kcal | 13.8g | 7.9g | 2.7g | 15.5g | 13.1g | 0g | 2.4g |

# HONEYCOMB

## DIPPED IN GLOSSY MELTED CHOCOLATE

Making honeycomb is a bit like magic: one minute you've got a hot caramel, then within a few seconds of adding the baking soda you've got a sprawling frothy concoction rising up the sides of the pan. It's great fun and super-delicious.

MAKES 20–25 PIECES

25 MINUTES

½ tablespoon baking soda

2⅓ cups superfine sugar

4 heaping tablespoons liquid honey

7 oz quality milk and/or dark chocolate (70%)

optional: shelled pistachios, dried cranberries, freeze-dried raspberries, popping candy

Line a deep baking pan (12 x 10 inches) with parchment paper. Measure out your baking soda and put it in a little dish next to the stove—you'll need to work quickly once the sugar reaches the right temperature. Put the sugar, honey, and 3 tablespoons + 1 teaspoon of water into a medium-sized, deep, heavy-bottomed pan. Stir, then heat to 300°F on a candy thermometer. Do NOT be tempted to touch or taste the caramel—it will burn you. It's best to keep kids and pets out of the room while you make this.

As soon as the caramel reaches the right temperature, turn the heat off and add the baking soda, whisking quickly and carefully to combine it. It will froth right up, but that's normal. Carefully pour the mixture straight onto your lined pan, but don't touch it or tilt the pan—you want to keep it still so you don't knock the bubbles out, and remember it's still super-hot! Leave to one side to cool completely.

Once cool, crack the honeycomb into bite-sized pieces (saving any smaller bits for sprinkling over puds, or use them in my Chocolate log—see page 256). You can leave the honeycomb plain, but I think it's at its best dunked in melted chocolate. Simply snap up and melt the chocolate in a heatproof bowl over a pan of gently simmering water. I find the easiest thing to do is to dunk, then place the pieces on a wire cooling rack to set. Whether you half dip or fully submerge is up to you. You can also follow the dunk with a dip into finely chopped pistachios or dried cranberries, freeze-dried raspberries, or even popping candy. Have fun with it!

This will keep for up to 2 weeks in an airtight container, or slightly longer if you opt for the full glossy chocolate dunk.

| CALORIES | FAT | SAT FAT | PROTEIN | CARBS | SUGARS | SALT | FIBER |
|----------|-----|---------|---------|-------|--------|------|-------|
| 178kcal | 6.3g | 3.9g | 1.2g | 30.5g | 30g | 0.3g | 1g |

# HOT CHOCOLATE

## MY EPIC MIX

◇◇◇◇◇◇◇◇◇◇◇◇◇◇◇◇◇◇◇◇◇◇◇◇◇◇◇◇◇◇◇◇◇◇◇◇◇◇◇◇◇◇◇◇◇◇◇◇◇◇◇◇◇◇◇◇◇◇◇◇◇◇◇◇◇◇◇◇◇◇◇◇◇◇◇

This is off the scale. It's so simple to make and is much better than the store-bought stuff, which probably hasn't got much chocolate in it anyway. I don't want you to feel cheated, I want you to have the real thing . . . life's too short not to.

**MAKES 1 BIG JAR
(24 SERVINGS)**

**10 MINUTES**

7 oz quality dark chocolate (70%)

10 tablespoons quality unsweetened cocoa powder

5 tablespoons Horlicks powder

5 tablespoons cornstarch

5 tablespoons confectioner's sugar

2 pinches of ground cinnamon

This is my go-to hot chocolate recipe. The quantities I've given you here make one really lovely jar that'll benefit whoever's lucky enough to receive it for months. The quantities are really easy to scale up (or down!), so it's easy to make a big batch of this and divvy it up between friends and family, or make a bonkers big jar to last someone an entire year! Whatever you do, follow the easy method for making the mixture, and be sure to share the instructions I've given you below on how to make a tasty cup of deliciously thick hot-chocolaty heaven.

To make the hot chocolate mix, finely grate the chocolate into a bowl. Add all the other ingredients and a good pinch of sea salt, mix well, then decant into jars.

For each portion of hot chocolate, you'll need 1 heaping tablespoon of mixture and **⅔ cup of whole milk**. Simply pour however much milk you need into a pan and bring to a steady simmer over a medium heat. Whisk in your hot chocolate mix and leave it to bubble away for a few minutes, or until you achieve a gorgeous, thick, almost claggy texture, which will be totally knockout. Pour into your mugs, and enjoy. This is absolutely irresistible teamed with Churros (see page 272).

### ONE FOR THE GROWN-UPS

Add a splash of brandy or Cointreau for a festive finish.

| CALORIES | FAT | SAT FAT | PROTEIN | CARBS | SUGARS | SALT | FIBER |
|---|---|---|---|---|---|---|---|
| 75kcal | 4.2g | 2.5g | 1.4g | 7.6g | 5.3g | 0.1g | 1.4g |

# LEMON CURD

## SMOOTH, SILKY, & SPIKED WITH LIMONCELLO

Lemon curd is a lovely gift and a great condiment to have in the fridge. It's super-simple and fun to make, and of course tastes way better than your average jarred stuff, especially with an added hit of limoncello—it is Christmas, after all!

**MAKES 2 LBS**
**50 MINUTES**
**PLUS CHILLING**

6 lemons

14 oz granulated sugar

6 large eggs

1⅓ cups unsalted butter

3 tablespoons limoncello

Finely grate the zest of 3 lemons into a large heatproof bowl, then squeeze in the juice from all 6 lemons—you want about ¾ cup in total. Stir in the sugar and sit the bowl over a pan of gently simmering water for about 15 minutes, or until all the sugar granules have dissolved, stirring occasionally. Remove the bowl and leave to cool for a few minutes, leaving the pan of water on the heat.

In a separate bowl, beat the eggs, then gradually whisk them into the lemon mixture until combined. Sit the bowl back over the pan for another 15 minutes, or until the mixture is thick enough to coat the back of a spoon, whisking regularly. Whisk in the butter, until melted, followed by the limoncello. Remove from the heat and leave to cool, then cover and pop into the fridge overnight to thicken.

Divide between cute little sterilized jars (see page 312), label up, and get gifting! It will keep for up to 2 weeks in a cool place. Enjoy it on scones, or simple toast, spooned over Pannacotta (see page 236), or in my Amalfi cake (see page 284).

### MIX IT UP

This recipe is a wonderful base for you to experiment with all kinds of seasonal citrus fruit. Try removing a little lemon juice and replacing it with lime, clementine, blood orange, or even pink grapefruit juice. You'll get spectacular results.

| CALORIES | FAT | SAT FAT | PROTEIN | CARBS | SUGARS | SALT | FIBER |
|----------|-----|---------|---------|-------|--------|------|-------|
| 122kcal | 6.5g | 3.7g | 1.5g | 14.5g | 14.5g | 0.1g | 0g |

# CHILI SAUCE

## HEAVENLY, HOMEMADE, & BRILLIANT WITH JUST ABOUT ANYTHING

Simple as this recipe is, it took me months of testing to get it just right. It has provided me, and the recipients of this lovely gift, with bags of pleasure. It's a beautiful thing—take it, make it, gift it, enjoy it—I know you'll love it.

**MAKES APPROX.
8 CUPS**

**1 HOUR
PLUS COOLING**

4 onions

4 cloves of garlic

20 fresh mild red chiles

olive oil

4 teaspoons chili powder

2 lbs ripe tomatoes

1¼ cups cider vinegar

heaping ⅓ cup superfine sugar

2 cups unsweetened apple juice

Peel the onions and garlic, pull the stalks off the chiles, then chop it all, either patiently by hand or in a food processor. Place a large casserole pan on a low heat with 2 tablespoons of oil, tip in the chopped veg, and cook for around 10 minutes, or until soft but not colored, stirring occasionally.

Stir the chili powder into the pan, then chop and add the tomatoes, followed by the vinegar, sugar, apple juice, ¾ cup + 5 teaspoons of water, and a good pinch of sea salt and black pepper. Bring to a boil, then simmer for 15 minutes, stirring occasionally.

Carefully pour the mixture into a blender, pop the lid on, and cover with a kitchen towel, then, holding it in place, blitz until silky smooth. If you like your chili sauce with a bit of texture, you can absolutely leave it as it is. I prefer it lovely and smooth, so I pass it through a fine sieve to get a nice pouring consistency—add a splash of boiling kettle water to loosen, if needed. Either way, have a taste and season to absolute perfection. This is a make or break moment: give the sauce attitude—it's a condiment to be dribbled over things, so it needs to pack a punch.

Divide between sterilized jars or bottles (see page 312), label up, and get gifting. It will keep for up to 6 weeks in a cool, dark place. Once opened, keep in the fridge and use within a couple of weeks. Trust me, once you taste it, it won't last long!

### MIX IT UP

Feel free to blend different types of chiles in this recipe—I particularly like to swap in jalapeño or Scotch bonnets. But obviously use your common sense—if you go for super-hot chiles like Scotch bonnets, you can reduce the amount by up to a half or the sauce will blow your head off!

| CALORIES | FAT | SAT FAT | PROTEIN | CARBS | SUGARS | SALT | FIBER |
|---|---|---|---|---|---|---|---|
| 13kcal | 0.3g | 0g | 0.2g | 2.4g | 2.2g | 0g | 0.3g |

HOT

# PICCALILLI

## PINEAPPLE, CAULIFLOWER, APPLE, MANGO, & CHILES

My ultimate piccalilli celebrates my favorite part of the recipe, the incredible harmony between pineapple and cauliflower, as well as that amazing array of spices. This, my friends, will become a year-round staple in your fridge.

MAKES APPROX. 4½ LBS
1 HOUR 25 MINUTES

2 lbs cauliflower

2 cloves of garlic

2-inch piece of fresh gingerroot

4 fresh red chiles

olive oil

2 heaping tablespoons black mustard seeds

2 tablespoons ground turmeric

2 teaspoons ground cumin

1 whole nutmeg, for grating

2 tablespoons English mustard

¼ cup all-purpose flour

2 cups white wine vinegar

2 eating apples

2 ripe mangos

1 ripe pineapple

4 fresh bay leaves

6 tablespoons superfine sugar

Cut the cauliflower into ¾-inch florets, finely dice the stalk (discarding the tough end bit), and place it all in a large bowl with 2 handfuls of sea salt. Pour in just enough water to cover it all, and leave in a cool place for 1 hour.

Peel and finely chop the garlic and ginger, and finely slice the chiles. Put a large pan or stockpot on a medium heat with 2 tablespoons of oil. Fry the mustard seeds, turmeric, cumin, and the finely grated nutmeg for 1 minute. Reduce to a low heat and add the garlic, ginger, and chiles, along with the mustard, flour, and a splash of vinegar. Stir well to make a thick paste, then gradually stir in the rest of the vinegar and ¾ cup + 5 teaspoons of water, stirring until smooth. Core the apples, peel and pit the mangos, then peel and core the pineapple. Chop it all into ½-inch chunks, chucking it into the pan as you go. Add the bay and sugar, and stir for 2 minutes.

Drain the cauliflower well and stir into the pan. If it looks a little thick, add a splash of water to loosen. Cook for 10 to 15 minutes, or until just softened and starting to release some juice. Taste, season to perfection, divide between sterilized jars (see page 312), label up, and get gifting. It will keep for up to 6 weeks in a cool, dark place. Once opened, keep in the fridge and use within a couple of weeks.

| CALORIES | FAT | SAT FAT | PROTEIN | CARBS | SUGARS | SALT | FIBER |
|----------|-----|---------|---------|-------|--------|------|-------|
| 17kcal | 0.4g | 0.1g | 0.4g | 2.8g | 2.6g | 0.1g | 0.2g |

# PEAR PICKLE

## MRS OLIVER'S FAVORITE SPICY RECIPE

My mum's delicious spiced pear and apple pickle is wonderful and can be used in so many different ways, from cheese platters to sandwiches, to spice up a gravy, or with hot or cold meats. It's the perfect gift, for a loved one or for yourself!

**MAKES APPROX. 4½ LBS**
**2 HOURS 20 MINUTES**
**PLUS COOLING**

4 fresh red chiles

2 large red onions

½ a bulb of garlic

4-inch piece of fresh gingerroot

4 cardamom pods

1 heaping tablespoon black
    peppercorns

2 teaspoons fenugreek seeds

3 tablespoons sunflower oil

3 tablespoons yellow mustard
    seeds

2 teaspoons ground cumin

1 tablespoon ground turmeric

4½ lbs pears

2 lbs Bramley, Granny Smith,
    or other tart cooking apples

14 oz dark muscovado or dark
    brown sugar

2 cups cider vinegar

Seed and finely slice the chiles, then peel and finely chop the onions, garlic, and ginger. Crack the cardamom pods in a pestle and mortar and pick just the inner seeds into the mortar, discarding the husks. Grind the seeds with the peppercorns and fenugreek seeds until fine. Put a very large pan on a medium heat to get nice and hot. Put the oil and mustard seeds into the pan, then, as soon as the seeds start to pop, add the crushed cardamom mixture, the cumin, turmeric, and 1 tablespoon of sea salt. Stir and cook for 2 minutes, then add the chiles, onions, garlic, ginger, and a splash of water. Cook gently for 5 minutes, or until softened, stirring occasionally, while you peel, core, and chop the pears and apples, adding them to the pan as you go. Stir in the sugar, vinegar, and 6 tablespoons of water. Bring to a simmer, then cook on a low heat for around 2 hours, or until you have a sticky, jammy pickle, stirring occasionally.

While the pickle is cooking, sterilize your jars (see below). Once cooked, divide between sterilized jars, label up, and get gifting. It will keep for up to 6 weeks in a cool, dark place. Once opened, keep in the fridge and use within a couple of weeks.

### HOW TO STERILIZE JARS

To sterilize jars, lids, and a spoon for dividing up your wares, either submerge them in a very large pan of boiling water for 10 minutes, then leave to dry, or put them through the hottest cycle of your dishwasher.

| CALORIES | FAT | SAT FAT | PROTEIN | CARBS | SUGARS | SALT | FIBER |
|----------|-----|---------|---------|-------|--------|------|-------|
| 24kcal | 0.4g | 0.1g | 0.2g | 5.1g | 5g | 0.1g | 0.5g |

# Super-fantastic

## SALADS

# SPINACH & BACON SALAD

## PINE NUTS, PICKLED ONIONS, & CRISPY CROUTONS

Classic, comforting, and simple, this is all about getting the details spot-on—fresh salad and spinach leaves, crisp smoky bacon, a delicious, bright, smooth dressing, and, of course, those crunchy bacon-fat croutons. This is hard to beat.

SERVES 4

20 MINUTES

6 thick rashers of smoked bacon

olive oil

2 heaping tablespoons pine nuts

12 x ½-inch-thick slices of
    French baguette

6 medium pickled onions, and
    2 tablespoons liquor from
    the jar

2 teaspoons Dijon mustard

quality extra virgin olive oil

4 large handfuls of baby spinach

1 handful of seasonal salad leaves

Slice the bacon into thin lardons and put into a large frying pan on a medium heat with 1 tablespoon of olive oil. Fry until golden, adding the pine nuts for the last minute, then scoop out with a slotted spoon onto a plate, leaving the tasty bacon fat behind. Toast the bread slices in the fat until beautifully golden on both sides.

Meanwhile, finely slice the pickled onions. In a large bowl, mix the pickled onion liquor with the mustard, ¼ cup of extra virgin olive oil, and a pinch of black pepper. Pick through, wash, and spin-dry the spinach and salad leaves, then gently pile them on top. Add the crispy bacon, pine nuts, and pickled onions, then lightly toss everything together with your fingertips, picking the salad up and sprinkling it back down from a height a few times—doing it this way means it's perfectly dressed but you avoid bruising the leaves. Add the croutons and tuck in.

### MIX IT UP

A couple of ideas to tweak this salad: a tiny amount of crumbled blue cheese or feta would be very nice, but you don't need to add much to make a difference. Similarly, some matchsticks of seasonal orchard fruit such as apple or pear would be a joy.

| CALORIES | FAT | SAT FAT | PROTEIN | CARBS | SUGARS | SALT | FIBER |
|---|---|---|---|---|---|---|---|
| 402kcal | 25.2g | 4g | 10.2g | 35.9g | 3.4g | 2g | 2.9g |

# CRISPY CAMEMBERT PARCELS

## WINTER SALAD & CRANBERRY DIP

This is one of my speedy favorites—if you're working quickly you can have it on the table in just 15 minutes, though of course feel free to take your time. Crispy pastry filled with oozy cheese and a tangy cranberry dip, what's not to love?

**SERVES 4**

**15 MINUTES**

### PARCELS

7 oz Camembert cheese

3½ oz shelled walnut halves

1 bunch of fresh chives (1 oz)

1 lemon

4 sheets of phyllo pastry

olive oil

### DIP

2½ oz unsweetened dried cranberries

1 pinch of ground cloves

½ teaspoon ground ginger

½ cup port

### SALAD

balsamic vinegar

extra virgin olive oil

1 red endive

1 green endive

1 eating apple

2½ oz watercress

1 pomegranate

Put the Camembert into a food processor with the walnuts and half the chives. Finely grate in the lemon zest and blitz until combined. On a clean surface, fold each sheet of phyllo in half widthways. Add a quarter of the mixture across the bottom of one folded sheet in a sausage shape, then loosely roll it up like a long cigar. Repeat until you have four parcels. Put a large frying pan on a medium heat. Brush each parcel with a little olive oil and put into the hot frying pan, turning till golden and crispy all over.

Meanwhile, put the cranberry dip ingredients into a small pan on a medium heat and leave to bubble away while you finely slice the remaining chives and scatter them over a large platter. Drizzle the platter with balsamic and extra virgin olive oil, squeeze over half the lemon juice, and add a pinch of sea salt and black pepper. Trim, then finely slice the endive bases and click the delicate leaves apart. Coarsely grate the apple, then add to the platter with the endive and watercress.

Blitz the cranberry dip mixture in a blender until smooth (adding a splash of water to loosen, if needed), then pour onto a small platter and serve with the parcels for dipping. Toss the salad with the dressing at the table, then cut the pomegranate in half, hold it cut-side down in your fingers over the salad, and bash the back with a spoon so the seeds tumble on top. Delicious.

| CALORIES | FAT | SAT FAT | PROTEIN | CARBS | SUGARS | SALT | FIBER |
|---|---|---|---|---|---|---|---|
| 600kcal | 32.5g | 9.6g | 19.2g | 51.5g | 23.8g | 1.7g | 3.4g |

# WINTER SLAW

## CARROT, APPLE, CABBAGE, RADISHES, DRIED FRUIT, & ALMONDS

◇◇◇◇◇◇◇◇◇◇◇◇◇◇◇◇◇◇◇◇◇◇◇◇◇◇◇◇◇◇◇◇◇◇◇◇◇◇◇◇◇◇◇◇◇◇◇◇◇◇◇◇◇◇◇◇◇◇◇◇◇◇◇◇◇◇◇◇◇◇◇◇◇◇◇◇◇◇◇◇◇◇◇◇

When made with love and care, this simple slaw is a total celebration of the season, embracing lots of lovely veg. It's super-healthy, and is wonderful with both hot and cold dishes, so it's great to have up your sleeve over the festive period.

SERVES 12 AS A SIDE
25 MINUTES

1 red onion

2 large carrots

2 eating apples

½ a red cabbage (1 lb)

½ a white cabbage (1 lb)

1 heaping tablespoon whole-grain mustard

¼ cup white wine vinegar

extra virgin olive oil

1 bunch of radishes

½ a lemon

3½ oz flaked almonds

3½ oz dried fruit, such as sour/tart cherries, cranberries, blueberries

1 bunch of fresh Italian parsley (1 oz)

The combo of veg and fruit here will give you a delicious-tasting slaw, but it's the pride you take in the slicing and shredding that will really give this slaw the edge when it comes to amazing texture. Peel the onion and carrots, core the apples, and click off any tatty outer leaves from the cabbages. Using the finest blade on your food processor or a mandolin (use the guard!), finely slice the onion, then place in a large bowl and toss with the mustard, vinegar, ¼ cup of oil, and a pinch of sea salt and black pepper—this will just take the raw edge off the onion.

Finely slice the cabbages and pile into the bowl on top of the onion and dressing. Switch to a julienne or fine grating cutter and shred the carrots and radishes, scattering them into the bowl as you go. Shred the apples, tossing them with the lemon juice to prevent them discoloring, then pile into the bowl.

Lightly toast the almonds, chop up the dried fruit, and scatter those into the bowl. Roughly chop the top leafy half of the parsley and sprinkle that in, too. At this point, you can transfer it to the fridge, unmixed, ready to toss together later, if you want to get ahead. When you're ready to serve, use your clean hands to toss and scrunch the slaw together well, then taste and season to perfection.

Delicious served with Jerk ham (see page 44), Bubble & squeak (see page 198), my Toad in the hole (see page 176), or grilled meats, fish, and other salads.

### MIX IT UP

I've given you a suggestion for what veg and fruit to use here, but feel free to swap in whatever you've got—anything fresh and crunchy will work a treat, from pears to celery to fennel and even Brussels sprouts!

| CALORIES | FAT | SAT FAT | PROTEIN | CARBS | SUGARS | SALT | FIBER |
|----------|-----|---------|---------|-------|--------|------|-------|
| 162kcal | 10.4g | 1.2g | 3.8g | 14.2g | 13.5g | 0.4g | 3.2g |

# ROASTED CARROT & AVO SALAD

## ORANGE DRESSING, WINTER LEAVES, SEEDS, & TOASTED CIABATTA

This fantastic Moroccan-style salad gives roasted carrots and avocado some serious attitude. With crunchy ciabatta croutons to add contrast, plus spice, seeds, sour cream, and a tasty citrus dressing, you've got a winner on your hands.

**SERVES 4**
**50 MINUTES**

1 lb small mixed-color carrots, heirloom if you can get them

1 teaspoon cumin seeds

1 small dried red chile

1 clove of garlic

4 sprigs of fresh thyme

extra virgin olive oil

1 tablespoon red wine vinegar

1 orange

2 large ripe avocados

4 x ½-inch-thick slices of ciabatta

¼ cup mixed seeds

2 handfuls of mixed winter salad leaves, such as Treviso, radicchio, arugula, baby kale

1 cup of sprouting cress

¼ cup sour cream

Preheat the oven to 350°F. Wash the carrots, then parboil in a pan of boiling salted water for 10 minutes, or until almost cooked through. Meanwhile, smash up the cumin seeds, chile, and a pinch of sea salt and black pepper in a pestle and mortar until fine. Peel and add the garlic, strip in the thyme leaves, pound into a paste, then muddle in 2 tablespoons of oil and the vinegar.

Drain the carrots well, tip them into a bowl, and, while they're still steaming hot, pour over the dressing, tossing until well coated. Tip the carrots into a roasting pan, halve and add the orange (its sticky juice will add great flavor to the dressing later), and roast for 25 to 30 minutes, or until nicely golden.

Just moments before the carrots are ready, halve, pit, and peel the avocados, then cut them into wedges lengthways and place in a big bowl. Remove the carrots from the oven and add them to the avocados. Using tongs, carefully squeeze the hot, sticky orange juice over the carrots, then add around three times as much oil and a good pinch of seasoning and delicately toss together. Toast or grill your ciabatta slices, and toast the mixed seeds in a frying pan on a medium heat until smelling fantastic. Get a big platter out, or individual plates if you prefer, and get your gang round the table.

Tear the toast into bite-sized pieces and toss with the carrots and avo. Pick through, wash, spin-dry, and tear in the salad leaves, snip over the cress, then lightly toss and transfer to your platter or divide between your plates. Spoon over the sour cream, sprinkle over the toasted seeds, and tuck in.

### EMBRACE YOUR LEFTOVERS

This is a great vehicle for using up leftover Glazed carrots (see page 132)—warm them through in the oven so you still have that lovely hot element.

| CALORIES | FAT | SAT FAT | PROTEIN | CARBS | SUGARS | SALT | FIBER |
|---|---|---|---|---|---|---|---|
| 367kcal | 30.6g | 6.9g | 7.2g | 20.5g | 10.6g | 1.4g | 1g |

# RETRO LAYERED SALAD

## MARIE ROSE SHRIMP, PASTA, DRESSED CRUNCHY VEG, & CHEESE

Dare I say it, this is a slightly tacky dish, inspired by those molded salads you can pick up in Marks & Spencer's. This little beauty is fun to make and brings back lots of happy childhood memories for me—I hope you love it as much as I do.

**SERVES 6–8**
**1 HOUR**
**PLUS CHILLING**

½ an English cucumber

1 heaping teaspoon dried dill

2 tablespoons white wine vinegar

8 oz dried mini pasta shells

15 ripe cherry tomatoes

olive oil

1 tablespoon balsamic vinegar

1 x 11-oz can of sweetcorn

2 scallions

extra virgin olive oil

cayenne pepper

½ an iceberg lettuce

3 cups sprouting cress

14 oz cooked peeled shrimp

2 large carrots

½ a bunch of fresh basil (½ oz)

3½ oz Red Leicester cheese

MARIE ROSE SAUCE

2 tablespoons tomato ketchup

4 heaping tablespoons
mayonnaise

Worcestershire sauce

brandy

Tabasco sauce

½ a lemon

Cut the cucumber into ½-inch dice, toss in a bowl with a pinch of sea salt and black pepper, the dill, and white wine vinegar, then leave to pickle. Cook the pasta in a pan of boiling salted water according to the package instructions, then drain and refresh under cold running water. Meanwhile, cook the tomatoes in a non-stick frying pan over a low heat with a splash of olive oil and a pinch of seasoning for 10 to 15 minutes, or until golden and soft, then squash and push through a coarse sieve into a bowl. Add the drained pasta and balsamic vinegar and toss to coat. Drain the sweetcorn and place in a separate bowl, trim, finely slice, and add the scallions, drizzle with a little extra virgin olive oil, add a pinch each of black and cayenne pepper, then mix. To make the Marie Rose sauce, mix the ketchup and mayo with a splash each of Worcestershire sauce and brandy, a few drips of Tabasco, and the lemon juice, then taste and season to perfection.

Line a 9½-inch-wide mixing bowl with a double layer of plastic wrap, letting it hang well over the edges. Spoon the sweetcorn into the base and pat down into an even layer. Finely slice the lettuce and scatter half into the bowl. Snip 2 cups of cress on top, taking the time to arrange it with the leaves facing out. Scatter over the shrimp, then spoon over the Marie Rose sauce and spread out in an even layer. Peel and coarsely grate over the carrots, then layer the dressed pasta on top. Pick over most of the basil leaves, then evenly grate over the Red Leicester and scatter over the remaining lettuce. Press everything down with your hands, then spoon over the cucumber and its dressing. Fold in the plastic wrap to seal the salad, then get yourself a plate that just fits inside the dish, place on top, and add something heavy like a pestle and mortar to weigh it down. Pop it into the fridge for at least 2 hours, or overnight, if you want it for the next day.

When you're ready to serve, turn out the layered salad—think sandcastle—and carefully peel away the plastic wrap. Snip over the remaining cup of cress, scatter with the remaining basil leaves, and drizzle with a little extra virgin olive oil. Serve as is, or as part of a bigger buffet spread.

| CALORIES | FAT | SAT FAT | PROTEIN | CARBS | SUGARS | SALT | FIBER |
|---|---|---|---|---|---|---|---|
| 390kcal | 11.7g | 4.6g | 21.2g | 50.2g | 10.8g | 2.4g | 5.1g |

# WALDORF SALAD

## ROASTED GRAPES, CRUSHED WALNUTS, ROQUEFORT, & CREAMY DRESSING

I love this evolution of the classic Waldorf salad with sweet roasted grapes and a yogurty dressing, making it more interesting, healthier and even more delicious to share with friends and family as a main, or as part of a bigger feast.

SERVES 4–6
50 MINUTES

1 lb seedless grapes

olive oil

2 sprigs of fresh rosemary

3½ oz shelled walnut halves

1 French baguette

1 lemon

1 teaspoon English mustard

2 tablespoons white wine vinegar

4 heaping tablespoons plain
  yogurt

1 bunch of fresh chives (1 oz)

2 Romaine lettuces

2 red endive

2 stalks of celery

½ a bunch of fresh tarragon (½ oz)

2½ oz Roquefort cheese

extra virgin olive oil

Preheat the oven to 350°F. Wash the grapes, removing any stalks, then place them on a roasting pan, drizzle with olive oil, and strip over the rosemary leaves. Roast for around 35 minutes, or until golden and sticky. Roughly chop the walnuts, scattering into the grape pan to lightly toast for the last 5 minutes, and warm your French baguette alongside at the same time.

To make your dressing, squeeze the lemon juice into a large serving bowl, add the mustard, vinegar, and yogurt, and mix together. Finely chop the chives, stir most of them into the dressing, then taste and season to perfection. Click apart the lettuce leaves and tear into the bowl on top of the dressing. Trim, then slice the endive bases and click the delicate leaves apart and add to the bowl. Trim, finely slice, and add the celery, and pick over the tarragon leaves, ready to toss together at the last minute.

Leave the grapes to cool for a few minutes, then add to your salad bowl with the walnuts, making sure you scrape in any sticky goodness from the base of the pan. Gently toss it all together, crumble over the Roquefort, and drizzle lightly with extra virgin olive oil (new season's, if you've got it). Sprinkle over the remaining chives from a height, and serve right away with the warm baguette on the side. A good glass of French red wine is always going to be enjoyable here, too.

| CALORIES | FAT | SAT FAT | PROTEIN | CARBS | SUGARS | SALT | FIBER |
|---|---|---|---|---|---|---|---|
| 442kcal | 20.7g | 5.1g | 13.7g | 54g | 18.2g | 1.4g | 4.1g |

# PORK & RICE SALAD

## GRANNY SMITH APPLES, WALNUTS, HONEY, & THYME

◇◇◇◇◇◇◇◇◇◇◇◇◇◇◇◇◇◇◇◇◇◇◇◇◇◇◇◇◇◇◇◇◇◇◇◇◇◇◇◇◇◇◇◇◇◇◇◇◇◇◇◇◇◇◇◇◇◇◇◇◇◇◇◇◇◇◇

Inspired by the Caribbean classic rice and peas, I created this really exciting rice salad of my own, embracing all the flavors of a good roast pork dinner, with honey, apple, and herbs. It's perfect hot, but also delicious served cold.

**SERVES 6**

**1 HOUR 10 MINUTES**

1½ lbs pork belly, skin off, bone out

olive oil

2 fresh bay leaves

2 sprigs of fresh rosemary

3 Granny Smith apples

1¾ oz shelled walnut halves

2 tablespoons liquid honey

4 sprigs of fresh thyme

1 orange

1½ cups mixed basmati and wild rice

2 tablespoons cider vinegar

2 scallions

1 bunch of fresh Italian parsley (1 oz)

Preheat the oven to 350°F. Use your sharpest knife to slice the pork belly into ¾-inch-thick slices, then across into ¾-inch chunks. Place 2 tablespoons of oil in a large ovenproof frying pan on a medium-high heat. Add the diced pork, the bay, and rosemary. Season well with sea salt and black pepper, then cook for 20 minutes, or until the pork is dark golden and crispy, stirring regularly. When done, remove and discard the herbs, then pour most of the fat into a jam jar, cool, and place in the fridge for tasty cooking another day. Leave the pan on the heat.

Quarter and core the apples, then cut into rough chunks about the same size as the pork. Add the apples to the frying pan with another 2 tablespoons of oil, roughly crumble in the walnuts, and add the honey. Strip in the thyme leaves, squeeze in the orange juice and stir well. Transfer the pan to the oven for around 20 minutes, or until the mixture turns gorgeous and dark golden—keep a close eye on it and take it out as soon as it's perfect. Basically you want to be almost getting nervous that it's going to burn, then you know you're at exactly the right point.

Meanwhile, cook the rice in a pan of boiling salted water according to the package instructions, then drain and leave to steam dry. Take the frying pan out of the oven and carefully tip the pork, apples, and walnuts onto the rice. Stir the vinegar into the hot pan with a wooden spoon, scraping up all those lovely sticky bits from the bottom—that's where all the flavor is. Once you've got it all looking delicious, tip the rice and pork mixture back into the frying pan. Trim and finely slice the scallions, finely chop the top leafy half of the parsley, and stir both into the rice. Taste and season to perfection, adding a little more vinegar, if needed. Serve straight away, at room temperature, or leave to cool, cover, and pop into the fridge to have cold the next day—great as part of a buffet.

| CALORIES | FAT | SAT FAT | PROTEIN | CARBS | SUGARS | SALT | FIBER |
|----------|-----|---------|---------|-------|--------|------|-------|
| 548kcal | 28.2g | 6.2g | 19.1g | 57.9g | 15.7g | 0.9g | 1.8g |

# WARM CRISPY DUCK SALAD

## GNARLY TOASTS, WINTER LEAVES, & CLEMENTINE DRESSING

This is a cross between a warm salad and an open sandwich. Whack it in the middle of the table and let everyone tear it up. Gnarly, spiced toasts, a robust winter salad, and crispy duck—heaven. I can promise you there'll be nothing left.

**SERVES 6**

**3 HOURS**

1 x 4½-lb whole duck

olive oil

1 tablespoon Chinese five-spice powder

2½ oz dried sour/tart cherries

red wine vinegar

2 cloves of garlic

2 sprigs of fresh rosemary

6 large, thick slices of sourdough bread

6 clementines

liquid honey

extra virgin olive oil

2 red endive

2 white endive

3 oz watercress

4 sprigs of fresh mint

Get your meat out of the fridge and up to room temperature before you cook it. Preheat the oven to 350°F. In a large roasting pan, rub the duck all over with 1 tablespoon of olive oil, the Chinese five-spice, and a pinch of sea salt and black pepper. Roast for 2 hours, or until the duck is crispy and cooked through. Just cover the cherries with boiling kettle water to rehydrate them.

After 2 hours, transfer the duck to a board. Leaving about ¼ cup behind, skim the rest of the fat from the pan into a jam jar, cool, and place in the fridge for tasty cooking another day. Stir 2 tablespoons of vinegar into the pan with a wooden spoon, scraping up all the sticky bits from the base, then crush in the unpeeled garlic through a garlic crusher. Strip in the rosemary leaves, then use the bread to wipe up all those flavors. Lay the bread slices juicy-side up in the pan, drain and sprinkle over the rehydrated cherries, and place in the oven for around 10 minutes, or until golden.

To make the dressing, finely grate the zest of 2 clementines into a small bowl and squeeze in the juice of 3. Mix in ¼ cup of vinegar, a pinch of salt and pepper, a drizzle of honey, and ¼ cup of extra virgin olive oil. Have a taste and check the balance—you want it to be slightly too acidic and salty.

Trim, then finely slice the endive bases, and click the delicate leaves apart. Put them into a large bowl with the watercress. Peel the remaining clementines and slice them into rounds, then pick and slice the mint leaves.

Pull all the crispy skin off your duck. Take the pan of bread out of the oven and quickly pull the skin apart over the top. Return to the oven for 5 minutes, while you use two forks to pull and shred every last bit of meat off the bone. Spoon a few tablespoons of the salad dressing over the shredded meat to stop it drying out.

Halve the toasts lengthways, then criss-cross them on your plates. Toss the shredded meat, the remaining dressing, and the salad leaves, clementine slices, and mint leaves together, pile on top of the toasts, and serve right away.

| CALORIES | FAT | SAT FAT | PROTEIN | CARBS | SUGARS | SALT | FIBER |
|----------|-----|---------|---------|-------|--------|------|-------|
| 596kcal | 39.3g | 10g | 19.9g | 41.1g | 16.1g | 1.3g | 2.1g |

# FIFTEEN CHRISTMAS SALAD

### THE PERFECT SEASONAL COMBO, INSPIRED BY MY LONDON RESTAURANT

With sweetness, bitterness, crunch, and softness, this is a brilliant combo. Fresh, juicy clementines, smoky speck, creamy mozzarella, salty Parmesan, fragrant mint, peppery arugula, bitter Treviso, and sticky balsamic. Delicious.

**SERVES 4**

**15 MINUTES**

2 x 4½-oz balls of buffalo mozzarella

1 lemon

4 clementines

extra virgin olive oil

2 handfuls of arugula

1 Treviso or radicchio

½ a bunch of fresh mint (½ oz)

4 slices of speck (smoked prosciutto)

Parmesan cheese

thick balsamic vinegar

Get out four pretty serving plates and tear half a ball of mozzarella onto each plate. Sprinkle from a height with a pinch of sea salt and black pepper, then finely grate a scraping of lemon zest over each portion. Peel the clementines, slice into ¼-inch-thick rounds, and divide between the plates.

Squeeze the lemon juice into a large bowl, add 2 tablespoons of oil and a pinch of salt and pepper, and mix well. Pick through, wash, and spin-dry the arugula and Treviso or radicchio, and tear into the bowl. Pick, slice, and add the mint leaves (reserving the baby leaves for garnish), then gently toss it all together to coat.

On a chopping board, lay out a slice of speck, pile a quarter of the dressed leaves on top, and wrap it up. Place the salad parcel on one of the plates, and repeat. Shave over a little Parmesan, sprinkle over the baby mint leaves, and finish with a few drips of good balsamic vinegar. Eat immediately!

### MIX IT UP

Clementines are super-festive here, but you can absolutely swap in blood oranges, peaches, pears, or figs, if you fancy.

| CALORIES | FAT | SAT FAT | PROTEIN | CARBS | SUGARS | SALT | FIBER |
|----------|-----|---------|---------|-------|--------|------|-------|
| 294kcal | 22.8g | 11g | 17.3g | 6g | 5.3g | 2.3g | 1.2g |

# DIPS,
# BITES,
## & handheld nibbles

# BAKED CAMEMBERT

## TEAR 'N' SHARE SPONGY ROSEMARY ROLLS

These are loads of fun to make, look pretty, taste great, and usually everyone's got a Camembert or similar-style cheese hanging around at Christmas, so this is a fantastic way to enjoy it. Gooey, creamy, tempting, and packed with flavor.

SERVES 15

1 HOUR 15 MINUTES
PLUS PROVING

3 cups strong bread flour,
 plus extra for dusting

2¾ cups strong whole-wheat
 bread flour

1 x ¼-oz package of dried yeast

unsalted butter

½ cup bread crumbs

3 x 8-oz round Camembert
 cheeses

6 sprigs of fresh rosemary

3 small cloves of garlic

1–2 fresh red chiles

olive oil

Put the flours, yeast, and 1 teaspoon of sea salt into a large bowl. Make a well in the middle and gradually pour in 2¼ cups of tepid water, stirring and bringing in the flour from the outside to form a rough dough. Knead on a clean flour-dusted surface for 10 minutes, or until smooth and springy. Place in a lightly greased bowl, cover with a clean damp kitchen towel, and proof in a warm place for 2 hours.

Grease a large nice-shaped ovenproof pan with butter, then evenly scatter over the bread crumbs. Leaving a ½-inch rim around the edge, cut the rind off the top of each Camembert (reserving two of the boxes). Pick the tip off each rosemary sprig and poke into the soft cheeses, then peel the garlic, finely slice with the chiles, and poke those in, too. Sprinkle each cheese with a pinch of sea salt and black pepper, then place one cheese in the center of the pan. Divide the dough into three pieces, then each of those into 10, giving you 30 in total. One-by-one, roll each piece into a ball and place on the pan, building out from the Camembert in a circular motion, like in the picture. Leave to proof for another hour, again covered with a damp kitchen towel.

Preheat the oven to 350°F. Strip the rest of the rosemary leaves into a little pile, toss with a little oil, and scatter over the dough. Sprinkle with a good pinch of sea salt from a height, then bomb over tiny bits of butter, which will melt into the bread as it cooks. Bake for 30 minutes, or until the Camembert is gooey and the bread is risen and cooked through. Bang the pan in the middle of the table, and dive in—elbows at the ready, this one's hard to resist. And what's great is that you know you've got two cheeses in reserve, ready to bake. As soon as you serve the first Camembert, bake the second one in its box on a pan for about 20 minutes, then decant onto the bread pan, repeating again with the remaining cheese, as and when needed. Guaranteed happy customers, all round.

| CALORIES | FAT | SAT FAT | PROTEIN | CARBS | SUGARS | SALT | FIBER |
| --- | --- | --- | --- | --- | --- | --- | --- |
| 270kcal | 13.4g | 7.9g | 15g | 24.3g | 0.4g | 1.2g | 2.1g |

# TARAMASALATA

### SILKY SMOKED COD'S ROE, LEMON, & CAYENNE

I really believe this is one of the most beautiful, decadent, and delicious dips you can make, and it's a wonderful excuse to celebrate exciting veg in all their different colors, shapes, and sizes on the side, for some epic dunking.

**SERVES 10**

**10 MINUTES**

7 oz white bread
(without crusts)

2 large lemons

2 pinches of cayenne pepper

½ a clove of garlic

6 tablespoons cold-pressed
extra virgin olive oil

3½ oz smoked cod's roe

Tear the bread into chunks and place in a mixing bowl. Pour over 6 tablespoons of cold water and leave for 1 minute. Squeeze the lemon juice into a blender with the cayenne, then peel and add the garlic and pour in the oil. Roughly chop the cod's roe and add on top. Squeeze the bread really well to get rid of any excess water, then add to the blender. Liquidize to a very fine, silky purée, adding a small splash of water to help it along, only if it needs loosening.

Taste the taramasalata and season to perfection with sea salt and black pepper, if needed. Spoon onto a platter and drizzle with a little extra oil. If making ahead, loosen with a splash of water before serving, if needed—it can thicken over time.

Delicious served with crunchy seasonal veg to provide contrast to the smooth silky taramasalata. Trim or slice radishes, fennel, kohlrabi, and carrots into bite-sized morsels that are a pleasure to eat, pick baby green and purple kale leaves, and click apart endive, serving on the side for dunking. Also good with warm buttered bread, grilled crostini drizzled with oil, nice crackers, or crispbreads.

### JAZZ IT UP

If you've got an extra piece of smoked cod's roe, freeze it to use another day. This makes it perfect for grating over things, like I've done in the picture here, adding a great sweet, smoky, kinda bitter-salty flavor to the dish.

| CALORIES | FAT | SAT FAT | PROTEIN | CARBS | SUGARS | SALT | FIBER |
|----------|-----|---------|---------|-------|--------|------|-------|
| 150kcal | 10.6g | 1.6g | 3.8g | 10.5g | 0.6g | 0.7g | 0.6g |

# SAUSAGE ROLL MANIA

EACH RECIPE MAKES 20 SAUSAGE ROLLS

### SWEET SQUASH & CHEDDAR

Preheat the oven to 350°F. Roast a **2½ lbs squash** whole for 1 hour 30 minutes, or until soft. Leave to cool, then halve lengthways and remove the seeds and skin. Roll out **12 oz of cold all-butter puff pastry** to 20 x 8 inches and brush all over with **beaten egg**. Crumble over **6 vac-packed chestnuts** and sprinkle with **1 tablespoon of unsweetened dried cranberries**, gently pressing them into the pastry. Finely grate over **1¾ oz of Cheddar cheese**, evenly fork over the squash, leaving a 1-inch border at one long edge, then season and roll up like a Catherine wheel. Brush with more egg, then slice 1 inch thick and lay on a non-stick pan. Grate over more cheese, then toss the leaves from 1 **sprig of fresh rosemary** in a little **olive oil** and sprinkle over. Bake now or freeze for another day. Bake in a preheated oven at 350°F for 30 minutes, turn, then bake for 10 minutes, or until golden.

### GARLIC MUSHROOM & THYME

Peel and finely chop **4 cloves of garlic** and place in a large pan on a medium-high heat with **2 tablespoons of unsalted butter**, the leaves from **6 sprigs of fresh thyme**, and a pinch of sea salt and black pepper. Stir, while you chop **1¼ lbs of mixed mushrooms**, adding them to the pan as you go. Cook for 40 minutes, or until dark and nutty. Cool, then finely chop and mix with **1 large egg** and **¾ cup of bread crumbs**. Roll out **12 oz of cold all-butter puff pastry** to 20 x 6 inches and shape the filling down the middle. Brush the exposed pastry with **beaten egg**, fold it over the filling, and gently press out any air. Trim, use a flour-dipped fork to crimp and seal the edge, then brush it all with more egg and scatter over **1 heaping tablespoon of raw sesame seeds**. Slice 1 inch thick and lay on a non-stick pan. Bake now or freeze for another day. Bake in a preheated oven at 350°F for 30 minutes, or until golden.

### SAUSAGE, SAGE, & MUSTARD

Roll out **12 oz of cold all-butter puff pastry** to 20 x 6 inches. Squeeze the meat out of **14 oz of Cumberland sausages**, and shape down the middle of the pastry. Tear over **12 fresh sage leaves**, finely grate over a little **nutmeg**, and add dots of **English mustard**. Brush the exposed pastry with **beaten egg**, fold it over the filling, and gently press out any air. Trim, use a flour-dipped fork to crimp and seal the edge, brush it all with more egg, and scatter over **1 heaping tablespoon of raw sesame seeds**. Bake now or freeze for another day. Halve and bake on a non-stick pan in a preheated oven at 350°F for 30 minutes, or until golden.

### BOLD BLACK PUDDING

Roll out **12 oz of cold all-butter puff pastry** to 20 x 6 inches. Discarding the skin, shape **10 oz of quality soft black pudding** down the middle of the pastry, then use your hands to squeeze and mold it into more of a round shape. Brush the exposed pastry with **beaten egg**, then fold it over the filling and gently press out any air. Trim, use a flour-dipped fork to crimp and seal the edge, then brush it all with more egg, and scatter over **1 heaping tablespoon of raw sesame seeds**. Slice 1 inch thick and lay on a non-stick pan. Bake now or freeze for another day. Bake in a preheated oven at 350°F for 30 minutes, or until golden.

| CALORIES | FAT | SAT FAT | PROTEIN | CARBS | SUGARS | SALT | FIBER |
|----------|-----|---------|---------|-------|--------|------|-------|
| 123kcal | 7.7g | 4.2g | 3.1g | 10.4g | 1.3g | 0.4g | 0.7g |

THESE VALUES ARE AN AVERAGE OF THE FOUR RECIPES ABOVE

# SMOKED SALMON BLINIS

## MINI SOFT FLUFFY PANCAKES & TOPPING IDEAS GALORE

We make these every Christmas when guests are arriving. It's generally a job that me and Dad do—while greeting people with a drink you can also be knocking out a few freshly cooked blinis, adding simple toppings as you go. Yum.


**MAKES 30 BLINIS**

**15 MINUTES
PLUS TOPPINGS**

1 cup self-rising flour

1 large egg

olive oil

1 cup reduced-fat (2%) milk

unsalted butter

For the blinis, place the flour and a pinch of sea salt in a large mixing bowl. Make a well in the center, crack in the egg, and add 1 tablespoon of oil, then beat into the flour. Gradually whisk in the milk until you've got a lovely, smooth batter.

Put a large non-stick frying pan on a medium heat and add 1 small knob of butter. Once hot and the butter's melted, add tablespoons of batter to the pan to make your blinis. Cook for 1 minute on each side, flipping over when they turn golden on the bottom and get little bubbles on top. The first batch always helps you figure out your temperature control, so adjust it up or down if needed. Transfer the cooked blinis to a plate, and continue with the remaining batter until it's all used up. Top with your favorite combos, season to perfection, and enjoy.

### TEAM WAVES OF QUALITY SMOKED SALMON WITH . . .

- Cucumber peeled into ribbons, placed proudly on top of a little cream cheese with a fine grating of lemon zest

- Peeled and finely shaved raw baby beets, a squeeze of lemon juice, and a pinch of fresh tarragon

- Cooked beets blitzed with cream cheese until smooth, topped with a fine grating of fresh horseradish root

- Cream cheese loosened with a little lemon juice, and a sprinkling of salmon caviar to add an extra pop of flavor

- A dollop of sour cream and a sprinkling of chopped fresh chives and finely sliced tender asparagus

- Puréed avocado and a little jarred jalapeño, a dollop of sour cream, and a few freshly picked cilantro leaves

### GET AHEAD

Make the batter the night before, then simply leave covered in the fridge until needed, whisking up well before use.

# WELSH RAREBIT

### CIABATTA, SILVERSKINS, CORNICHONS, & CHILI JAM

I don't know anyone who doesn't go mad for Welsh rarebit—it's essentially just posh cheese on toast! This recipe is great, as you can make the rarebit topping in advance and simply keep it in the fridge, ready to spread, bake, and go.

SERVES 12

40 MINUTES

**RAREBIT**

4 large eggs

10 oz crème fraîche

1 heaping teaspoon English mustard

7 oz mature Cheddar cheese

Worcestershire sauce

2 x 9-oz loaves of nice ciabatta

**PARTY FARE**

1 jar of chili jam

1 jar of baby cornichons

1 jar of silverskin pickled onions

3½ oz watercress

Separate the eggs, then whisk the egg yolks with the crème fraîche and mustard (put the egg whites into a sandwich bag and pop in the freezer for making meringue another day—see page 222). Finely grate and stir in the cheese, then season to perfection with sea salt, black pepper, and a good few drips of Worcestershire sauce. Cover, and put into the fridge for up to 2 days, or until needed.

When you're ready to cook, preheat the oven to 350°F. Halve the ciabattas lengthways, place on a large baking sheet and pop into the oven for 10 to 15 minutes to crisp up. Take out the pan, then divide and spread the rarebit mixture evenly across the ciabatta halves, randomly stabbing them with a regular butter knife to encourage the rarebit to penetrate the bread. Return to the oven for another 10 to 15 minutes, or until they're golden and bubbling.

Slice up the rarebit and serve with chili jam, cornichons, silverskin pickled onions, and picked watercress leaves for a bit of crunch and contrast. Delicious.

| CALORIES | FAT | SAT FAT | PROTEIN | CARBS | SUGARS | SALT | FIBER |
|----------|-----|---------|---------|-------|--------|------|-------|
| 315kcal | 20.1g | 11.3g | 10.8g | 24.4g | 2.2g | 1g | 1.5g |

# Party stations

Keep your party simple, and you'll have the time to enjoy it, too. Set up stations where people can help themselves—Silky pâté (see page 32) next to loaves of bread and a toaster or a vat of Party squash soup (see page 100) with a stack of cups and a ladle. Prep stuff ahead, ready to heat and go, such as my Welsh rarebit (see page 346), Baked Camembert (see page 336), and fun Sausage roll mania (see page 342).

# QUESADILLAS

## SWEET RED ONIONS, BRUSSELS SPROUTS, & PECORINO

These tasty bites of deliciousness are about celebrating the humble Brussels sprout in all its glory, in a delightful homemade tortilla that has incredible texture. These quesadillas also make a great lunch for four lucky people.

**MAKES 12 TRIANGLES**

**50 MINUTES**

2 red onions

8 oz Brussels sprouts

2 tablespoons unsalted butter

½ teaspoon cumin seeds

¼ teaspoon smoked paprika

6 sprigs of fresh thyme

1 lime

5 oz pecorino or Parmesan cheese

4 tablespoons plain yogurt or sour cream

hot chili sauce

### QUINOA TORTILLAS

1½ cups quinoa

1 heaping teaspoon fennel seeds

1 level teaspoon baking powder

olive oil

You can obviously use regular flour or corn tortillas, if you prefer, but to make these delicious quinoa tortillas, blitz the quinoa, fennel seeds, and baking powder with 1 tablespoon of oil in a blender until fine, shaking regularly. Once you have a fairly fine flour, remove 2 heaping tablespoons for dusting. Tip the rest into a bowl and slowly add enough water to turn it into a firm-ish dough. Knead for 1 minute, then divide it into four equal-sized balls. Use some of the reserved flour to generously dust a clean surface, then press out a piece of the dough with your hand. Dust the top with more flour, then gently roll out to the thickness of a beer mat. Because there's no gluten in the dough it may crack, but you can easily pull a bit off the side to patch up any holes. Use an 8-inch cake pan, lid, or plate to cut out each perfect round, then cook them in a hot dry frying pan as and when they're rolled, for 1 minute on each side. Place on a clean kitchen towel and cover until needed.

For the filling, peel the onions, wash and trim the sprouts, clicking off any tatty outer leaves, then run them through the fine slicing attachment of your food processor. Place in a large non-stick frying pan on a medium heat with the butter, cumin seeds, and paprika. Strip in the thyme leaves, cover, and cook for 10 minutes, stirring occasionally. Remove the lid and fry for 10 minutes more, or until golden and caramelized, still stirring occasionally, then add a good squeeze of lime.

Lay your tortillas on a flat surface and use half the cheese to add a good grating to just half of each tortilla. Divide up the sprout filling and sprinkle on top of the cheese, then grate over the rest of it. Fold the tortillas in half and press together. Cook two at a time in your frying pan on a medium heat until golden and crisp on both sides and the cheese has melted. Place on a board, cool for 1 minute, then slice each triangle into three and serve with yogurt or sour cream spiked with chili sauce, plus lime wedges for squeezing over. Yum.

| CALORIES | FAT | SAT FAT | PROTEIN | CARBS | SUGARS | SALT | FIBER |
|---|---|---|---|---|---|---|---|
| 168kcal | 8.9g | 4.3g | 7.4g | 15.6g | 2.8g | 0.8g | 1.8g |

# SAMOSA CIGARS

## BEAUTIFUL CURRIED VEG, LENTILS, & CHICKPEAS

I've always loved samosas, and rolled up like this into cigar shapes, they're the perfect appetizer or finger food for parties and gatherings, plus they're simple to put together. I find them equally delicious torn over a salad for a nice lunch.

MAKES 18 CIGARS
1 HOUR 30 MINUTES
PLUS COOLING

10 cardamom pods

6 cloves

2 teaspoons Madras curry
   powder

2 cloves of garlic

1¼-inch piece of fresh gingerroot

1 onion

2 medium carrots

½ a bunch of fresh cilantro
   (½ oz)

2 tablespoons unsalted butter

heaping ⅓ cup red lentils

1 x 15-oz can of chickpeas

¾ cup frozen peas

1 lemon

6 sheets of phyllo pastry

olive oil

4 sprigs of fresh mint

Crack the cardamom pods in a pestle and mortar and pick just the inner seeds into the mortar, discarding the husks. Finely grind the seeds with the cloves and a pinch of sea salt into a dust, then mix in the curry powder.

Peel the garlic, ginger, onion, and carrots, then finely chop with the cilantro stalks (reserving the leaves in a bowl of cold water). Place it all in a large pan on a medium-low heat with the butter and two-thirds of the spice mix. Cook for 10 minutes, or until soft and lightly golden, stirring occasionally. Stir in the lentils and the chickpeas (juice and all), and add enough water so everything is just covered. Simmer on a low heat for 40 minutes, or until the lentils are cooked through and it's thick and delicious, stirring occasionally. Remove from the heat, taste, and season to perfection. Stir in the frozen peas and leave to cool. Once cool, finely chop and stir through the cilantro leaves, along with the lemon juice.

Unroll your phyllo. Lay the sheets out in front of you, with the long edges nearest to you. Lightly brush them all with oil and sprinkle over most of the remaining spice mix from a height, then cut each sheet into three fat strips, giving you 18 in total. Divide up the filling, placing 1 level tablespoon near the bottom of each strip. One at a time, shape the filling into a neat cylinder, leaving a ¾-inch border at the bottom and sides. Fold in the sides and loosely roll them up (to prevent them from cracking), sealing the edges with a little oil. Repeat until they're all wrapped up, spacing them out on an oiled baking sheet as you go. Brush with a little more oil and scatter over the rest of the spice mix, then chill until needed.

Bake in a preheated oven at 350°F for 15 to 20 minutes, or until crisp, golden, and hot through, then serve sprinkled with baby mint leaves and with dips of your choice on the side. I like to blend ripe mango flesh with yogurt for one dip, and cucumber, fresh mint, and yogurt for the other. Just remember to season your dips to perfection before you serve them.

| CALORIES | FAT | SAT FAT | PROTEIN | CARBS | SUGARS | SALT | FIBER |
|----------|-----|---------|---------|-------|--------|------|-------|
| 100kcal | 2.5g | 0.9g | 3.9g | 15.6g | 2.4g | 0.3g | 1.9g |

# BAKED BUNS

## STUFFED WITH WINTER RAGÙ

◇◇◇◇◇◇◇◇◇◇◇◇◇◇◇◇◇◇◇◇◇◇◇◇◇◇◇◇◇◇◇◇◇◇◇◇◇◇◇◇◇◇◇◇◇◇◇◇◇◇◇◇◇◇◇◇◇◇◇◇◇◇◇◇◇◇◇◇◇◇◇◇◇◇◇◇◇◇◇◇◇◇◇◇

These baked buns are delightful and delicious. They make fantastic handheld food at a party, or as part of a buffet, and work a treat served like a Cornish pasty with a salad. People will go crazy over them—give them a go, you won't regret it.

**MAKES 20 BUNS**

**1 HOUR 30 MINUTES PLUS PROVING**

**FILLING**

1 lb Winter ragù (see page 190)

Worcestershire sauce

HP sauce

**BUNS**

1 x ¼-oz package of dried yeast

1 tablespoon superfine sugar

3⅔ cups strong bread flour, plus extra for dusting

½ cup unsalted butter (cold)

¾ cup reduced-fat (2%) milk

1 large egg

If you haven't done so already, make up a batch of Winter ragù (see page 190). For the ideal filling consistency, making it a day or more in advance is helpful.

To make the buns, stir the yeast and sugar into ⅔ cup of tepid water and leave for 10 minutes. Place the flour and a really good pinch of sea salt in a bowl, dice and add the butter, then use your thumbs and forefingers to rub the butter into the flour until you have a crumble consistency. Make a well in the middle, pour in the yeast mixture, along with the milk, then gradually mix into the crumbs, bringing them in from the outside. When it starts to come together, knead with clean hands on a clean flour-dusted surface for 5 to 10 minutes, or until smooth, silky, and elastic. Divide into 20 even-sized balls (about 1¾ oz each), space them 2 inches apart on a flour-dusted surface, cover with a clean damp kitchen towel, and leave to proof for up to 2 hours, or until nicely puffed up.

Now it's time to give your ragù a bit of extra attitude, and make sure it's the perfect filling consistency. You want it just a little saucy, so if you've made it ahead it'll probably be spot-on, but if you've cooked up a fresh batch, it's worth draining off a little liquid. Taste your cool ragù and tweak it with Worcestershire and HP sauces, so it'll pack a punch when stuffed into your buns. One-by-one, flatten each dough ball, add a heaping dessertspoon of ragù to the center, then pull the sides of the dough up around the ragù, pinching them together as you go. At this stage you could freeze the buns, ready to bake another day.

When you're ready to cook, let your buns come up to room temperature, brush them with beaten egg, and place them on baking sheets lined with parchment paper. Bake in a preheated oven at 350°F for 25 to 30 minutes, or until puffed up, golden, and the filling is hot through. Good with English mustard.

| CALORIES | FAT | SAT FAT | PROTEIN | CARBS | SUGARS | SALT | FIBER |
| --- | --- | --- | --- | --- | --- | --- | --- |
| 123kcal | 2.1g | 0.6g | 5.8g | 20.9g | 2.6g | 0.2g | 2.9g |

# FOUR PARTY DIPS

### SPANISH STYLE
#### RED PEPPERS, HAZELNUTS, & PARSLEY

Drain **1 x 16-oz jar of large peeled red peppers**, quickly pat them dry with paper towel and place in a blender. Trim, roughly chop, and add **2 scallions**, along with the leaves from **½ a bunch of fresh Italian parsley (½ oz)**, **1 tablespoon of sherry vinegar**, and **1 tablespoon of extra virgin olive oil**. Toast **2½ oz of hazelnuts** in a frying pan on a medium heat until smelling fantastic, then tip into the blender and blitz it all until smooth. Taste and season to perfection, then decant into a bowl and drizzle with a little more **extra virgin olive oil**.

### GUACAMOLE
#### SMASHED AVO, SCALLIONS, & CHILE

Trim **1 scallion** and seed **1 fresh red chile**, then finely chop them on a large board. Pit **3 perfectly ripe avocados** and scoop the flesh onto the board, halve and add **6 ripe cherry tomatoes**, and pick over the leaves from **½ a bunch of fresh cilantro (½ oz)**. Keep chopping and mixing until lovely and smooth, mashing it with a fork to help it along, if needed. Taste and season to perfection with sea salt, black pepper, **extra virgin olive oil**, and a squeeze of **lime juice**, then scrape into a bowl. You could also do this one in a food processor.

### CREAMY BLUE CHEESE
#### GREEK YOGURT & A HUM OF GARLIC

In a bowl, mix **1 cup of Greek yogurt** with **2 teaspoons of white wine vinegar** and **1 dash of Worcestershire sauce**. Melt **3½ oz of blue cheese** in a small pan on a medium heat, then stir into the spiked yogurt. Crush in **½ a clove of unpeeled garlic** through a garlic crusher, mix well, then taste and season to perfection. Decant into a bowl—I like to crumble a little **more blue cheese** on top—and drizzle with a little **extra virgin olive oil**.

### SILKY HUMMUS
#### CHICKPEAS, TAHINI, & YOGURT

Tip **1 x 19-oz can of chickpeas**, juice and all, into a blender. Add **2 heaping teaspoons of tahini**, **2 tablespoons of plain yogurt**, **½ a peeled clove of garlic**, **the juice of 1 lemon**, and **1 pinch of cayenne pepper**, then blitz until smooth. Taste and season to perfection, then decant into a bowl. Toast **1 good pinch of cumin seeds** in a frying pan on a medium heat until smelling fantastic, then tip on top and drizzle with a little **extra virgin olive oil**.

#### SERVING IDEAS GALORE

As well as making delicious dips for dunking everything from crunchy seasonal crudités and crackers to breadsticks and toast soldiers, all these dips would work a treat used as a topping for crostini or bruschetta.

| CALORIES | FAT | SAT FAT | PROTEIN | CARBS | SUGARS | SALT | FIBER |
|----------|-----|---------|---------|-------|--------|------|-------|
| 49kcal | 4g | 0.9g | 1.2g | 2g | 0.9g | 0.3g | 0.5g |

THESE VALUES ARE AN AVERAGE OF THE FOUR RECIPES ABOVE

# Foodie decorations

We tend to buy a few new decorations every year, but also have fun making them with the kids. You can slice up citrus fruits and let them dry out on a non-stick baking sheet in a low oven for 2 to 3 hours, then tie them up with ribbons; string up fresh chiles by their stalks for a brilliant pop of color (plus once they dry out you can keep them in jars to use in your cooking); or even make strings of popcorn (see page 360). Have fun—the kids will love seeing what they've made out on display.

# PERFECT POPCORN

## SPICED CHRISTMAS SUGAR

The megamix of spices and flavors in this festive sugar creates a wonderful tutti frutti vibe that's totally irresistible when teamed with hot popcorn. Use leftover sugar to spice up puds, such as baked fruit or Churros (see page 272).

(see page 272)

**MAKES 2 LBS OF SUGAR**
**15 MINUTES**
**PLUS DRYING**

**SPICED SUGAR**

3 fresh bay leaves

2 oranges

2 lemons

1 whole nutmeg, for grating

1 vanilla bean

6 whole cloves

½ teaspoon ground cinnamon

2 lbs superfine sugar

**FOR 1 LARGE BOWL OF POPCORN**

olive oil

2 tablespoons unsalted butter

4½ oz popcorn kernels

3 tablespoons Spiced sugar

It's so easy to make this flavorsome sugar that you may as well do a big batch, which will last for months. Tear the bay leaves into a food processor, discarding the stalks. Finely grate in the orange and lemon zest, and half the nutmeg. Halve the vanilla bean lengthways and scrape out the seeds, then add both bean and seeds to the processor with the cloves and cinnamon, and blitz up well. Add the sugar and blitz again to distribute all that flavor. There's quite a bit of moisture in the citrus zest and vanilla bean, so pour the sugar onto two large baking sheets, spread it out evenly and leave it to dry out for a few hours. Once the sugar is dry, push and rub it through a sieve to catch any larger pieces of spice. Discard anything left behind in the sieve, then pop the sifted sugar into an airtight container.

To make the popcorn, put 1 tablespoon of oil and the butter into a large pan over a high heat. Once the butter has melted, stir in the popcorn kernels until well coated. Put the lid on straight away and leave it for a few minutes to get going. As the corn starts to pop, hold the lid firmly in place with a kitchen towel and give the pan a shake every 30 seconds or so, to make sure all the kernels get popped. Put 3 tablespoons of Spiced sugar into a large bowl, and, when the popcorn is ready, quickly toss it into the bowl so the hot popcorn picks up those lovely flavors. Remove any unpopped kernels and serve right away, or, if you need a get-out-of-jail-free card, leave the popcorn to cool and bag it up as a last-minute gift. If the sugar settles at the bottom of the bag, just give the bag a little shake before tucking in.

| CALORIES | FAT | SAT FAT | PROTEIN | CARBS | SUGARS | SALT | FIBER |
|---|---|---|---|---|---|---|---|
| 132kcal | 5.7g | 2.3g | 1.7g | 18.8g | 6.8g | 0g | 1.3g |

# The cheeseboard

Come Christmas, I don't know anyone who doesn't have an array of different cheeses lined up in the fridge, ready for a bit of after-dinner indulgence or to take center stage at a party. Here's my advice on how best to celebrate the wonderful world of cheese.

## CHOOSING YOUR CHEESE

Variety is key, so if you're shopping, try to get to a good cheese shop and ask their advice on what to choose. The most useful thing to remember is that you want to take your guests on a journey from milder, fresher cheeses such as Cheshire and Red Leicester, up to a good Cheddar, then into your blue cheeses like Stilton, finishing with the creamier varieties such as Brie or Camembert. This will mean you can taste and appreciate each cheese as you go.

## PRESENTATION

Use a nice big wooden board, a piece of granite, or even designate a little table as your cheese area—this is a centerpiece that everyone will get excited about. I like to position the cheeses in the way you want your guests to enjoy them, numbering them with flags to guide them from the mildest, youngest cheeses through to the more complex, stronger, smellier ones. Stick little names in the cheeses, too, so your guests know what they're trying.

## CHEESEBOARD ETIQUETTE

Whether host or guest, certain rules apply. With a rinded cheese, when taking your portion, slice from the rind to the center, rather than cutting across the nose—it ripens from the outside in, so the flavor profile differs at either end. With blue cheese this is exaggerated further, so you get less blue on the outside and more acidity in the center. Slice wisely and you'll be sure of maximum enjoyment!

## A BIT ON THE SIDE

In terms of vehicles, I believe in keeping your bread, crackers, oatcakes, or crispbreads simple, so you can let the cheese do the talking. On the condiment front, most seasonal fruits and jams complement cheese really well—think apples, pears, clementines, grapes, figs, or even dried raisins and dates. Quince membrillo, chutneys, marmalades, jams, pickles, and preserves can all serve you well, so have a cupboard raid and see what you can pair up.

## KEEPING YOUR CHEESE HAPPY

Chilling cheese in the fridge reduces its flavor, so if you've got a room that isn't centrally heated, store the cheese in there so it stays cool but not cold. It's happiest wrapped in parchment paper, or even aluminum foil, so unpack and re-wrap it once you get it home, if you need to. You absolutely want to enjoy your cheeses at room temperature, but don't put them in a room that's too hot for too long before serving or you risk them drying out or melting—covering them with a slightly damp, clean kitchen towel will help.

## A CHEESE-FRIENDLY TIPPLE

As a rule of thumb, it's generally easier to pair white wines, or even pale ales, porters, stouts, and ciders, with British cheeses. Vin Santo, Marsala, and sweet wines work really well with blue cheeses, and stinkier cheeses make good combos with whisky, where the pungency of the cheese can keep up with the strength of the alcohol.

## CHEESEBOARD CURVEBALLS

Pair something like a fresh, young Lancashire cheese with your Christmas cake, to give you a bit of relief from the richness. Another favorite of mine is to drizzle a piece of Cheddar with some good honey, then sprinkle with a little pinch of freshly ground coffee—it's a festive flavor mash-up and will totally challenge perceptions.

# Perfect

# DRINKS

In the pages that follow, you'll find a bunch of utterly delicious cocktails that are easy to knock together at home. Each recipe makes one drink, but they're easy to scale up, and some make brilliant batch cocktails, too. I've taken advice from ultimate cocktail maestro J Rivera, my head bar manager at Fifteen London, to make sure these deliver on the flavor front, every time. Of course, if you can do things like squeezing your lemons in advance so you can simply measure out what you need, when you need it, that's only going to make your life easier. And having a bit of cocktail kit to work with will help you look the part. Have fun!

# WHITE RUSSIAN

3 tablespoons Grey Goose vodka

5 teaspoons coffee liqueur

5 teaspoons heavy cream

Shake the vodka and coffee liqueur together over ice, then strain well into a glass with more ice. Vigorously shake up the heavy cream, then gently pour it into the glass over the back of a spoon so it forms a layer on top.

# HOT
# BUTTERED RUM

1 tablespoon unsalted butter

6 tablespoons + 1 teaspoon unsweetened cloudy apple juice

3 tablespoons Bacardi 8 rum

5 teaspoons apricot brandy

3 whole cloves

1 whole nutmeg, for grating

1 orange

Melt the butter in a small pan on a low heat, stir in the apple juice, rum, brandy, and cloves, then finely grate in 1 scraping each of nutmeg and orange zest. Pour into a heatproof glass, discarding the cloves, and serve warm with extra grated nutmeg and zest.

# FISH HOUSE PUNCH

5 teaspoons Bacardi 8 rum

5 teaspoons Earl Grey tea (cold)

2½ teaspoons Cognac

2½ teaspoons apricot brandy
   liqueur

2 teaspoons Spiced sugar syrup
   (see below)

½ a lemon

1 orange

### SPICED SUGAR SYRUP

¼ cup demerara sugar

1 stick of cinnamon

1 star anise

2 cloves

What's great about this recipe is that it's super-easy to scale up, so it's perfect if you want to make a big bowl of punch for everyone to enjoy at a party.

To make the spiced sugar syrup, place the sugar in a small pan with 2 tablespoons of water, the cinnamon stick, star anise, and cloves. Place on a medium-high heat and bring to a boil, leave bubbling away until the sugar has dissolved, then remove from the heat and leave to cool, discarding the spices. This quantity will give you enough syrup for roughly six cocktails, but you can easily scale up, keeping the syrup in an airtight jar for a few weeks.

For your punch, simply stir the rum, tea, Cognac, liqueur, 2 teaspoons of sugar syrup, and the lemon juice together over ice for 10 seconds, then strain well into a glass with more ice. Use a vegetable peeler to add a strip of orange peel to garnish, and enjoy.

# MANHATTAN

3 tablespoons rye whiskey

2½ teaspoons Martini Rosso (red vermouth)

2½ teaspoons dry vermouth

2 dashes of orange bitters

1 orange

Stir the whiskey, vermouths, and bitters together over ice, then strain well into a chilled Martini glass. Use a vegetable peeler to add a strip of orange peel to garnish.

As the main cocktail mixture here is entirely made up of booze (we like that), it means this is the perfect cocktail recipe to batch up, either to get ahead for a party or to give as a gift to some lucky friends or family. If you're serving up multiple drinks at once, just remember that ice melts quickly and it's still advisable to stir it up in smaller batches, so you don't dilute the mix too much.

# PINK PEPPER NEGRONI

5 teaspoons Bombay Sapphire gin

5 teaspoons Martini Rosso (red vermouth)

5 teaspoons Campari or bitter liqueur

5 whole pink peppercorns

1 blood or regular orange

These quantities make one delicious cocktail, but as you need to leave this to steep overnight, it's well worth making a big batch to get ahead for a party, or for gifting. And, of course, if you want to make a classic Negroni, leave out the peppercorns and steeping stage.

To flavor your Negroni, simply mix the gin, vermouth, Campari or bitter liqueur, and peppercorns together and leave overnight, or for a couple of days, so the flavors infuse, leaving you with a light, sweet, bitter, spicy dimension to your cocktail. Stir into a glass of ice and add a nice slice of orange to garnish.

# WINTER
# OLD FASHIONED

# ROB ROY

¼ cup quality bourbon

1 teaspoon maple syrup

2 dashes of chocolate bitters

1 orange

Simply place the bourbon, maple syrup, and bitters (you could also use Angostura or orange bitters, if you prefer) in your glass with some chunky ice and stir gently for 25 seconds, or until combined, being mindful not to shard the ice. Use a vegetable peeler to add a strip of orange peel to garnish.

3 tablespoons blended Scotch whisky

4 teaspoons Martini Rosso (red vermouth)

1 dash of Angostura bitters

1 or 2 ripe cherries

Simply stir the whisky, vermouth, and bitters together over ice, then strain into a glass. Garnish with a cherry or two.

# HOT TODDY

1 lemon

3 tablespoons blended Scotch whisky

3 teaspoons liquid honey

1 stick of cinnamon

Squeeze 4 teaspoons of lemon juice into a heatproof glass, add the whisky and honey, then stir in ¾ cup + 1½ tablespoons of boiling kettle water until the honey has dissolved. Serve garnished with a cinnamon stick and a slice of lemon.

# FESTIVE BELLINI

4 teaspoons peach purée or crème de pêche (peach liqueur)

4 teaspoons orgeat syrup (almond syrup)

½ a lemon

Prosecco

Shake the peach purée or liqueur, orgeat syrup, and 3 teaspoons of lemon juice together over ice, then strain into a Champagne flute. Top up with chilled Prosecco.

# PARTY PROSECCO

## LOTS OF FUN & FRUITY IDEAS

Bubbly Prosecco is the perfect party drink and can easily be pimped in all sorts of fruity ways to create a bounty of enticing cocktails to impress your guests and liven up the party. I hope this lovely page will give you lots of inspiration.

5 MINUTES
PLUS CHILLING

If you want a super-simple way to keep your party interesting on the drinks front, whether you're entertaining a handful of people or a bigger crowd, then look no further than this colorful page of joy. Prosecco is super-popular, and as such you'll often find it on offer in the shops these days. Look out for the best deals, take advantage of its popularity, and stock up ahead of the party season, ready to rustle up drinks as the host or to take with you when you get invited elsewhere. Just be sure to take along something from the list below to pimp that ride and get the party started with a bang!

First up, as host, as well as chilling the Prosecco you'll get a lot of thanks for popping your glasses in the freezer for about an hour before you use them, so they're super-chilled and keep your drinks nice and cold, too. When you're ready to serve up, simply line up your glasses and get squeezing, spooning, and pouring with fresh fruit or liqueurs. You can go bold with one flavor in each, or mix and match to find your favorite combos.

THINGS THAT WILL ALWAYS WORK A TREAT ARE . . .

- Freshly squeezed clementine, blood orange, or grapefruit juice

- The sweet, tangy flesh scooped out of a wrinkly passion fruit

- Pomegranate seeds or a fresh squeeze of their juice

- Fresh seasonal berries for garnish or smashed into a tasty purée

- Fruity liqueurs, such as St-Germain elderflower, crème de cassis, or Cointreau

- A splash of sloe gin or a dash of Campari

- A few dashes of interesting bitters, such as lavender, pomegranate, or citrus blends

# FROZEN GRAPES & GRAPPA

## GOOD-QUALITY CHOCOLATE & A SMILE

5 MINUTES
PLUS FREEZING

My mate Mr David Loftus, my food photographer for a long time, obviously loves food as he spends half his life taking pictures of it. When we were in Italy shooting a few years back, he said I should freeze my grapes—which immediately made me think he was a raving heathen! God knows what my friends the grape-pickers would say. Why on earth would you get beautiful fresh grapes, then freeze them?

But . . . of course, it was a fantastic idea and I admit I was completely wrong!

When David brought the frozen grapes outside for us to eat, it was an incredibly hot and sweltering day and just what we needed to cool us down. And that's the brilliant thing about this amazingly simple dessert: it's super-refreshing, so it works a treat at any time of the year, particularly during the festive period when you may be in need of a pud that provides a cool contrast to the rich indulgence of all that wonderful Christmas food. To be honest, you could even serve up the grapes on their own as an interlude between courses, if you're having a big feast.

Over in Italy, David had managed to get hold of some nice sweet fragola grapes, which are a joy to eat but quite rare in supermarkets. A good muscat grape or any other grape variety that you enjoy eating would also work well. As soon as the grapes start to freeze, all the flesh and juice inside turns into a sort of popsicle-type sorbet, while the outside remains firm and beautifully frosted.

For me, the best way to eat frozen grapes is after a meal, with a few bits of good-quality chocolate and a nice glass of grappa or Vin Santo. If, like me, you are a bit skeptical about this dessert, please try it—it's super-cool. Well done, Dave!

# Festive spirit

Cut the top off an 2-liter plastic bottle or carton, sit your 700ml bottle of spirits inside, then shove herbs, holly leaves, citrus zest, berries, whatever you fancy, down the sides and top up with water. You'll need to clear enough space in your freezer to carefully stand it upright for a few hours before laying it flat to save space, so it's best to make these well in advance (don't worry—spirits don't freeze). When you're ready to serve, simply run the sleeve quickly under a tap and slide the plastic off. You'll have a perfect ice wrap around the bottle to keep it cold for your party, and it'll look incredible, too.

# Get creative with crackers

Jazz up some store-bought ones by adding better gifts, funnier jokes, and personalized name tags for your lucky guests or, even better, make your own . . .

To start, you need a sheet of letter-size paper—use colored paper, newspaper, pages from comics, wrapping paper, hand-drawn pictures, whatever you fancy. Lay a sheet flat with the longer edge in front of you.

Place a toilet-roll tube in the middle of the longer edge and secure it in place with a bit of sticky tape.

Poke through a cracker snap (you can buy these online), taping it to the toilet-roll tube on one side.

Make up and write out your joke, and pop it into the tube with a paper hat and the toy or treat of your choice.

Add an extra toilet-roll tube on each side of your middle one, threading the cracker snap ends through them.

Roll up the paper around the tubes, pinch together at either side of the middle tube, gently squeeze and twist, then tie a piece of string or ribbon around to secure it in place and remove the tubes from either end.

Add a name tag if you've personalized the contents, and there you have it—your very own homemade cracker!

# *Guide to*
# ROASTING MEAT

To help you get your roast meat spot-on every time, I've created a chart that covers all the big hitters, including turkey, duck, goose, chicken, beef, pork, and, last but not least, lamb.

Before you start, there are a few extra things to take into consideration. First and foremost, buy the best-quality meat you can afford—remember, it's better to trade up on the welfare front and choose a slightly smaller bird or piece of meat than to opt for poor quality. Buy from a butcher if you've got one locally, and don't be afraid to ask them where their meat comes from and the standards and welfare the animals were raised in—if you don't get the answers you're looking for, vote with your feet and try somewhere else.

Another key thing to remember is to take your meat out of the fridge an hour or two before you want to cook it (depending on its size) so that it can come up to room temperature—this way, it'll cook more evenly. All the timings I've shared on the following pages are based on cooking your meat from room temperature. Turkey timings are based on a higher-welfare bird, so you'll need to up the times (see page 56) for a standard bird.

The resting stage is similarly important and should never be skipped. This is what will give you super-tender, juicy meat, so I've suggested timings for each type of meat, too.

It's good to bear in mind that all ovens will vary slightly and they're not always the temperature that they say they are! A lot of you will be used to the quirks of your own oven, but if you want to be doubly sure you're cooking at the right temperature, get yourself an oven thermometer and adjust the heat accordingly.

And, of course, although I've given you timings to work from, you'll need to rely on your instincts, too. The height, width, and type of pan you use, whether it's covered or uncovered, and things like adding a splash of stock, booze, or a veg trivet, or if you cook more than one thing in your oven at once, can all mean you'll need to make slight adjustments. That's why I've included extra notes, so you'll know what to aim for.

| MEAT | CUT | WEIGHT | TEMPERATURE |
|------|-----|--------|-------------|
| **TURKEY** | WHOLE | 9–11 lbs | 350°F |
| | | 11–13 lbs | |
| | | 13–15 lbs | |
| | | 15–17½ lbs | |
| | | 17½–20 lbs | |
| | | 20–22 lbs | |
| **DUCK** | WHOLE | 4½–6½ lbs | 350°F |
| **GOOSE** | WHOLE | 9–11 lbs | 350°F |
| **CHICKEN** | WHOLE | 2–3 lbs | 350°F |
| | | 3–4½ lbs | |
| | | 4½–6½ lbs | |

| COOK TIME | REST TIME | EXTRA INFO |
|---|---|---|
| 2 HOURS 15 MINUTES to 2 HOURS 30 MINUTES | 1 HOUR 30 MINUTES | To check it's cooked, the simplest way is to stick a knife into the thickest part of the thigh—if the juices run clear, it's done (you want to reach an internal temperature of 150°F for a top-quality bird, such as Paul Kelly's turkeys, or 160°F for a supermarket higher-welfare or standard bird) |
| 2 HOURS 30 MINUTES to 3 HOURS | | |
| 3 HOURS to 3 HOURS 30 MINUTES | 2 HOURS | |
| 3 HOURS 30 MINUTES to 4 HOURS | | |
| 4 HOURS to 4 HOURS 15 MINUTES | | |
| 4 HOURS 15 MINUTES to 4 HOURS 30 MINUTES | | |
| 2 HOURS | 30 MINUTES | This is a slow-roast method—the meat will be soft and tender, but not pink |
| 3 HOURS 30 MINUTES | 30 MINUTES | This is a slow-roast method—the meat will be soft and tender, but not pink (you'll know it's ready when the leg meat falls easily off the bone) |
| 1 HOUR 15 MINUTES to 1 HOUR 30 MINUTES | 30 MINUTES | To check it's cooked, the simplest way is to stick a knife into the thickest part of the thigh—if the juices run clear, it's done (you can also pinch the thigh meat—if it comes away easily from the bone, you're good to go) |
| 1 HOUR 30 MINUTES to 2 HOURS | | |
| 2 HOURS to 2 HOURS 30 MINUTES | | |

| MEAT | CUT | WEIGHT | TEMPERATURE |
|------|-----|--------|-------------|
| | **FORERIB, FRENCH TRIMMED** (and without chine bone or cap meat) | 2-bone → 4½–6½ lbs | |
| | | 3-bone → 6½–9 lbs | 350°F |
| | | 4-bone → 9–11 lbs | |
| | | 5-bone → 11–13 lbs | |
| **BEEF** | **TOPSIDE** | 2–3 lbs | Full whack 475°F then 350°F |
| | | 3–5 lbs | |
| | **LOIN, RIB BONE IN, SKIN ON** (chine bone removed) | 4½–6½ lbs | Full whack 475°F then 350°F |
| | | 6½–9 lbs | |
| | | 9–11 lbs | |
| | **BELLY** | 4½–6½ lbs | 350°F |
| **PORK** | **SHOULDER, BONE IN** | 6½–9 lbs | Full whack 475°F then 325°F |
| | | 9–11 lbs | |
| | **SHOULDER, BONE IN** | 4½ lbs | 350°F |
| **LAMB** | **LEG** | 4½ lbs | 425°F |
| | **RACK** | 5-bone | 350°F |
| | | 7-bone | |

| COOK TIME | REST TIME | EXTRA INFO |
|---|---|---|
| 1 HOUR 30 MINUTES | | ADD 20 MINUTES |
| 2 HOURS | This will give you meat that ranges from well done at either end, to medium-well and medium-rare as you reach the center. If you prefer your meat well done ... | ADD 30 MINUTES |
| 2 HOURS 15 MINUTES | | ADD 40 MINUTES |
| 2 HOURS 30 MINUTES | AT LEAST 30 MINUTES | ADD 45 MINUTES |
| 15 MINUTES at full whack, then reduce the temperature for 1 HOUR 15 MINUTES to 1 HOUR 30 MINUTES | | ADD 15 MINUTES |
| 15 MINUTES at full whack, then reduce the temperature for 1 HOUR 30 MINUTES to 2 HOURS | | ADD 20 MINUTES |
| 30 MINUTES at full whack, then reduce the temperature for 1 HOUR | | Some people cook pork blushing pink, but these timings are for cooked through, but still juicy. For the best crackling, score the skin with a sharp knife (into the fat, but not the meat) and rub with a little sea salt before roasting |
| 30 MINUTES at full whack, then reduce the temperature for 1 HOUR 30 MINUTES | | |
| 30 MINUTES at full whack, then reduce the temperature for 1 HOUR 45 MINUTES | 30 MINUTES | |
| 2 HOURS to 2 HOURS 30 MINUTES | | These joints are best cooked low and slow, but don't worry, the wonderful fat inside will keep the meat super-juicy, plus it gives your crackling lots of time to crisp up |
| 30 MINUTES at full whack, then reduce the temperature for 2 HOURS 30 MINUTES | | |
| 30 MINUTES at full whack, then reduce the temperature for 3 HOURS | | |
| 4 HOURS | | This joint is best cooked low and slow, but don't worry, the wonderful fat inside will keep the meat super-juicy |
| 1 HOUR 15 MINUTES | 30 MINUTES | ADD 15 MINUTES |
| 25 MINUTES | | This will give you blushing, juicy meat. If you prefer your lamb well done ... |
| | | ADD 10 MINUTES |
| 30 MINUTES | 10 MINUTES | ADD 15 MINUTES |

# NUTRITION AT CHRISTMAS

"Christmas is the ultimate special occasion. It's a time for celebration, for getting together with family and friends, and for enjoying ourselves. A lot of that revolves around food, and in a book like this, the job of our team is to make sure that every recipe Jamie writes is the best it can be, without compromising on the point of the dish in the first place. Every book has a different brief, and by nature most of the recipes in this book are indulgent, and therefore not to be enjoyed every day. In order for you to be able to make informed choices, we've published the nutritional content for each recipe on the recipe page itself, including figures per serving for calories, fat, saturated fat, protein, carbohydrates, sugars, salt, and fiber, giving you a really easy access point to understand what you're eating. Remember that a good, balanced diet and regular exercise are the keys to a healthier lifestyle."

**Eretia O'Kennedy—Head of Nutrition, RNutr (food)**

For more information about our guidelines and how we analyze recipes, please visit jamieoliver.com/nutrition. For a quick reference list of all the dairy-free, gluten-free, and vegan recipes in this book, please visit jamieoliver.com/christmas-cookbook.

# INGREDIENTS ROUND-UP

## FOOD STANDARDS

For me, there's no point in eating meat unless the animal was raised well and it was at optimal health. Choosing grass-fed animals where possible, which have been free to roam and haven't lived in a stressful environment, is essential—it makes total sense to me that what we put into our bodies should have lived a good life, to in turn give us goodness. It's about quality over quantity, so please choose organic, free-range, or higher-welfare meat and responsibly sourced fish whenever you can.

With eggs, always go free-range or organic, and do the same for anything containing egg, such as mayo and pasta. Please choose organic stock and bouillon cubes, too.

With staple dairy products, such as milk, yogurt, and butter, I honestly couldn't endorse more the trade-up to organic. It is slightly more expensive, but every time you buy organic you vote for a better food system. Embrace seasonal produce to get it at its cheapest, and at its best.

## SWAP-INS

You'll notice throughout the book that sometimes I've given you very specific recommendations for ingredients. This doesn't mean you can't substitute your own personal favorites; they're just the things that I believe will elevate your dish to that extra-special place. So, for example, when I've suggested a certain type of wine for the base of a sauce or stew, the idea is that you can enjoy a glass of that wine when you serve up, too, safe in the knowledge that it's going to be a brilliant companion to your finished dish.

## A NOTE ON FREEZING

Let food cool before freezing, and break it down into portions so it cools quicker and you can get it into the freezer within 2 hours of cooking. Make sure everything is well wrapped, meat and fish especially, and labeled for future reference (and to avoid freezer roulette!). Thaw in the fridge before use. Generally, if you've frozen cooked food, don't freeze it again after you've reheated it.

# Hungry for more?

For handy nutrition advice, as well as videos, features, hacks, tricks, and tips on all sorts of different subjects, and loads of brilliant tasty recipes, plus much more, check out jamieoliver.com and youtube.com/jamieoliver.

jamieoliver.com

# Thank you

## WITH BELLS ON

With every book I write, I tend to do the thanks page last, so I can make sure everyone who's played a part gets a mention. But with it being Christmas, that wonderful yearly event we can't get enough of, and one that I've been creating content for, for over 17 years now, this thanks page is a little bit special. I'll tell you why: there are a LOT of incredibly talented, brilliant people out there—some who I still see and work with every day, and others who've long flown the nest—all of whom by their input over the years have contributed to the heart and soul of this book. You wonderful lot have helped me hone and perfect my ideas, culminating in this bumper book that I really am very proud to be sharing.

It's a funny old thing, the thanks page, because it really does mean such a lot to each and every individual and team that appears here. And rightly so, because every single one of you—and I wish I could fit more of you in by name—deserves to be thanked. Without the love, support, creativity, patience, and commitment of you lovely bunch, I wouldn't be able to do what I do. So, whether you're named here or not, I hope you know how much I appreciate you.

So, first and foremost, thank you to my brilliant family and friends, because let's face it, that's what this time of year is all about. To Jools, kids, Mum, Dad, Anna, Mrs N., the don Mr Gennaro Contaldo, and all the gang.

To my dear chum and long-suffering photographer, "Lord" David Loftus, thank you. We've done a lot of new stuff for this book, and boy is it beautiful, but it's also such a pleasure to see so much of our history peppered throughout the archive shots, too.

To my talented food team, who are a constant source of inspiration, and always ready to get stuck elbow-deep into Christmas, whatever the time of year. To old-timers and my closest book allies Ginny Rolfe, Pete Begg, and Bobby Sebire. Christmas is a great time for reflection, and looking back on what we've done together, I can't help but wonder what we'll all be doing to support each other come another 20 years . . . let's start an old people's home and grow old together. To the rest of the wonderful motley crew that make up my amazing food team—thank you—Abigail "Scottish" Fawcett, my original Greek sister Georgina "Sparkly" Hayden, my conscience Christina Mackenzie, super-dedicated Phillippa Spence, one-of-a-kind Jodene Jordan, wonderfully mad Maddie Rix, lovely Elspeth Meston, sweet Rachel Young, and my Aussie mate Jonny Lake, as well as handy festive helpers Francesa Paling, Becca Sulocki, Lisa Harrison, and Isla Mackenzie. Big shout out to the rest of the extended food-team family, super-creative Sarah "Tiddles" Tildesley, got-my-back Joanne Lord, organization whiz Laura James, my new Greek sister Athina Andrelos, world-traveler and hair-flicker Daniel Nowland, and the one-and-only Helen Martin. Thank you to genius Barnaby Purdy on my art team, and to lovely ladies Ella Miller and Sam Graves for all your help trawling the archives for the old shots.

On nutrition, thank you to ever-patient Eretia O'Kennedy and Rozzie "Batch" Batchelar, overseen from afar by the boss Laura Matthews. There's no escaping the fact that this is an indulgent old book, but the values you've instilled in me still ring true even in these recipes, so thank you for helping me to make the recipes be the very best they can be, without going off the charts!

Big thank you to my brilliant words girls, my illustrious editor Rebecca "Rubs" Verity, testing-maestro Bethan O'Connor and gang, for making sure I'm as clear and helpful as can be, and ensuring that everything from the color of the ribbons (and the fact there's two!) to how to describe (or not to describe!) something is always spot-on.

To the rest of my truly fantastic team that support me in the creation of the book and beyond, headed up by my brother-in-law Mr Paul Hunt, cactus-collector and media extraordinaire Claudia Rozencrantz, and, of course, secret agent Louise "Chewbacca" Holland. To everyone on my personal team, especially chicken-lover Sy Brighton and Amelia Crook, my book marketing and PR gang, including the leader-of-the-pack Claire Postans, Laura Jones, Ben Lifton, and Peter Berry, all the digital and social crew, the girls in legal led by Giovanna Milia, Therese MacDermott and the finance team, the IT boys, and everyone else who supports us in getting this book out there! One of the things I'm always grateful for is the enthusiasm of my team of office testers—you guys make a real and valuable contribution to the success of these recipes, so thank you.

So on to the wonderful team at Penguin Random House UK. I know you've wanted me to do this book for some time, so Tom Weldon—happy Christmas, my friend! Thank you for letting me wait until now. The time was right. To everyone at Penguin who contributes to the success of my books, led by the always glamorous and supportive Louise Moore, thank you. John Hamilton—

I'm proud to have known you and called you a mate before those tattoos came along. Juliette Butler—big thanks, and sorry for making your life dramatic. To all the wonderful guys in the PR, marketing, and comms teams, led into the fray by super-ladies Clare Parker, Bek Sunley, and Elizabeth Smith. To always lovely Chantal Noel, Anjali Nathani, Khan Lawrence, and the rest of the diligent rights team. To Martin Higgins and all the sales gang—big shout out to you lot for getting the book out there! And last but not least, to Nick Lowndes, my old friend Annie Lee, and Jill Cole, Caroline Pretty, and Caroline Wilding.

A massive shout out to Mr James Verity (lead designer and champion of leopard skin—maybe an idea for next year's cover?), Mark Arn, and the guys at creative agency Superfantastic. Thank you for helping me to have fun navigating 17 years' worth of Christmas stuff, and creating this Christmas bible that I know we'll take great pleasure in seeing on the shelves, year after year.

You'll see throughout the book many of the crazy haircuts I've had over the years on my various TV shows, so thank you to Jay Hunt and all the guys at Channel 4 for continuing to support me in helping the public have stress-free Christmases. New ideas champ Zoe Collins, super-resourceful, lovely Katie Millard, and razor-sharp Sean Moxhay—we've done a fair few Christmas shows together, thank you for your boundless enthusiasm on an annual basis. This year, thank you to Emily Kennedy and Jo Thornhill for heading up what I know is set to be an epic production. And a massive thanks to all the crew who have helped with my shows over the years. A lot of you have come back year-on-year and become great friends, and every show is a joy to film. I hope we'll be doing it for many years to come!

And finally to Lima O'Donnell, Julia Bell, and Abbie Tyler for making me look presentable. I know my wife appreciates it (just don't cut my hair!).

# INDEX

Recipes marked V are suitable for vegetarians